Aftershocks

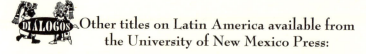

SERIES ADVISORY EDITOR: LYMAN L. JOHNSON,
UNIVERSITY OF NORTH CAROLINA AT CHARLOTTE

The cover of a book on the 1906 Valparaíso, Chile, earthquake, published in Santiago within four months of the event. (ALFREDO RODRIGUEZ ROZAS AND CARLOS GAJARDO CRUZAT, *La catástrofe del 16 de agosto de 1906 en la República de Chile* [SANTIAGO: BARCELONA, 1906]).

Aftershocks

Earthquakes and Popular Politics
in Latin America

Edited by
JÜRGEN BUCHENAU
and
LYMAN L. JOHNSON

University of New Mexico Press ✢ Albuquerque

LIBRARY OF CONGRESS CATALOGING-IN-PUBLICATION DATA

Aftershocks : earthquakes and popular politics in Latin America /
edited by Jürgen Buchenau and Lyman L. Johnson.
p. cm. — (Diálogos)
Includes index.
ISBN 978-0-8263-4623-0 (pbk. : alk. paper)
1. Earthquakes—Political aspects—Latin America—History.
2. Earthquakes—Social aspects—Latin America—History.
I. Buchenau, Jürgen, 1964– II. Johnson, Lyman L.
QE535.2.L29A34 2009
980—dc22
2009013455

DESIGN AND LAYOUT: MELISSA TANDYSH
Composed in 10/13.5 Janson Text Lt Std
Display type is Bernhard Modern Std

To Anabel and Sue

Contents

PREFACE

Like many good ideas in general, the idea for this book came from a child. On a cold December afternoon in 2004, seven-year-old Nicolas Buchenau was engrossed in watching television. When his father attempted to tear him away and invited him to a game of basketball on the patio, Nicolas indignantly drew his attention to what he was watching. As the horrendous scenes of the Indian Ocean tsunami flickered across the screen, he asked his father "Why don't you ever work on natural disasters? Like earthquakes, tsunamis, floods? You should write a book about that."

The result of this conversation is the present book, compiled in the knowledge that a project on natural disasters in Latin America is best done in collaboration. We thank our collaborators for their hard work in writing seven essays that explore earthquakes across two and a half centuries and in seven different areas. We especially thank Sam Martland for providing the image used in the cover art for the book, and all those who joined us at a panel on Latin American earthquakes at the Latin American Studies Association meeting in San Juan, Puerto Rico, in March 2006.

We also appreciate the interest and encouragement of Clark Whitehorn, editor in chief of the University of New Mexico Press, who provided much valuable advice throughout the publication process.

Charlotte, November 2008

Introduction

Earthquakes and Latin American Political Culture

JÜRGEN BUCHENAU AND LYMAN L. JOHNSON

✝ SUNDAY MAY 31, 1970, BEGAN AS A NEAR PERFECT DAY IN THE TOWN of Yungay, Peru, a provincial capital of approximately twenty thousand people. A cloudless sky revealed the twin snow-covered peaks of Mount Huascarán, Peru's tallest mountain, towering above the valley. In the morning, townspeople attended Mass and most then went to the town's lively market, a center of commercial activity for the surrounding region. In the afternoon, most of the town's residents were indoors listening to the broadcast of the first game of the World Cup soccer tournament in Mexico City when the first tremors began. Many remained glued to their radios. Disaster struck at 3:24 p.m. As the earth shook and the roar overwhelmed the radio commentaries, the town's residents fled to the streets. Survivors would later testify that the earthquake began as a swaying motion that knocked many off their feet and then gave way to a series of violent shocks that destroyed most of the buildings in Yungay. The worst was yet to come.

The powerful quake, which affected much of northern Peru, leveled buildings and left the population exposed in the streets of Yungay and

Site of the Yungay plaza showing the remains of the cathedral walls and four palm trees buried to a depth of five meters. The ridge overtopped by the Yungay debris lobe is visible in the distance. The wreckage in the right middle ground consists of a smashed bus and truck (IMAGE 23, PERU, 1970, U.S. GEOLOGICAL SURVEY PHOTOGRAPHIC LIBRARY; ALL USGS PHOTOS CAN BE FOUND AT HTTP://LIBRARYPHOTO.CR.USGS.GOV/EARTH.HTM).

nearby villages such as Ranrahirca. Some ten minutes later huge blocks of ice shaken loose from the high peaks that line the valley swept down on the vulnerable survivors. A wave of boulders dislodged from mountain sides long deforested to provide firewood for the region's poor indigenous population then followed. Finally, a massive wall of water and mud that escaped from high mountain lakes rushed over the flattened town, leaving behind thousands of tons of mud. Only a few thousand residents of Yungay and the nearby countryside ultimately survived the catastrophe, but an exact toll is difficult to measure because census takers had always undercounted the region's indigenous population. One foreign missionary in the area at the time of the quake reported the day after, "Yungay no longer exists."[1]

Yungay was not alone in experiencing the destructive power of this seismic event. Across northern Peru the earthquake and related avalanches and mudslides claimed a total of approximately 70,000 lives, injured another 140,000 people, and left 500,000 survivors homeless.[2] Anthropologist Anthony Oliver-Smith has labeled this complex of seismic events and succeeding avalanches and mudslides the worst natural disaster in the recorded history of Latin America.[3] His summary judgment emphasizes both the material and human destruction of this terrible event in a region that had suffered an earthquake that cost 2,000 lives just seven years earlier. It also places the experience of Yungay in the broader context of Latin America's long and intimate experience with natural disaster. If this was the worst natural disaster in the region's history, it was at the same time only one of hundreds of powerful natural disasters that destroyed lives and property, disrupted economies, and undermined governments. This book is an effort to provide a broad introduction to the prevalence and meaning of these events in the history of Latin America.

The Yungay earthquake of 1970 had significant repercussions at the national and international levels: the Peruvian government, then under the control of the nation's military, made the town a test case for its economic reconstruction efforts, directing national and international disaster relief efforts for the area and providing some emergency housing.[4] The government's efforts often had a hard edge. Threatening to relocate the inhabitants to other areas if they did not cooperate with the reconstruction effort, the government managed to instill a sense of common purpose in the Yungaínos, who struggled together to subsist in the disaster area. The scale and intrusiveness of government efforts also served to remind these provincials that ultimate political authority resided in Lima.

The catastrophe also attracted large-scale international relief efforts. Sixty nations sent aid in the days following the disaster, including medical teams from France, Italy, the United States, and South Africa. U.S. relief efforts included a $10 million grant to the Peruvian government. Revolutionary Cuba and the Soviet Union, among the United States' chief rivals in the Cold War, also sent substantial amounts of aid. The Soviets not only provided a strong medical presence, they also sought to demonstrate a commitment to the developing world by shipping prefabricated homes to Yungay. Despite good intentions, socialist architecture proved a poor fit in the Andes.[5] In the twentieth century there have been numerous examples of forceful large-scale relief efforts by outsiders in Latin America, but, as in Yungay, these forms of aid have often ignored local preferences or proven inappropriate or badly administered.

A year after the quake, more than twenty thousand residents of the Yungay region still lived in provisional housing. In a region where residents traditionally constructed housing of adobe or even thatch, national and international agencies commonly made temporary housing from aluminum and fiberboard sheeting. Some quake survivors referred to the camps constructed by relief agencies and the Peruvian government as "stables."[6] The reconstruction of Yungay itself moved at a snail's pace. Residents became so angry with Peruvian officials in charge of reconstruction that they threatened to tie them up and send them out of town mounted on burros. Among the many irritations experienced by residents was the decision by Peruvian relief officials to knock down the few surviving buildings to facilitate the construction of new streets and waterlines. International efforts proved flawed as well. One batch of clothing sent by the Alliance for Progress included used band uniforms donated in Austin, Texas.

Over the past two decades, growing numbers of historians and other social scientists have studied the impact of natural disasters in Latin America. Academic authors have examined floods, droughts, and hurricanes, as well as earthquakes and tsunamis. Much of this literature is narrative in nature, focusing on the terrible human costs accumulated in the wake of these destructive events and directed toward illuminating the large drama of political reaction and rebuilding. The testimonies of survivors and other firsthand accounts routinely provide the foundation for these studies.[7] Other scholars have argued that natural disasters provide a particularly efficacious opportunity to examine the social, cultural, and political structures of a society, because disaster strips away the routines and everyday understandings that obscure or conceal relations of hierarchy and power. Historical examinations of earthquakes, in particular, have demonstrated a convincing utility to reveal Latin America's social constructions, culture, and politics as well as its belief systems, religious practices, and superstitions.[8]

Among the natural disasters that have battered Latin American societies, earthquakes have gained a special place in the public imagination due to their destructiveness. The largest earthquake ever recorded in human history occurred in Chile in 1960, 9.5 on the Richter scale. While hurricanes have claimed nearly seventy thousand lives and caused enormous amounts of property destruction in the twentieth century, earthquakes have cost close to two hundred thousand lives and totaled much greater material loss. Earthquakes have also earned a special place in the region's consciousness. As in Yungay in 1970, the presumed substantial and solid foundation of all human activity, the earth itself, moves and shakes, undermining and subverting human ambition and achievement, bringing low the monuments of religion, politics, and the economy, as well as the humble homes of the poor. It is no wonder that most of the region's native peoples presumed that earthquakes were manifestations of divine will. Charles Darwin, perhaps the perfect representative of nineteenth-century science, recorded his reaction to a powerful quake that struck Chile in 1835. Darwin wrote, "A bad earthquake at once destroys the oldest associations; the world, the very emblem of all that is solid, has moved beneath our feet like a [thin] crust over a fluid." He went on to say, "One second of time has created in the mind a strong idea of insecurity, which hours of reflection would not have produced."[9]

Earthquakes not only sweep aside the built environment, leveling the homes of rich and poor alike, they destroy the physical settings of government and commerce. They also disrupt, if not dismantle, the social processes that organize and direct societies and cultures. As villages, towns, and cities attempt to recover from earthquakes, long-settled arrangements among families, classes, and institutions are tested and challenged in profound ways. Even where old structures and forms are reestablished following an earthquake, new meanings and new institutions can be developed as the society's experience of disaster transforms both expectations and behaviors. The physical destruction caused by an earthquake, like the one that crushed Yungay in 1970, forces political institutions and political actors to demonstrate their legitimacy and efficacy in new and challenging ways. In these unusual circumstances, governments and individual leaders can crumble just like buildings brought down by the powerful tremors of the initial seismic event.

This predictable, even inevitable, connection between earthquakes and politics originates in the material interface of nature and human society, the built environment. While earthquakes themselves can take thousands, even tens of thousands, of lives, these terrible costs have always been prepared by the accumulated result of prior societal action, the political processes that locate and concentrate human populations. These patterns of population concentration and building practices establish the conditions where lives are lost. Human beings as political actors forge social and economic relations that pull populations together in dense arrays. Governments lay out streets, direct construction, and regulate the essential rhythms of every society. Economies distribute wealth in ways that determine the resilience or vulnerability of businesses and homes. When disasters strike, governments act quickly to organize life-saving efforts and determine reconstruction priorities that commonly reflect class organization and political affiliations. These decisions multiply or limit the loss of life and pace of recovery. As the shock of the event wears off, survivors always assess blame, judge political decisions, and live with consequences. Every earthquake trails behind itself a path of political judgment.

One broadly experienced outcome of earthquake relief in Latin America is that government institutions and politicians are forced into closer proximity with the governed. In these moments of turmoil and destruction, the agents of government are, in effect, forced into the street to invent policies and allocate resources in highly public settings. With bureaucratic functions interrupted, police and judicial authorities forced out of their routines, and markets dismantled, the personal qualities of political leaders, qualities stripped of the contextual supports that sustain them in normal times, are revealed in a stark light that invites comment and criticism.

In the wake of disaster, this forced intimacy of rulers and ruled predictably leads to a more hostile and more combustible political environment, where a society's formerly routine decisions and procedures face critical scrutiny. This was certainly true following the destructive quakes of 1976 in Guatemala, 1972 in Nicaragua, and 1970 in Mexico, but it was also present in colonial Peru in 1746 and independence-era Venezuela in 1812. In all these cases, a new and larger public discussed the competence and legitimacy of political leaders and political institutions in the context of relief efforts and rebuilding. In these circumstances, few public officials escaped without criticism. In all the cases discussed in this collection, the disposition of police and military assets, for example, were understood to be decisions about whose property would be protected and whose would be sacrificed. Survivors commonly read the priorities established for construction as either recognizing and reinforcing or ignoring or challenging preexisting hierarchies of wealth and power.[10] Decisions to rebuild a cathedral or church before a court or administrative building were commonly understood as reinforcing or undermining institutional authority.

In the colonial era, viceroys, judges, and other administrators often expressed exasperation when faced by public criticism or civil disorder following a natural disaster. Administrators who had risen in the colonial bureaucracy through their careful cultivation of powerful mentors and their equally careful selection of marriage partners were exposed in unfamiliar ways by these calamities to popular demands for immediate and decisive action, action outside the comfortable confines of imperial policies or established local custom. They also typically lacked adequate local fiscal resources. Some waited for directions from Spain while others invented policies and found resources without consultation. Both reactions could be dangerous, because delay might further provoke local resentment, and the appropriation of the king's resources without permission might ruin a promising career. Spanish authorities in secondary cities like Quito or Guatemala City, regardless of their skill or competence, were even more dependent on decisions and resource allocations made at a distance. Viceroys, the highest level of colonial administration, were as jealous as the king in protecting their prerogatives and funds.[11]

By the end of the nineteenth century, many republican governments were more muscular and ambitious than their colonial antecedents. The leaders of new nations were also more accustomed than colonial-era administrators to the use of public ritual and direct communication with electorates. As a result, they reacted quickly in the wake of earthquakes to secure public favor and direct popular opinion in support of their actions. Nevertheless, even experienced politicians routinely found themselves mercilessly criticized for their responses to the destructiveness of these disasters. In these moments of extreme stress, perceptions of administrative incompetence and individual selfishness or allegations of corruption, real or imagined, could lead to public demands for regime change. The failure of the Estrada Cabrera government in Guatemala to provide housing and employment following the earthquake of 1917 or to deal with the epidemics that followed, for example, led to working-class support for the opposition.[12] Even the long-established dictatorship of the Somoza family in Nicaragua found it difficult to recover from popular reactions to its policies and to well-founded reports of corruption in the administration of international aid (see the essay by Paul Dosal in this collection).

No postdisaster decision was more likely to produce conflict than the decision to relocate a population to a new site. These discussions proved more politically disruptive and difficult to manage than any other. Much of Mexico, Central America, and the Andean region is situated in zones of intense seismic activity. As a result, many of the region's towns and cities have borne multiple seismic blows. Earthquakes repeatedly struck colonial Chile, Peru, Ecuador, and Guatemala. While colonial author-ities poorly understood the geology of their situation, they did realize that some locations were apparently more subject to earthquakes than others. With the second or third experience of earthquakes, authorities were inevitably drawn into discussing relocation. In colonial Guatemala, Ecuador, and Peru, imperial authorities initiated or reacted to discussions of relocating populations to more stable sites. Because relocation to a new site potentially undermined existing property rights and unsettled hierar-chies of wealth and power, even determined Spanish administrators were routinely thwarted by local elites determined to protect their economic and social advantages, regardless of the cost and risk attached to future seismic threats.

In the national period, these debates had a more potent popular char-acter because competing voices over relocation or other policy issues sought and found audiences and allies in the mass media. Factions were formed, leaders were found, and mobilizations developed in the streets and other public places. In this collection, contributors examine in detail debates over the possible relocation of cities destroyed by earthquakes in twentieth-century Guatemala, Argentina, and Nicaragua. It is clear from these cases that these debates about relocation should be seen by historians as struggles over power. Earthquakes shake loose the political arrange-ments and accommodations that have held firm for years, if not decades. The pressing needs of the emergency push aside the habits and routines so useful to legitimacy. In place of these comfortable patterns that work reliably in normal times, survivors, in the wake of earthquakes and other disasters, press for immediate actions, judging politicians and political institutions almost daily.

The experience of earthquake and recovery typically play out within well-worn categories, guided by the everyday structures of human society. Nearly everywhere, survivors and more distant observers look for mean-ing, often finding God's hand directing the destruction and selecting the victims. In Yungay the earthquake and avalanches and mudslides devas-tated urban residences of the whites and mestizos who had long benefited from Peru's exploitation of the indigenous, while sparing many indige-nous villages located at higher altitudes on less desirable land. This caused some to ask if this was not a judgment of God. Religious interpretations were more prevalent in the colonial era, where the imputation of religious

Statue of Christ at Cemetery Hill overlooking Yungay, which,
together with four palm trees, is all that remains of the city
(IMAGE 7, PERU, 1970, U.S. GEOLOGICAL SURVEY PHOTOGRAPHIC LIBRARY).

significance to earthquakes was routine. As Charles Walker's and Stuart
McCook's essays in this volume demonstrate, many inhabitants of Lima
and Caracas interpreted the respective earthquakes of 1746 and 1812 as
evidence of God's wrath.

In both cases, this religious dimension implied a critique of the ways
of life of the governing classes—in the first case, the wealthy and corrupt leadership of the viceregal capital of Peru, and, in the second case,
the secular independence movement of Simón Bolívar. Religious leaders
reminded the inhabitants of both cities to turn their backs on their godless leadership and return to a righteous path, presumably one under their
own tutelage. At a time when popular expectations of government earthquake relief remained relatively low (and when the colonial government
responded to the immediate needs of the population as well as it could; at

least in the major cities), popular protest chiefly manifested itself along religious lines.[13] As McCook argues, disasters were seen as divine punishment for earthly sins.

In Lima, a baroque city in which the wealthy ostentatiously displayed their fortunes, the earthquake/tsunami of 1746 not only killed approximately 10 percent of the capital's population but also afforded the deeply religious majority of the population a chance to lash out at what they perceived as decadence and sinfulness. For example, both groups and individuals blamed the earthquake on the risqué clothing of elite women, the decadence of the religious orders, and the conspicuous consumption of the rich. Not for nothing was Lima known as the City of Kings—by far the most opulent city of the Andes. Ten years later, as Walker relates, a Franciscan priest announced at Mass that a small group of nuns had experienced premonitions in which great balls of fire would strike the City of Kings as a manifestation of God's wrath, and that the earthquake had been merely a warning to the residents of Lima to mend their ways. This priest and others placed the 1746 earthquake in the context of a long list of calamities in the surrounding region that included an earlier earthquake, an epidemic, social revolts, and crop failures. According to the priest and like-minded clergy, the calamity was only one in a series of punishments for a licentious city that had turned away from God.

In Caracas at the beginning of the nineteenth century, calamity struck at the time of an independence movement many saw as precipitous and misguided. On Holy Thursday 1810, the city's elites had deposed the Spanish captain general. This event had marked the first step toward the declaration of Venezuela's independence from Spain during the following year—a step supported by a creole urban elite faction but not a large-scale, grassroots movement. Hence opposition to independence erupted immediately, and Caracas could not gain control of royalist strongholds such as Coro and Maracaibo. Two years later, another earthquake hit on Holy Thursday, striking a city set to celebrate both its independence movement and Holy Week. When disaster hit on the anniversary of the first step toward independence, the symbolic potency was not lost on the factions battling for supremacy in Venezuela. As a result, the royalist opposition attempted to politicize the event, claiming that the earthquake was evidence of God's wrath for having rebelled against a divinely ordained king. Meanwhile, most of the patriots—and first and foremost, their leader, Simón Bolívar—insisted that the earthquake was an act of nature that had nothing to do with the politics of the day. As McCook demonstrates, citizens personalized the disaster as punishment for their own sins rather than regard it as a condemnation of political structures. Therefore, the discourse surrounding the earthquake was overtly religious and, at best, covertly political. The archbishop, for example, likened Caracas to the biblical cities of Sodom and Gomorrah—cities destroyed by God's wrath for the sins of their inhabitants. In particular, the archbishop hinted at the patriots' decision to allow freedom of worship as one of the sins to be punished by God. Thus, one way in which the earthquake damaged the independence movement was by redirecting popular attention toward divine explanatory models rather than the secular, progressive-minded mentality advocated by the patriot elite.

In both Lima and Caracas, postdisaster religious discourse therefore served to discredit modernity in colonial cities. In contrast, the authors of four chapters on the twentieth-century earthquakes in Valparaíso, Chile (1906); San Juan, Argentina (1944); Managua, Nicaragua (1972); and Mexico City (1985) note the decreased role of religious explanations in the popular political discourse, and a correspondingly greater engagement with the secular state and its obligation to provide effective relief to the victims. The only exception to this trend was the Guatemala City earthquake of 1976, which occurred against a backdrop of competing secular, Catholic, and evangelical Protestant explanations.

The destructiveness of earthquakes also reveals existing social and economic fault lines, giving rise to new expressions of class conflict. The Holy Thursday earthquake in Venezuela highlighted class and racial differences that separated the radical creole proindependence faction and the mixed-race majority of the colony's population. The postcolonial leadership replaced many forms of legalized racial discrimination of the Spanish colony with new forms of prejudice, limiting suffrage to male, property-owning creoles, for example. Facing armed resistance from Spanish loyalists and starved for funds since the declaration of independence, the patriot treasury could not fund substantial relief efforts in the aftermath of the earthquake. Having raised popular expectations with the proclamation of a republic that supposedly existed to serve all of its citizens, the patriots could not meet these expectations and confronted widespread poor and middle-class protests in their own strongholds. In the case of the 1906 earthquake that severely damaged the port of Valparaíso, Chile, Samuel Martland demonstrates that the Chilean authorities feared strikes and a general social uprising in the wake of the destruction. As a result, the government harshly cracked down on suspected and convicted criminals. To be sure, the Valparaíso case also showed the possibility of class harmony in the aftermath of disaster, as observers noted that rich and poor citizens worked together to care for the injured, provide basic services, and rebuild their city. The difference in this case was an energetic government that noted the potential for social disruption in Chile's premier port city and provided prompt assistance, while in Venezuela in 1812 a weak government facing an armed opposition dropped the ball.

Earthquakes can therefore sometimes provide new opportunities for hitherto disadvantaged groups. In the case of Lima, the women who claimed to have experienced the premonitions about the balls of fire that would destroy their city took center stage in an unusual degree of prominence for women in Lima's patriarchal society. Judges of the inquisitorial court paid rapt attention as women recounted dreams in which fire falling from the sky destroyed their city. Although some of these women may have appeared in court coerced by authorities, it is likely that the premonitions expressed genuine anxiety about the future, shared by a group excluded from power. In the aftermath of the Mexico City earthquake of 1985, looters took what they could not have stolen otherwise. In addition, the quake served as a catalyst for political mobilization of the city's middle classes— and particularly of the residents in the worst stricken area near the Plaza de las Tres Culturas in Tlatelolco. As Louise Walker demonstrates, the earthquake led left-leaning middle-class residents to compare their plight to those of the revolutionaries of Nicaragua and El Salvador, who in the former case were besieged by a U.S.-backed force composed primarily of former Somoza supporters, and in the latter case by a repressive government backed by right-wing death squads. In the words of Mexican intellectual Carlos Monsiváis, the earthquake marked the emergence of civil society in Mexico City.

One of the greatest reasons for the widespread social, cultural, and political impact of earthquakes is that they do not affect all inhabitants equally. In revolutionary Venezuela of 1812, the tremor primarily damaged areas held by Simón Bolívar's patriot government, while the royalist strongholds emerged unscathed. As a result, the earthquake helped shift the balance in the military conflict between the two sides toward the royalists and contributed to the emergence of Francisco de Miranda's dictatorship in Caracas—an authoritarian regime that served only to alienate more citizens from the patriots. Likewise, the Valparaíso earthquake of 1906 disproportionately affected the wealthy, who lived near the quake-prone coast rather than up in the hills. In contrast, the mansions of the rich built on volcanic soil withstood the Mexico City quake of 1985, and the disaster largely spared the shantytowns of that city, while the poorly constructed condominiums of Tlatelolco collapsed to bury part of the middle class. All three of these examples differ from the experience of the Yungaínos. There no one, whether rich or poor, could escape the virtually complete destruction brought on by the 1970 earthquake, although some indigenous villages nearby were spared.

Earthquakes have also helped undermine the established political order since colonial times. In the 1740s, the Inquisition in Lima tried the priest who had revealed the religion-based premonitions of the destruction of the city, and the case led to confrontations among both high clergy and politicians, pitting Archbishop Pedro de Barroeta against Inquisitor Mateo de Amusquíbar, whom the archbishop blamed for circulating the premonitions and stirring up fear among the local population. In the 1810s, the earthquake in Venezuela shook up the patriot government, dividing former allies and strengthening loyalist opponents.

Politics became an even more central part of historical processes affected by earthquakes after the consolidation of the Latin American nation-states in the late nineteenth century. Mark Healey's chapter on the San Juan earthquake of 1944 highlights the fact that this earthquake brought the poverty and underdevelopment of Argentina's rural periphery into stark relief and led to proposals to address this problem, including those of Juan and Evita Perón and their populist political allies. Just like in Mexico City forty years later, the earthquake exposed faulty building construction that had exacerbated the human cost of the disaster. The calamity thus helped spark a national conversation on political and social reform that would continue for the rest of the decade.

As Paul Dosal relates, the 1972 quake in Managua exposed the corruption and repression of the Somoza clan—a family of dictators that had ruled Nicaragua for thirty-five years. It also undermined the long-standing U.S. support for a dynasty founded by Anastasio Somoza García, a West Point graduate about whom U.S. president Franklin D. Roosevelt had once reportedly said, "Somoza may be a son of a bitch, but he's *our* son of a bitch." By 1972, Somoza's younger son, Anastasio Somoza Debayle, was in power. When the gang of the younger Somoza sold blood supplies his government had received from the Red Cross for its own benefit, the president alienated the foreign public opinion crucial for the survival of his regime, forcing U.S. president Richard Nixon to repeat Roosevelt's old mantra. This response indirectly helped pave the way for the Nicaraguan Revolution of 1979, which toppled the Somoza clan after forty-two years of rule. To be sure, as historian Matilde Zimmermann reminds us, the failure of postdisaster relief in Managua did not lead to any widespread condemnation in Nicaragua, particularly among the lower classes.[14] But the inefficient and even cynical response of the Nicaraguan government proved decisive in turning the middle classes, once staunch defenders of the Somoza regime, into passive bystanders when the socialist Sandinista movement challenged the vintage dictatorship.

Virginia Garrard-Burnett develops this connection between natural disaster and political discontent further, arguing in her chapter on the 1976 earthquake in Guatemala that an earthquake can also serve as a detonator of revolution. In this case, it was a major enabling element in the left-wing guerrilla warfare that challenged the brutal Guatemalan military regime that had come to power with U.S. assistance more than two decades earlier. In the aftermath of the quake, the guerrillas found it far easier to recruit, and rebel groups greatly expanded their base of operation. Likewise, the popular church in Guatemala—and particularly those members of the clergy associated with liberation theology—viewed the earthquake as a call for social justice and the building of a new society. In response, the Guatemalan military undertook scorched-earth tactics against indigenous villages and took their brutal campaign of repression to new heights. By all accounts, the period 1978–83 represented the bloody climax of repression in Guatemala under military rule.

Likewise, Walker demonstrates that the 1985 earthquake in Mexico City highlighted graft in both the relief effort and construction industry. Mexico at this time was ruled by the Partido Revolucionario Institucional (PRI), an official revolutionary party that had been in power since 1929 under three different names. The PRI claimed to represent the aspirations of the Mexican Revolution of 1910, a movement that began with the goal of overthrowing dictator Porfirio Díaz but ended up as an effort to seek wide-ranging social change, including labor reform and the parceling out of hacienda land among landless campesinos. However, the party had lost credibility for its handling of the student opposition in 1968, when police killed hundreds of peaceful protesters at the Plaza de las Tres

Culturas in Tlatelolco, and of the 1982 debt crisis, a consequence of the heavy indebtedness of the Mexican government that ended in the curtailment or abolition of many government programs to help the poor. In Mexico City, the 1985 earthquake further shook the public's confidence in their government and hence contributed to the PRI's first-ever loss at the presidential polls fifteen years later. The government had abolished the city's Prevention of Disasters and Management of Risk office one year prior to the earthquake and had developed a top-secret plan that it refused to divulge when the political opposition demanded that it be revealed so that the leadership could be held accountable. The PRI leadership in Mexico City had also conspired with corrupt contractors to build structurally inadequate apartment complexes that collapsed like houses of cards when the quake hit.

Finally, earthquakes offer a chance to rebuild human settlements along the prevalent spirit of the day or to build sturdier architecture better equipped for absorbing seismic shocks. The Bourbons rebuilt eighteenth-century Lima as a modern city; the elites of Valparaíso constructed an art nouveau city on the rubble of a colonial one; the Argentine city of San Juan reemerged in the age of modernism; and the quaint town of Yungay got rebuilt in the style of the 1970s with prefabricated cookie-cutter homes. Other regimes did not take advantage of the opportunity provided by the rebuilding of cities. For example, the Valparaíso leadership learned little from the disaster of 1906 and reconstructed the city with the same type of structures that had collapsed in the earthquake.

The essays that follow permit the reader a glimpse of the broad regional significance of this phenomenon. Earthquakes have been common occurrences in most Latin American nations. Five present-day Latin American nations have experienced more than ten severe earthquakes since Spanish colonization: Chile (eleven), Colombia (sixteen), Ecuador (ten), Mexico (seventeen), and Peru (eighteen). In addition, there were more than twenty-two significant earthquakes in Central America. Indeed, it is no coincidence that the U.S. anthropologist Eric Wolf labeled the ancient Mesoamericans the "sons of the shaking earth," in reference to the significance of earthquakes in Central American and southern Mexican history.[15]

More than anything, the comparative analysis of earthquakes and other natural disasters reveals the human role in shaping the interaction with our environment. Our built environment exacerbates the damage in human and economic terms, and disasters become political events because our species judges the quality of our institutions in part by their response to emergencies. Earthquakes therefore lay bare essential economic, political, and social structures, providing space for popular movements to question and reshape them.

✛ NOTES ✛

1. This description of the event closely follows the report published in the *New York Times* (H. J. Maidenberg, "U.S. Envoy Surveys Peru from Air and Finds Chaos," June 5, 1970).

2. A year after the quake the *New York Times* estimated that forty thousand to fifty thousand had died in the immediate area of Yungay (Juan de Onis, "Year Later, Peru Still Battles Quake Damage," June 2, 1971).

3. Anthony Oliver-Smith, *The Martyred City: Death and Rebirth in the Andes* (Albuquerque: University of New Mexico Press, 1986), ix–11. See also Barbara Bode, *No Bells to Toll: Destruction and Creation in the Andes* (New York: Charles Scribner's Sons, 1989), for the experiences of another U.S. anthropologist who worked in the area following the quake.

4. See also Bode, *No Bells to Toll*; and "La catástrofe sísmico de mayo de 1970," *Boletín de la Sociedad Geográfica de Lima* 89 (1969–70): 3–32, for the destructive consequences of this event.

5. Bode, *No Bells to Toll*, 97, 235–39.

6. de Onis, "Year Later."

7. As an example, see Porfirio Barba Jacob, *El terremoto de San Salvador: narración de un superviviente, 1917* (Bogotá, Colombia: Villegas, 2001); and Elena Poniatowska, *Nothing, Nobody: The Voices of the Mexican City Earthquake*, trans. Aurora Camacho de Schmidt (Philadelphia: Temple University Press, 1995).

8. This is not the place to provide a comprehensive list of publications. Among many meritorious works are Franco Fernández Esquivel, *Terremoto: los terremotos de Cartago en 1910* (Cartago, Costa Rica: Uruk, 1995); Martha Fernández García, *Ciudad rota: la Ciudad de México después del sismo* (Mexico City: UNAM, 1990); Lawrence H. Feldman, *Mountains of Fire, Lands That Shake: Earthquakes and Volcanic Eruptions in the Historic Past of Central America, 1505–1899* (Culver City, CA: Labyrinthos, 1993); Cleto González Víquez, *Temblores, terremotos, inundaciones, y erupciones volcánicas en Costa Rica, 1608–1910* (Cartago, Costa Rica: Editorial Tecnológica de Costa Rica, 1994);

Jesús Emilio Ramírez, *Historia de los terremotos en Colombia*, 2nd ed. (Bogotá: Editorial Argara, 1969); and Charles F. Walker, *Shaky Colonialism: The 1746 Earthquake-Tsunami in Lima, Peru, and Its Long Aftermath* (Durham, NC: Duke University Press, 2008).

9. Quoted in Carmen Oquendo-Villar, "Pinochet: General Earthquake," *Revista, Harvard Review of Latin America*, Winter 2007, 52.

10. In the Yungay region a left-leaning Catholic priest complained that the Peruvian government did not include a broad land reform to improve the lot of the rural poor. See de Onis, "Year Later."

11. See André Saint-Lu, "Movimientos sísmicos, perturbaciones psíquicas y alborotos sociopolíticos en Santiago de Guatemala," *Revista de Indias* 42, no. 169/70 (1982): 545–58.

12. Oscar Guillermo Peláez Almengor, *La nueva Guatemala de la Asunción y los terremotos de 1917–18* (Guatemala City: Universidad de San Carlos, 1994).

13. Charles F. Walker, "Shaking the Unstable Empire: The Lima, Quito, and Arequipa Earthquakes, 1746, 1783, and 1797," in *Dreadful Visitations: Confronting Natural Catastrophe in the Age of Enlightenment*, ed. Alessa Johns (New York: Routledge, 1999), 138.

14. Matilde Zimmermann, *Sandinista: Carlos Fonseca and the Nicaraguan Revolution* (Durham, NC: Duke University Press, 2000).

15. Eric Wolf, *Sons of the Shaking Earth: The Peoples of Mexico and Guatemala; Their Land, History, and Culture* (Chicago: University of Chicago Press, 1964).

CHAPTER ONE

Great Balls of Fire

Premonitions and the Destruction of Lima, 1746

CHARLES F. WALKER

❧

✠ ON OCTOBER 28, 1746, AT 10:30 P.M., A MASSIVE EARTHQUAKE RIPPED open Lima, the capital of the viceroyalty of Peru. It shattered buildings, hurtling adobes, beams, facades, balconies, and the heavy bells that graced churches upon its victims. The wall that surrounded much of the city also toppled over. It damaged most of the city's approximately seventy-five churches, convents, and monasteries; one exaggerated report calculated that only twenty-five houses remained standing.[1] The viceroy, José Manso de Velasco, described Lima as "a frightening place, like a war scene put to the sword and set to fire, its beautiful buildings turned into piles of dirt and stones."[2] This bustling, multiracial city of fifty thousand, the heart of Spain's territories in South America, lay in ruins.

A two-hundred-mile stretch of the Nazca tectonic plate had lurched under the continental plate about a hundred miles off the coast of Peru. As the underwater fault surged, it not only sent shockwaves but also pushed up parts of the sea floor. This prompted waves that moved across the Pacific at jet airplane speeds. The waves magnified in power and height as they reached shore, merging in a looming, destructive tower of water. Eerie

18

sounds of water receding indicated imminent horrors just before the wave hit. This fifty-foot mass of water struck Lima's port, Callao, at 11:00 p.m., half an hour after the earthquake. The tsunami obliterated the city, leaving little evidence of what had been a bustling commercial hub and the centerpiece of Peru's defenses. Less than two hundred of Callao's five thousand to six thousand residents survived. Some had found themselves inland at the time of the tsunami while others had miraculously stayed afloat on driftwood or even on a large painting of Saint Joseph, or clung to the top of the one bastion of Callao's perimeter wall that withstood the wave. Lima merchants who had houses or warehouses in the port had trouble identifying the location of their property—nothing remained.[3]

Although estimates of the number of dead in Lima range from 1,300 to 15,000, a total of 5,000, or about 10 percent of the population, appears to be a reasonable calculation. This number includes the thousands who died in the epidemics after the catastrophe, when water was scarce and sanitation appalling.[4] Hundreds of aftershocks, the gruesome discoveries of buried bodies or cadavers washed up on the beaches, the sounds of tumbling buildings, the stench of rotting human and animal flesh, a crime wave, and the shortage of food and water made life miserable. The viceroy worked efficiently to ensure sufficient food and water and to find emergency shelter. He worried that Lima's precise urban code, set in stone by the Spaniards in 1535, would be lost if people remained dispersed in gardens, plazas, and outside of the city's tumbled-down walls. For his efforts, he was given the title of Conde de Superunda (Count Over the Waves). He drafted an elaborate plan to rebuild Lima along enlightenment or absolutist urban ideas of the eighteenth century. His program to "rationalize" the city and to centralize power in his office, however, met broad opposition from almost all of the city's residents and corporate groups, including the patrician upper class, the Catholic Church, and the multiracial lower classes.[5]

The debates about how to rebuild Lima were inextricably linked to discussions and controversies about the earthquake's origin. A few erudite souls discussed natural causes, replicating the worldwide division in this era before plate tectonics between those who blamed subterranean gases and those who stressed water seeping underground and weakening the earth.[6] The vast majority of Lima's inhabitants, however, saw it as a sign of God's wrath, angry at the city's well-known decadent ways. In speeches, masses, processions, and publications, groups and individuals denounced the immorality of Lima and suggested how to correct it. They reproached women's independent ways and risqué clothing as well as the decadence of the religious orders with particular vehemence. Guilt and fear about the prospect of further divine wrath due to Lima's errant behavior paralyzed much of the population. Some took consolation in the belief that the punishment could be prevented if they amended their sinful ways. Divine rather than natural explanations of earthquakes have their advantages.

Concerns about God's wrath and Lima's decadence did not begin with the earthquake. This eminently baroque city had a long history of religious figures beseeching the city's population to change its behavior and to take heed of telluric warnings. Most of Peru's prominent colonial saints or images—San Francisco Solano, Santa Rosa de Lima, El Señor de los Milagros, and others—had their own earthquake miracle stories and had equated these catastrophes with God's displeasure. In the eighteenth century, fears about divine wrath mixed with widespread concern about the decline of Lima's economic and political importance. A citywide panic after the earthquake prompted by religious women's premonitions takes us into this world of fear, apprehension, and recrimination.

Cloistered Voices

On November 7, 1756, ten years and ten days after the earthquake, the Franciscan priest Joaquín Parra gave Mass in his order's main church, San Francisco. The first Sunday of each month was dedicated to the Sacred Heart of Christ and usually attracted a large and prominent crowd. Among those present were Mateo de Amusquíbar, the head of the Peruvian Inquisition, and the eminent lawyer Manuel de Silva y la Banda. Father Parra stunned the audience and prompted a citywide panic and years of judicial wrangling as he described the premonitions of a small group of nuns and other religious women. All had a common theme: due to its inhabitants' licentious ways and disregard for previous warnings, the City of Kings, as Lima was known, would soon be the victim of God's wrath in the form of balls of fire falling from the sky. Although forewarned, few if any would survive the flames. While spreading the blame widely, the nuns targeted the failings of the religious community, particularly the orders, and the sinful customs of the city. The 1746 earthquake was seen as an unheeded warning, a staggering first blow. News about the Mass spread through the city's well-developed rumor and gossip circuits, bringing to the surface profound fears shared by most of the population. Father Parra himself became the subject of an extended inquiry, as the Inquisition, the archbishop, and the Franciscans fought over who should try him for disseminating these possibly heretical visions.

Parra's trials shed light on the usually hidden struggles among these different institutions. The inquisitor Amusquíbar locked horns with the irascible archbishop, Pedro de Barroeta. The Franciscans, in turn, gingerly attempted to keep the investigation internal and thus shield Father Parra from the judicial arms of the Inquisition and the Archbishopric. Much more interesting, however, are the premonitions themselves and the panic that they prompted. The Inquisition records include detailed accounts of both the nuns' painful experience of these visions and their chilling content. Each woman envisioned different forms of God's wrath, including various types of fireballs, fire-breathing bulls, and wretched demons who obscenely taunted women. They also encountered a mournful Jesus walking the streets of Lima, talking statues and images, and messages in the sky. Their visions display immediate obsessions as well as more enduring fears and nightmares.

The premonitions defined a cycle that began with the severe and obvious warning of the 1746 earthquake and would end with even more devastating catastrophes. All of the visionaries saw the earthquake and tsunami as earth-shattering warnings that had not been heeded. The cycle also included revolts that had taken place in Lima and in the nearby Andes in 1750, the ongoing Juan Santos Atahualpa uprising in the jungle to the east, and, across the Atlantic, the Lisbon earthquake that had taken place on November 1, 1755, just over a year before Parra's Mass. Yet the nuns' accounts also reflected longer-term concerns or patterns. The nuns shared with many of the city's residents the belief that Lima had been hexed since the late seventeenth century. The 1687 earthquake, subsequent agricultural decline (what was called "sterility of the fields"), the 1718–1723 epidemic that killed over two hundred thousand people, and intermittent pirate attacks were also signs of God's rising anger with the City of Kings.

The 1680s to 1750s had witnessed constant discussions about Lima's sinful ways and their relationship with its decline. It lost its political hegemony in South America with the creation of the New Granada (1739) and, subsequently, Rio de la Plata viceroyalties (1776), while the emergence of Atlantic ports such as Buenos Aires threatened Callao. Its population had grown slowly in the eighteenth century. Economic and political worries surfaced in the premonition panics. While modern analysts might see these premonitions and widespread fear as a manifestation of the concerns about the waning position of the city and a display of baroque religiosity, contemporaries, however, had the opposite explanation. They blamed the city's social and political stagnation and possible destruction on its sinful ways.

The debates over the premonitions transport us into the depths of the cloisters and the city's deep religious fervor. It is deliciously ironic that nuns—women who cloistered themselves or "retired" from the mundane world—provide us with these insights. While the voices of the nuns are filtered—the testimonies are almost all from their confessors—their premonitions and the deep concern about the implications of what they were saying for the safety of the city provide uniquely vivid testimony on eighteenth-century Lima. They bring to the fore concerns about the weakening division between sacred and mundane spaces.

Sins, Saints, and Earthquakes

Since Lima's founding in 1535, earthquakes, sins, and saints were so intertwined that much of what occurred in 1746 and 1755 seems almost timeless, possible in the sixteenth, seventeenth, or eighteenth centuries and beyond. Collective panics and public pleas for penitence and redemption were common in this pious city that seemed to have more than its share of "natural disasters." In 1664–1665, for example, anxious Lima inhabitants interpreted comets as signs of impending divine punishment.[7] The 1755 events formed part of a perceived cycle of crises dating from the late seventeenth century. Luis Miguel Glave deems 1680–1693 the highpoint of "baroque fatalism" in Peru, listing a shocking array of epidemics, famine, earthquakes, and other maladies.[8] The wall surrounding the city embodied the growing anxieties of its residents, the fears of baroque Lima.[9] In the same year that the wall was completed, 1687, a strong earthquake struck Lima. Writers in the eighteenth century, echoed in the twentieth, blamed the earthquake for Lima's agricultural decline, claiming that it had "sterilized" the land and forced open the door to Chilean competition, particularly for wheat. Eighteenth-century Lima residents experienced other signs of crisis, decline, and, for many, divine ire. An epidemic from 1718 to 1723 killed seventy-two thousand people just in the archdiocese of Lima; British ships attacked the coast in the early 1740s; rebellions began to occur in the hinterland; and Lima's political and economic weight vis-à-vis Mexico and its South American competitors declined.[10] Apocalyptic thought and stern counterreformation texts and evangelization reverberated in Lima, deepening the city's anguish and the residents' search for another sign of God's anger.

At the heart of the nun's premonitions was the decades-long debate about the sinful ways of Lima's inhabitants. This was the overwhelming message of their visions—that God had sent a severe warning in 1746 and was soon to inflict a much greater punishment. More than a manifestation of Lima's seeming political and economic decline, their visions focused on divine anger and the need for rapid redemption. Sermons and paintings that stressed the apocalyptic beliefs of Saint Augustine and Joachim of Fiora, both deeply rooted in the Americas, helped nourish these concerns about the end of the world.[11]

Since the Middle Ages, many believed that women had special communication powers and embodied true Christian piety. Saints such as Catherine of Siena (1347–1380) and Teresa of Avila (1515–1582) emerged in Europe and became important figures in the Americas. With the Counter-Reformation, the proliferation of the tales of saints and the fervent battles against the Protestant north had further encouraged a female religiosity that emphasized mystical experiences such as revelations and premonitions. Pierre Chaunu refers to a "feminization" of Counter-Reformation religiosity.[12] Since the Council of Trent (1543–1563), however, the Catholic Church had also attempted to rein in female mysticism, questioning medieval notions about women's particular sensitivity to God's message and discouraging nuns' and other women's physical, almost sensual, experience of the Lord.[13]

Female aesthetes—nuns, *beatas*, *alumbradas*, and others—had constituted a key element of Lima's population since its founding, venerated by many and intermittently challenged by the Inquisition. In the eighteenth century, the Bourbon regalist program revived the campaign against them. The divergent notions of female religiosity clashed in the anguish and trials over the 1755 premonitions. Many of the testimonies referred to the belief that women had a special gift and thus needed to be heeded. They shed light on the heterodoxy of female religiosity, which thrived in part because it took place offstage, in convents, worship houses, and processions, and was nurtured by popular culture. Archbishop Barroeta, however, dismissed this view, presenting the visions as a mere reflection of women's "weakness" and simplemindedness. He understood female mysticism as an unfortunate remnant of baroque and lower-class religious practices that needed to be extirpated.[14]

Who to Blame?

The news about Parra's sermon disseminated quickly throughout the city. For some, it was terrifying news; for others, it confirmed rumors about premonitions and signs of God's ire. One testimony provides insight into how the information spread: "[F]ull of very Christian fears, Manuel de Silva, being very persuaded and thus telling everything to everyone in his house, caused his wife great consternation, not shielding it from her despite the fact that she was very ill, and the news reached her very extensive family and from there to others, so that by that evening there was not a person who had not learned the news, affecting everyone differently according to the state of his or her conscience."[15] Authorities acted quickly, due in part to their concern about the panic and the threatened destruction of Lima but also due to their interest in avoiding blame and assuring that their institution judged Parra.

The archbishop of Lima, Pedro Antonio de Barroeta, sent two clerks on the following morning to summon Parra. He was out of Lima on the day of the Mass and would later be criticized for acting slowly. Barroeta was a controversial figure. Born in Ezcaray (La Rioja, Spain) in 1701, he arrived in Peru in 1748 and was archbishop until 1757. He fought incessantly against Manso de Velasco, writing hundreds of memos against the viceroy and his inner circle. The viceroy bitterly noted that Barroeta had conflicts with "almost all the Tribunals, and he filled the city with edicts and mandates, greatly confusing the residents."[16] Part of this was personal—Barroeta was a confrontational character who believed that Manso and his followers had slighted him since his arrival. He complained endlessly about etiquette breaches (how he was greeted, where he was seated at receptions, etc.) and attacked Manso's supporters with shockingly personal insinuations about dark-skinned lovers, black ancestors, and leprosy.[17] Beyond his own cantankerous nature, his countless written complaints also demonstrate his role as a stern reformer of the church. With the same vigor with which he took on the viceroy and the Inquisition, he battled the heterodox nature of Peruvian Catholicism, attempting to rein in the orders and homogenize religious practices. He campaigned against raucous processions and other religious celebrations, baroque sermons, profane music, sensual festivities, and other "excesses."[18]

The clerks found Parra on their second short trip from the cathedral to San Francisco and Barroeta interrogated him on that same day. He was accused of spreading false and dangerous revelations or rumors and thus prompting a panic. This accusation hinged on whether the nuns and the premonitions were trustworthy, the focus of the investigation. Parra was initially evasive about the identity of the religious women, invoking the secrecy of the confessional, where much of the information had been gleaned.

From the beginning, his defense rested on three points. First, he had consulted with "distinguished people," including Barroeta and the inquisitor Amusquíbar, before the Mass. Barroeta did not deny this but instead, as will be seen later, shifted the blame to Amusquíbar. Second, Parra explained that he was not "making public" (*publicar*) or "breaking the news" about the premonitions but instead simply commenting on something quite well known and much discussed to calm the nerves of the people. In other words, he was not the first person to bring people's attention to these revelations. Parra developed this linguistic self-defense, contending that he did not "*predicar*" (preach or advocate), but instead was simply "spreading the news [*notiziar, hazer saber*]."[19] He insisted that before his mass "rumors were spreading in the city about several punishments."[20] He had not prompted the commotion—it already existed and he was attempting to calm it. For example, some women were falsely claiming to have had the premonitions and Parra implied that he was trying to stem copycat visions.[21] Other testimonies confirmed the spreading rumors in the weeks before Parra's sermon. In noting his skepticism about a woman who claimed to have had premonitions about the 1746 earthquake as well as the catastrophe that Parra and others predicted, Friar Juan Garro observed, "this year rumors were more widespread than ever, and it might be that hearing them would have enlivened her imagination."[22]

Finally, Parra and other priests justified their actions in biblical terms, contending that they were simply transmitting God's will. Parra cited Saint Paul ("Do not quench the Spirit. Do not despise the words of prophets, but test everything; hold fast to what is good") and chapter 3 of the book of Amos to support the notion that God did not punish his kingdom without a warning. Parra, as well as his Franciscan brother Garro, cited textually the lines from Amos: "Surely the Lord God does / Nothing, / Without revealing

his secret / To his servants the prophet." Their reading of Jeremiah, chapter 5, made them wonder whether fire might be a mere symbol and that
another form of punishment such as the plague was what God intended for
Lima.[23] Parra used the Bible to support his announcement of the premonitions. He and the other priests believed that God sent warnings; they also
understood from their readings that the punishment would be gruesome.

On November 16, Barroeta excommunicated Parra due to the Mass
and his refusal to give names. He continued to interrogate him into early
1757. The Franciscans refused to recognize Barroeta's jurisdiction and
battled against the archbishop. The real dispute, however, was between
Barroeta and Amusquíbar. The archbishop accused the inquisitor of being
"the author or at least the principal promoter of the revelations, which
prompted great fear in the city, as well as much censurable behavior, in
light of the fact that someone of such rank and office would find himself mixed up in such flippancy [*ligereza*] and deeds of less reflexive people, above all nuns and *beatas*, who for their gender and weak condition,
are so prone to understanding any dream or fantasy as revelations." He
accused Amusquíbar of frequenting the convents and becoming too close
to Sor Andrea, a Capuchin nun "very tempted by everything to do with
Revelations."[24] Elsewhere, he asked whether Amusquíbar was the "spiritual son" of Parra "or at least his intimate confidante and friend."[25]

The Inquisition looked into these accusations, finding that Amusquíbar
as well as Father Gregorio Zapata had visited the Jesus, Maria, José Convent
of the Capuchin order and learned about Sor Andrea's visions of Lima
burning. Barroeta claimed that they had visited her before Parra's Mass,
passing secret papers and fostering rumors. They denied these charges,
contending that they had visited the convent after the Mass to find out
more about the premonitions.[26] Once again, Barroeta's battles combined
the personal with broader institutional reconfigurations. Barroeta clearly
disliked Amusquíbar and believed that he had fallen for foolish fantasies.
Yet he was also locked in battle with the Inquisition over jurisdictional
disputes. Throughout Spanish America, archbishops and the Inquisition
fought over the extent of the latter's control of "*causas de fe.*" Barroeta
battled particularly hard, publishing edicts that forced all ecclesiastics,
even the inquisitor, to receive his permission to take confession. He dis-
couraged them from visiting monasteries without a document verifying
his authorization.[27] He also limited the inquisitor's right to name officials.
The court of Fernando VI, as part of its attempt to rein in the Inquisition,

backed Barroeta on both accounts.[28] On the other hand, the Inquisition believed that the archbishop was overstepping and seconded the charge by the Franciscans that Barroeta was merely attempting to cover up his ineptitude in the premonition panic. They also joined in the accusations that Barroeta himself led an overly lavish lifestyle. Skirmishes between the two built up until they came to a head in the Parra trial.[29]

While including constant sniping between Barroeta and Amusquíbar, the inquiries focused on whether the premonitions were trustworthy, which would justify Parra's declarations, or rumor-induced fantasies. Parra abandoned his initial silent tactic and gave lengthy testimony about his spiritual daughter, the central figure in the premonitions and the trial, and provided the names of the different confessors, who then testified. The testimony is detailed but indirect—the nuns themselves rarely talk (Parra's nun does at one point), only their confessors. The reliability of such testimony is a question of debate but the trial records here support the view that the confessors and nuns could develop strong relationships and that the testimony could reflect the nuns' point of view. The priests professed great sensitivity to the nuns and, as will be seen, opened up the nuns' usually closed or cloistered physical and mental worlds.[30]

God Is Angry: Ashes as Punishment for Grave Sins

After some initial denials, Parra admitted that one of the nuns with premonitions was his own spiritual daughter. His testimony as well as that of others emphasized her extreme spirituality and the painful suffering her visions caused, qualities that added credence to her visions. She was about thirty-five years old, a *doncella* (unmarried virgin), from a good family. She had vowed chastity at nine and lived a simple, selfless life in an unnamed convent. She slept little, prayed more than three hours a night, and left the convent only for Mass or a religious obligation. One of her examiners, the Augustinian friar Diego de Aragón, mentioned that ten years before the devil had tried to tempt her ("against her chastity, with horrendous propositions, against the faith") but that she had pledged herself to the image of Our Lady of the Rosary and no longer suffered such temptations. Another priest said that he had never met such a pure soul, a compliment that left her worried that she would become vain.[31]

On August 14, 1756, the eve of the Assumption of the Virgin, she dreamed that God threw three flaming lances or arrows at each house in Lima "burning them all, leaving them in ashes as punishment for the grave sins committed, especially by members of the secular and regular ecclesiastic communities, including nuns." She woke up soaked in tears. The vision of Lima burning returned every time she prayed. She saw male and female saints pleading for Lima, including Saint Teresa and Saint Catherine of Siena, who "always accompanied her." She believed that the divine punishment would occur on the eve of a celebration for the Virgin Mary so her fears increased around these dates. After a "brother of hers, a theologian and a mystic himself" advised her to "empty her interior" and tell everything to her abbess or confessor, she decided to confide in Friar Parra. She worried, however, that she would end up in the Inquisition for being a "witch or delusional [*ilusa*]."[32]

The core of her premonitions, fire falling on Lima for the sins of the church, is found in virtually all of the other visions, which varied greatly in other details. Fire is, of course, a key Christian symbol. Passages from the New and Old Testaments declare that fire would be used in the final judgment of the Lord and in the punishment of the damned. The priests involved in this case joined in the centuries-long debate about whether the fire was metaphorical or not. Although the prevalence of adobe and brick houses rather than wood meant that fires were not the grave danger that they posed in other cities, it certainly had a prominent place in the city's mentality. For example, Ana María Pérez, a *mulatta* friend of Santa Rosa, noted how "God had wanted to bury this city in flaming spears [*palos*] for its sins but thanks to her [Santa Rosa] and another of the Lord's servants he had not done it."[33] The image of Christ with three lances was extensive in colonial Lima.[34]

After hearing the nun's confession, Parra met with a fellow Franciscan to ask how he should proceed. He told Parra that if she spoke in Latin, her premonitions would be certain. The next day, Parra was flabbergasted when in the midst of her prayers she clearly said *iratus est Dominus*, "God is Angry."[35] She explained that while praying, "I understood that God was angry, in the interior of my soul I felt a deep fear and at the same time I understood a few words: *iratus est Dominus* and I believed and understood that God was angry." This prompted a spiritual crisis in Parra as well and his encounters with her and his own revelatory experiences increased. The following day he suddenly burst out in tears at the altar, "with a sensitive pain in the heart." He spent a night praying with another priest and the following day the nun asked him about his prayers, as though she had been there. On October 31, the doncella suddenly had a "grave impulse" to go to the San Francisco church, where she met Parra. She described her pleas and prayers to God to not punish Lima, convincing Parra that "the revelation was certain, she had too much of a soul to be *alucinada*."[36]

The trial tells us much more about the methods for evaluating premonitions and visions than about the nun herself. The Augustinian father Aragón examined her to verify whether her visions could be trusted, inspecting to see if she were humble, virtuous, obedient, and consistent in her spiritual life. He also evaluated for any physical or external cause, probing to see

> if she had any stomach or head ailment, if she slept little, if she fasted too much, if she mortified herself excessively, if she were prone to dreams, visions, and fear of the demons, if she were frequently tempted by horrible *sugetaciones* or imaginations, if she had ever desired having revelations . . . if she suffered from melancholy, if she cloistered herself and was not prone to conversations, visits, and frequent commerce of people, if she read too many spiritual books, especially those that deal with revelations.[37]

Father Aragón confirmed her proper spirituality, discipline, and distance from negative influences, particularly questionable people and books. He noted that women require more scrutiny because their "simpler nature and susceptibility to impressions" made them prone to revelations and visions. Aragón embodied the cautious ambivalence toward female mysticism described earlier. Women's nature made them superior recipients of God's messages yet also made them susceptible to false impressions. The friar supported her, calling for further inquiry. He lauded her humility and benevolence, asserting "if she ever fools herself it is not her fault, but rather God's providence, who orders it for more humiliation and knowledge."[38]

Friar Aragón also evaluated the premonitions. He used two guidelines to verify them: if they contained elements known only to God and not to the "young woman" and if the vision or revelation lasted in her memory—divine warnings could not be ephemeral.[39] He noted that although choleric humors or another physical explanation could have provoked the fire dreams, the details about the lances and their target indicated that they were God's determinations. As to the second point, her continual visions and fear in the Virgin's festivals indicated that the premonitions were trustworthy. Even more convincing was her outburst in Latin. He cited Saint Thomas to argue that it could not have been the work of the devil, whose understanding did not have such a great reach. Aragón emphasized her repeated visions in Mass, her union with Parra and other priests, the depth or "penetration" of her prayers, and her discretion, as she confided only in her confessor, "admirable" in women who are generally "talkative and simple-minded." He judged that "God's spirit resides in her" and she was not delusional (ilusa). He finished by noting the similarities between her premonitions and those of the others: "although the devil can fool this or that person, it is difficult to believe that God would allow him to trick nine." He deemed her visions "frightening."[40] She had passed Friar Aragón's lengthy "discernment of spirits" test.

Fires and Bulls

The trial also reviewed other women with premonitions: eight nuns, two beatas, a "virtuous woman," a doncella, and a married woman of "known virtue." They constitute an insightful cross section of female religiosity in Lima, moving outside the walls of the city's convents and *beaterios*. Their premonitions and suffering illuminate how religion was lived and the fears that enveloped Lima. Although the 1746 earthquake represented in most cases the starting point, their visions moved farther back into the past, into the Peruvian interior, and across the Atlantic.

As was the case with Parra's charge, only the name of the confessor is provided. Fray Pedro Alcántara of the San Francisco de Paula order had a spiritual daughter whom he had known for twenty-five years. He emphasized her tolerance for pain and her dedication to serving others. In 1750, in the midst of an Indian conspiracy in the El Cercado neighborhood and in the Andean town of Huarochirí about thirty miles east of Lima, she broke out in profuse sweat, felt sudden anxiety, and pleaded that priests be spared from the violence. She had no way to know of these events—she only later learned about the uprising and the death of Spaniards by "those barbarians."[41] She and Fray Alcántara realized that at the very moment of the Spaniards' deaths, she had been praying to God for their salvation. On November 1, 1755, without understanding why, she found herself praying for suffering distant cities. Months later, she found out that it had been at the same time as the Lisbon earthquake on All Saint's Day.[42] Fray Alcántara noted that she "feels in her spirit notable sorrow for the disorder and scandalous profanity of this city and she has told me that in her prayers she experiences seeming lightning bursts, which distress her as she takes them to be signs of the Lord's anger with this city." Her pains and sorrow had begun with the 1746 earthquake and she had since begun to feel that Lima would be destroyed if radical changes were not made. She begged God for his mercy so that "the fire falls into the sea and mountains" and not on Lima.

Alcántara also told the story of a young woman he knew well, although he was not her confessor, who before October 28, 1746, saw in her dreams Lima devastated with "trenches filled with cadavers." Once, when she was deep in prayer the image of Jesus that she had in her room talked to her: "he lamented sadly that his creatures had hurt and offended him." She was so upset that she became ill. Fray Alcántara also discussed Doña María Ruíz Luna, a married woman who was the spiritual daughter of the Franciscan Fray Garro.[43] He described her with a long list of compliments, including "exemplary, of known virtue, heroic humility, and constant prayer." When she saw profane women, "she became inflamed in zealous defense of God's honor [*enardecida en el celo de la honra de Dios*]" and exclaimed in threatening fashion: "Our Lord, because of so many sins in this city, especially the obstinacy of these vices that scorn the divine wrath experienced in the ruin of the 1746 earthquake, will send fire to purify it of so much evil."[44]

The spiritual daughter of the Franciscan friar Joseph Antonio de Santiesteban, a nun in an undisclosed convent (non-Franciscan), led a life of tremendous self-discipline. He could find no sins in her conduct but described a unique style of prayer. She suffered "sweet and loving" ecstasy or rapture to the point that she had to be separated from the other nuns. She became impassioned and sobbed "tenderly" with abundant tears, becoming so tranquil as though "in a sweet, loving hug"; in these moments, she appeared "angelical." Besides this sensual form of worship, she punished herself brutally: she ate seeds and bark to get ill and applied hot wax, plants with thorns, and studded leather to her skin until she blistered and bled. Her torments were also internal and terrifying. Not only did the devil bother her, but she had visions of dead souls who asked for prayers. With one look she recognized people who were soon to die.[45]

Around the year 1750, in the midst of self-mortification (*disciplina de sangre*) in her convent cell, she looked out the window to see the San Cristóbal hill (to the north of the city, now in its very midst) on fire "with countless people of both sexes and social conditions hugging one another."

She thought that it was punishment for her own sins and she disciplined herself so brutally that she fainted. She believed that she had prevented the wrath of God, angry at Lima's affronts. Months later she had another "nightmare." She saw a large herd of bulls running the streets led by "many demons with ugly features and whips that made a thunderous din, who went along saying dishonest and horrifying things." The bulls smoldered and with one look incinerated countless passersby, who screamed dreadfully before dying. With the cross on his shoulder, Christ walked behind them, bleeding heartily and lamenting that nothing that he had done for the Lima population "made them refrain from offending him so much." The nun woke up soaked in tears and began to do her spiritual exercises. From that day on she cried for Lima. When bullfights were first held in the Acho bullring in the early 1750s, she asked Fray Santiesteban if they weren't the bulls of her nightmare.[46]

Fray Santiesteban passed on a story told by another priest who confessed "a soul of great contemplation," who three times had been "snatched in spirit and placed in the presence of the Supreme Judge Jesus Christ." The first time she saw that Jesus tried to burn Lima to the ground. She appealed to the Virgin Mary who responded, "my daughter, plead to God with me for Lima" and then kneeled in prayer. The second time she again saw fire falling on Lima and invoked the Virgin Mary. In the third, she saw fire in the form of "burning cotton balls" raining down on the city. She consulted with the Virgin, "our Queen," who recommended that she speak with "virtuous, zealous people who should plead for Lima and that its inhabitants make amends: she said that women's clothing, the bad lives of priests and the wife of his Majesty, the poor's clamor for justice and the widespread dishonesty and lasciviousness had irritated our Lord."[47] The Virgin's admonishment includes virtually the entire list of sinners (especially the religious community and profane women), as well as the sins that prompted God's wrath found in the other premonitions, including the scandalous clothing of women.

Friar Santiesteban closed his testimony with another story from his priest friend. He knew a "very holy and simple religious soul" who in 1748 lived in Huamanga (between Lima and Cuzco, today Ayacucho). She claimed that God had warned her several times about the imminent ruin of Lima and Callao, whose sins had given him no choice but to "scorch them." Twice in her prayers she saw Lima in flames as fire fell from the sky. The priest, Santiesteban's friend, was so moved by these stories that he returned to his hometown of Lima "full of terror." This case indicates how the fear moved from the nuns, to their confessors, and beyond. Everyone involved understood the 1746 earthquake as a prelude or warning, and dreaded that the balls of fire would fulfill the threat.

The major chaplain of the Concepcionist-observant convent Descalzas de San José, Friar Joseph González Terrones, testified about the visions of Mother Theresa de Jesús, a black veil nun and twice abbess of the convent. Since the 1730s she had perceived that God was indignant with the city's sensuality and blasphemy and that he would ruin it with a "formidable earthquake." She denounced the servants' dress in the convents, deeming them "profane and indecent." Weeks before October 28, on her deathbed (Llano Zapata claims that she was more than one hundred years old), she envisioned the city and its temples ruined, with nuns walking the streets and men roaming the inner sanctum of the convents. With tears in her eyes, she begged that people take to the streets to preach and enlighten people about the threat. Father González Terrrones consulted with others and they decided not to do anything, more to prevent a panic than due to skepticism about her premonitions.[48]

Mother Theresa de Jesús was the best known of the prophesizing nuns discussed here. Two Franciscan friars, Friar Luís Rodriguez and Parra himself, classified her as a successor to other holy people who had predicted Lima's earthquakes, such as San Francisco Solano and Father Galindo de la Merced (1687), as well as the fishermen who saw Panama City in flames from their boats fifteen days before the actual 1737 fire.[49] Llano Zapata, in one of his accounts of the earthquake, dedicated a paragraph to her. He noted her prediction that she would die before the earthquake, as she did just thirteen days before the catastrophe, and criticized the authorities for dismissing her warning due to her age.[50] Although Llano Zapata's account might have increased her reputation in Lima, she was already a well-known and feared figure. Fray González Terrones provided more anecdotes that no doubt fortified her fame.

One night, with González Terrones present, Father Nicolás Carrasco Palomino, the chaplain of the Discalced Trinitarians convent, went to the San José convent to take her confession. She told him that she would die in his hands and not in those of González Terrones. He laughed because he lived three blocks away while González Terrones lived in the convent. Weeks later, however, Carrasco Palomino gave her the last rites, as González Terrones had become ill. Both friars worried that this would mean that her prediction about the destruction of Lima would also turn out to be true, which the events of October 28 confirmed. But this was only one of several confirmations of her powers. She had tenaciously fought González Terrones's plan to build a *sala de profundis* in the convent, deeming it a waste of money and time. She prophesized that no matter how strongly built, it would be ruined in the earthquake. González Terrones went ahead with the project and, to the delight of the contractor and masons, paid to have it heavily fortified. The earthquake destroyed the new building, including the normally resilient wooden doors.

One night, weeks before the earthquake, nuns gathered around her cell to hear her predictions. Another nun, María Joseph de Mercedes, made fun of them. She was from the distinguished Jaúregui family—her sister was married to the prosperous merchant don Martín de Olavide, the father of Pablo de Olavide.[51] Mother Theresa heard her jibes and according to several nuns said, "don't laugh, I guarantee that the first news you hear after the tremor will be about the death of your people." María Joseph's sister and brother-in-law would be two of the most distinguished victims of the earthquake when their house crushed them.[52] Mother Teresa's story indicates that premonitions about the destruction of Lima took hold in the city before the 1746 earthquake. The aftershocks in the following months—430 in the three and a half months from October 28 until February 16, 1747—must have petrified Lima's population, who feared that each one could be the final punishment.[53]

Friar Carrasco Palomino, the surprised provider of Mother Theresa's last rites, told another story of one of "his religious women." One night in 1751, she saw large flames violently enter under the door frame and through the window of her convent cell. This vision lasted for fifteen minutes or more and she called a servant to accompany her. This woman stayed the night but saw nothing. The next night the nun observed that her cell lit up with the reflection of fire, but the servant again saw nothing. The third night the reflection was fainter so she did not call the servant. Her fear increased, however, a few days later when another nun told her that she had dreamed of flames falling from the sky, boiling the water in the baptismal font and filling the convent with "bits of fire." Fray Carrasco Palomino's testimony ended with those words.

Fray García de Moroña, a Dominican and chaplain of the Santa Rosa convent, referred to a doncella of "great purity" and frequent visions. She had proven her powers to him when he had asked her to pray that two women would commit themselves to spiritual exercises. She said that one would continue and the other would leave. She seemed to have been wrong as the one that she predicted would stay did not and vice versa. Soon thereafter, however, they reversed themselves. In the months before the earthquake she had night visions. She saw with horror that fire rained over the city ("a fine hail of fire"), inducing her to increase her daily prayers. Another night she saw Jesus on horseback in Lima, with his sword in hand, "as though he were threatening its inhabitants with a great punishment." She later saw Santa Rosa ("our glorious patron") humbly pleading before God and the Virgin for the salvation of Lima, "her patria." Santa Rosa "sheltered under her blanket all who came to her fearful of Divine justice." The young woman understood that Santa Rosa and the Virgin had postponed but not prevented the punishment; she lived petrified of its impending arrival.[54]

Friar García de Moroña gave other examples of premonitions and alarm. A "virtuous woman" whom he confessed knew a "servant of God" who had a Jesus figure that talked. It revealed that Lima was to be punished with fire and recommended that she "take refuge in a temple, because its angels will defend it and save all of the city's temples from the fire."[55] The "virtuous woman" also told about a priest who fled 40 or 50 leagues (120–150 miles) from Lima. There he confessed a doncella who had twice dreamed about the earthquake. She described it with such detail and exactitude that the priest was shocked to learn that she had never set foot in Lima. In the second dream, she returned to Lima to learn that God was going to punish it with "an even bigger earthquake." She saw "horrifying things such as huge trenches opening up in the ground and engulfing people." Her stories as well as those of the woman in Huamanga indicate that the fear spread far beyond Lima itself.

Fray Juan Garro, a Franciscan, told brief stories of two women who had passed away. Ana María de la Concepción, a beata of the Santa Rosa de Viterbo beaterio, saw in 1747, 1748, and 1749 (the year she passed away) that fire fell from the San Cristóbal hill and that the ocean tumbled into the city. María del Rosario, also called María Terrones, a *cuarterona* (daughter of a Spaniard and mestiza) whom Garro confessed, told him in 1749 that she was happy to die not only because she awaited the mercy of God but also "to miss the fire that my Lord Jesus Christ told me he was going to send down on the city." When the friar asked her when this would occur she answered ominously "soon."[56]

Garro also discussed a woman of "known virtue" who heard voices earlier in 1755, some when awake and others when asleep, that told her "I have to destroy this city of Lima with fire," although not specifying when. Another woman, who had lived for decades in a *recoleta*, or more reclusive monastery, in 1747 and 1748 had seen in the sky a powerful hand holding a sickle while a voice repeated "I must devastate this city." Another nun he confessed, who lived in a different convent than these women, dreamed in 1748 and 1749 that it rained fire on Lima. A fourth nun told him that God had told her that he wanted to "burn down" (*acabar con fuego*) Lima. Another had the same vision but with more detail: the fire fell in the form of "burning golden bread," making the city smell like roasting beef. Her prelate and confessor, the Franciscan friar Thomas de la Concha, examined her closely. Finally, Garro mentioned two pious women who confided in him that they had seen Lima burn down in their dreams. At this point, Garro conceded that rumors abounded about the destruction of Lima, which perhaps stimulated people's imagination and nurtured the abundance of similar visions. Nonetheless, Friar Garro cited the prophet Amos, as well as Saint Theodoret, and noted: "With his infinite commiseration and compassion God always warns the faithful before a universal punishment." He implied that he doubted some of these premonitions but did not reject the possibility of divine punishment.[57]

In his testimony, the Dominican friar and prior of the Santa Rosa convent, Gregorio de Mendoza, stressed that God often employed women and female saints to reveal his mysteries. He cited the role of Mary Magdalene in the resurrection of Christ, despite the fact that Saint Thomas and Saint Buenaventura were alive. He told the story of a "noble woman," an open-veiled (*de hábito descubierto*) beata and doncella, who months after the earthquake saw in her dreams abundant fire falling on the city with such force that the horrifying screams, groans, and howls "broke hearts." She used an unusual metaphor: countless gold-plated books thrown into the sky and tumbling down onto the city. Lima immediately fell into a nightmarish silence, as if there were no survivors. She saw lots of smoke and noted that the city smelled like "burnt meat." Not surprisingly, she could not forget this nightmare and lived in constant terror. What is surprising is that Friar Mendoza, when asked if he had heard of other people with such dreams, answered no.[58]

The Franciscan friar Rodriguez gave a brief account of a nun who had also correctly prophesized the 1746 disaster, including details such as the flooding of Callao and the gathering of displaced nuns in plazas. Since early 1747, whenever in prayer she sensed another imminent punishment. One time she saw fire falling from the sky and people kneeling and pleading for divine mercy when suddenly everything went silent. The smell of burning people spread and fire continued to fall like *"panes de oro batido"* (loaves of whipped gold). She told the friar that the vision had recurred a year before and that she understood that God wanted to "destroy voraciously" Lima.[59] Friar Rodriguez then told the story that most scared him. It indicated that not all of the visionaries were women.

He knew a deeply religious man who often seemed crazy but had extended periods of absolute lucidity in which he had "new enlightenment and intelligence about the things of God and the sacred mysteries." While praying one day prior to 1746 he saw that God and divine justice wanted to annihilate the city with fire. He was then transported to heaven where he begged the Lord to punish him, "this vile sinner," and save the people. He was turned over to the devil. In the months following the earthquake, he repeatedly cautioned that Lima had avoided punishment once but would not be so fortunate in the near future. He blamed the city's disorderly and profane customs for the impending punishment.

The Franciscan friar, Joseph de Pozo, told a story about a priest. One morning before dawn in 1753 or 1754, deep in prayer, he had a brief but clear vision of Lima with its temples standing but their towers tumbled over and the city otherwise flattened and without people. Relating this to the vision that he had six or seven months before the 1746 earthquake that proved to be correct, he came out of his "abstract" state of mind fearing that Lima would soon be greatly punished. Nuns were not the only ones in Lima receiving the disturbing warnings about impending doom.

Fears

The visions and premonitions that beset mid-eighteenth-century Lima are a wonderful entryway into the fears and mentalities of the era. A few of their common features are evident. They were not overtly political or subversive in nature such as those that starkly questioned power relations and prompted messianic or millenarian movements. Instead, they confirm Richard Kagan's point that "[t]he vast majority of medieval and Renaissance prophecies addressed religious issues. The dominant theme was the reform of the church, which was accused of corruption and immorality."[60] With the possible exception of Mother Theresa and her threatening rejoinder to the upper-class nuns who teased her believers, none of the nuns enjoyed or took advantage of their special knowledge. As Parra's nun best demonstrated, they suffered terribly with the visions, both in the painful reception of messages about an impending apocalypse as well as the ensuing anguish. Once they had the vision, they not only dreaded divine wrath but also guiltily reviewed their own sins to see if they were perhaps the culpable party.

The nuns and much of the rest of Lima believed that the 1746 earthquake had been a sign of God's wrath and that only a drastic change in the residents' behavior and piety could prevent an even more crippling punishment. Virtually all of the participants in the trial shared this view. The nuns understood their visions as messages from God while the priests cited the Bible to support the notion of prophetic warnings. In the trial, the inquisitors as well as the archbishop clearly assumed that women had a gift and that the warnings needed to be heeded. This interpretation revived—if it had ever died down—the decades-long debate and mass concern about Limeños's errant ways and the decadence of the church.

Dread and guilt permeated Lima. For most of the city's inhabitants, the 1746 earthquake had deepened their concern about God's wrath, confirming the subtext in decades of discussions about Lima's sinful ways and its wayward church: repent or calamity would strike. The nuns blamed the city, the church, and themselves for God's anger. Certain symbolic elements stand out. The premonitions expressed particular horror and concern about women in Lima, particularly their profane dress. The earthquake and the premonitions stimulated campaigns to tighten control of women's bodies, efforts that displayed fascinating notions about gender and race. This interpretation of the earthquake and the fear that it deepened shaped the city's rebuilding. No discussion or plan could avoid the issue of God's wrath and the search for its causes (the guilty sinners) and a solution.

What about the nuns and their visions? As was often the case in colonial Spanish America, the pitched jurisdictional battle, in this case between the archbishop and the inquisitor, ended up in a rather amorphous tie, with no apparent winner. The final sentence does not clearly favor one over the other.[61] Barroeta continued this and his many other battles until his transfer to Granada, Spain, in 1758. Franciscans managed to move Parra out of the limelight and his name and the case itself are not prominently mentioned in the newspaper, *La Gaceta de Lima*, or documentation from the era. In 1769 he was transferred to Chile.[62] We know nothing about the nuns. They presumably took solace that the devastating blow that they envisioned did not occur. The testimonies indicate that while they blamed themselves for the city's woes, they also recognized that their own efforts could detain God's ire. They no doubt continued to be troubled by their special insights into impending events and fearful of divine wrath, pained by their own sins as well as that of their city. Nothing in the record indicates a reprieve from that fate. What is clear is that the debates about the causes or nature of disasters shaped the physical, institutional, behavioral, and social reconstruction of Lima.

✤ NOTES ✤

1. Father Pedro Lozano, "Relación del terremoto que arruinó a Lima e inundó al Callao el 28 de octubre de 1746," in *Terremotos: colección de las relaciones de los más notables que ha sufrido esta capital*, ed. Manuel D. Odriozola (Lima: Aurelio Alfaro, 1863), 36. This essay is an abbreviated version of chapter 2 of my book, *Shaky Colonialism: The 1746 Earthquake-Tsunami in Lima, Peru and Its Long Aftermath* (Durham, NC: Duke University Press, 2008).

2. Conde de Superunda, *Relación de gobierno: Perú (1745–1761)*, ed. Alfredo Moreno C. (Madrid: CSIC, 1983), 259.

3. For descriptions of the event, see the accounts by José Eusebio Llano Zapata, Victorino Montero del Águila, Father Lozano, and the marquis of Obando, all republished in Odriozola, *Terremotos*.

4. I discuss these conditions at length in *Shaky Colonialism*.

5. This contentious aftermath is the focus of *Shaky Colonialism*.

6. On eighteenth-century notions of earthquakes, see John Gates Taylor, "Eighteenth-Century Earthquake Theories: A Case-History Investigation into the Character of the Study of the Earth in the Enlightenment" (PhD diss., University of Oklahoma, 1975).

7. Margarita Suárez, "Ciencia, ficción e imaginario colectivo: la interpretación de los cielos en el Perú colonial," in *Historia, memoria y ficción*, ed. Luis Millones and Moisés Lemlij (Lima: Biblioteca Peruana de Psicoanálisis, 1996), 312–19.

8. Luis Miguel Glave, *De rosa y espinas: economía, sociedad y mentalidades andinas, siglo XVII* (Lima: IEP/BCR, 1998), "baroque fatalism," 343; events, 343–66.

9. Pacheco Vélez calls them a "symbol of baroque plentitude." César Pacheco Vélez, *Memoria y utopía de la vieja Lima* (Lima: Universidad del Pacífico, 1985), 241. Juan Günther Doering and Lohmann Villena, *Lima* (Lima, Madrid: MAPFRE), 1992, 125–26.

10. For Lima's woes in the 1740s, see the nice summary in Guillermo Lohmann Villena, "Victorino Montero del Aguila y su 'Estado político del reyno del Perú' (1742)," *Anuario de Estudios Americanos* 31 (1974): 751–807. On the epidemic, see Adrian Pearce, "The Peruvian Population Census of 1725–1740," *Latin American Research Review* 36, no. 3 (2001): 69–104. For a strong overview of the Andes in the eighteenth century, see Kenneth Andrien, *Andean Worlds: Indigenous History, Culture, and Consciousness under Spanish Rule, 1532–1825* (Albuquerque, University of New Mexico Press, 2001), chaps. 7, 8; for rebellions, see O'Phelan Godoy, *Un siglo de rebeliones anticoloniales: Perú y Bolivia 1700–1783* (Cusco: Centro Bartolomé de Las Casas, 1988).

11. Ramón Mujica, "El arte y los sermones," in *El Barroco Peruano*, ed. Ramón Mujica (Lima: Banco de Crédito, 2002), especially see 219–38.

12. Quoted by Asunción Lavrin and Rosalva Loreto L., eds., *Monjas y beatas: la escritura femenina en la espiritualidad barroca novohispana, siglos XVII y XVIII* (Mexico City: AGN/Universidad de las Américas, 2002), intro., 12.

13. Antonio Rubial García, "Los Santos milagreros y malogrados de la Nueva España," in *Manifestaciones religiosas en el mundo colonial americano*, ed. Clara García Ayluardo and Manuel Ramón Medina (Mexico City: Universidad Iberoamericana, 1997), 55.

14. On visionaries in Lima, see Nancy van Deusen, *The Souls of Purgatory: The Spiritual Diary of a Seventeenth-Century Afro-Peruvian Mystic, Ursula de Jesus* (Albuquerque, University of New Mexico Press, 2004), 40–49.

15. Inquisición, n.d., leg. 1651, papeles sueltos, Archivo Histórico Nacional (hereafter AHN), Madrid.

16. Cartas y expedientes tramitados en el consejo, 1763, leg. 819, Archivo General de Indias (hereafter AGI), Lima.

17. On their conflict, see Pablo Emilio Pérez-Mallaína Bueno, *Retrato de una ciudad en crisis: la sociedad limeña ante el movimiento sísmico de 1746* (Sevilla: EEHA-CSIC/Instituto Riva-Agüero, 2001), 227–42; Moreno Cebrián, introduction to *Relación*, by Conde de Superunda, 52–56.

18. On Barroeta as a reformer, see Juan Carlos Estenssoro, "Modernismo, estética, música y fiesta: élites y cambio de actitud frente a la cultura popular, Perú 1750–1850," in *Tradición y modernidad en los Andes*, ed. Henrique Urbano (Cuzco: Bartolomé de Las Casas, 1992), 181–96.

19. Inquisición, November 16, 1756, leg. 1651, exp. 2, AHN; also found in Inquisición, n.d., leg. 2206, exp. 4, AHN.

20. Inquisición, leg. 1651, AHN.

21. Ibid., 6v.

22. Ibid., 7v.

23. Along with Amos and Saint Paul, the prophet Jeremiah, chapter 5, is also mentioned twice. Inquisición, leg. 1651, AHN, 2v., 18v.

24. Ibid.

25. November 7, 1756, leg. 807, AGI.

26. Inquisición, January 24, 1757, leg. 2206, AHN.

27. René Millar Carvacho, *La Inquisición de Lima: tomo 3 (1697–1820)* (Madrid: DEIMOS, 1998), 118.

28. Ibid., 118–19.

29. This theme is well covered by Pérez-Mallaína Bueno, *Retrato*, 182–87.

30. On this theme, I have followed Jodi Bilinkoff, "Confessors, Penitents, and the Construction of Identities in Early Modern Avila," in *Culture and Identity: Early Modern Europe (1500–1800). Essays in Honor of Natalie Zemon Davis*, ed. Barbara Diefendorf and Carla Hesse (Ann Arbor: University of Michigan, 1993), 83–100.

31. Inquisición, leg. 1651, AHN.

32. Ibid., 3.

33. Ramón Mujica, *Rosa limensis: mística, política e iconografía en torno a la patrona de América* (Lima: IFEA, FCE, BCR, 2001), 329.

34. Mujica, "El arte y los sermones," 227–28. Ramón Mujica relates the three lances to the diffusion of sermons by San Vicente Ferrer (1350–1419).

35. Inquisición, leg. 1651, AHN.

36. Her testimony is found in Inquisición, January 7, 1757, leg. 1651, pp. 80–83, AHN.

37. Ibid. On the discernment of spirits, see among many works, Anne Jacobsen Schutte, *Aspiring Saints: Pretense of Holiness, Inquisition, and Gender in the Republic of Venice, 1618–1750* (Baltimore: Johns Hopkins University Press, 2001), chap. 3.

38. Inquisición, leg. 1651, AHN.

39. See Schutte, *Aspiring Saints*, 47: "Visions from God are always glorious, pure, chaste, comforting, and lasting, whereas those from the devil are very often disgusting and frightening and always of short duration."

40. Inquisición, leg. 1651, AHN.

41. Ibid.

42. The Lisbon earthquake took place at approximately 9:30 a.m., 3:30 a.m. in Lima, an unusual time for a nun to be praying but certainly not impossible.

43. Inquisición, leg. 1651, AHN.

44. Ibid. Alcántara mistakenly refers to Joseph rather than to Juan Garro.

45. Ibid.

46. Although the Plaza de Acho was inaugurated in 1766, bullfights were held in the "pampa" there well before, particularly as fundraisers after the earthquake.

47. Inquisición, leg. 1651, AHN. King Ferdinand VI's wife, the Portuguese Barbara de Braganza, was unpopular in Spain.

48. José Eusebio Llano Zapata, "Carta o diario que escribió," in Odriozola, *Terremotos*, 104.

49. Espinsosa refers to "a religious woman from the Descalzas de San Joseph Convent" while Parra names her. Inquisición, leg. 1651, AHN, 44v, 50.

50. Llano Zapata, "Carta o diario," 104.

51. Paul Rizo-Patrón Boyle, *Linaje, dote, y poder: la nobleza de Lima de 1700 a 1850* (Lima: Pontificia Universidad Católica del Perú, 2000), 82.

52. On Pablo de Olavide and his family, see Marcelin Defourneaux, *Pablo de Olavide: El afrancesado* (Mexico City: Renacimiento, 1965); Pablo de Olavide and Estuardo Núñez, ed. *Pablo de Olavide: Obras selectas* (Lima: Banco de Crédito, 1987).

53. Llano Zapata, "Carta o diario," 81.

54. Inquisición, leg. 1651, AHN. On Santa Rosa, see Mujica, *Rosa limensis*; and Frank Graziano, *Wounds of Love: The Mystical Marriage of Saint Rose of Lima* (Oxford: Oxford University Press, 2004).

55. Inquisición, leg. 1651, AHN.

56. Ibid.

57. Ibid.

58. Ibid.

59. Ibid., 45v–46.

60. Richard Kagan, *Lucrecia's Dream: Politics and Prophecy in Sixteenth-Century Spain* (Berkeley: University of California Press, 1990), 86.

61. For a summary, see Millar Carvacho, *La Inquisición de Lima*, 121–22.

62. Virrey Amat, leg. 651, duplicado (via reservada), AGI.

CHAPTER TWO

Nature, God, and Nation in Revolutionary Venezuela

The Holy Thursday Earthquake of 1812

STUART McCOOK

Modern nations, careful of their own remembrance, snatch from oblivion the history of human revolutions, which is that of ardent passions, and inveterate hatred. It is not the same with respect to the revolutions of the physical world. They are described with the least accuracy, when they happen to coincide with the period of civil dissentions.

—Alexander von Humboldt, *Narrative of Travels*

If nature opposes us, we will struggle against her and force her to obey us.

—Simón Bolívar, March 26, 1812

✣ ON THE MORNING OF MARCH 26, 1812, VENEZUELANS BEGAN preparing for the Holy Thursday celebrations later that day. That particular Holy Thursday was more than just a religious holiday; it also marked an important political milestone for the young republic. Two years earlier, on Holy Thursday of 1810, the patriot *cabildo* of Caracas had deposed

43

the captain general appointed by Spain. This was the colony's first step toward declaring complete independence from Spain the following year. Although Venezuela was beset by many domestic and foreign problems, on that day, the houses of Caracas were adorned with flags, and the streets were filled with processions carrying crosses and religious banners. In the afternoon, devout *caraqueños* flocked to one of the city's many churches to attend Mass. Afterward, the *plaza mayor* in front of the cathedral was to be the scene of the day's most important ceremonies. Fusiliers and grenadiers waited in formation at the doors of the cathedral, ready to join the religious processions as they emerged from the cathedral after Mass.[1] Suddenly, tiles began to fall from the buildings, houses cracked, and "the earth began to move with a horrifying noise." A French eyewitness wrote that "shocks succeeded each other with incredible rapidity; and were so strong that persons standing and walking tottered, and were even thrown to the ground." Across the city "public houses, public buildings, and churches, tumbled down in all directions. Clouds of dust enveloped everything; and the crash of edifices, with their dead and wounded inhabitants, exhibited terrible spectacles on every side." Many who fell to their knees in prayer at the first tremor were crushed by falling buildings. In the Plaza San Jacinto, a journalist named José Domingo Díaz saw "the greater part of the temple collapse, and there also, amid the dust and the death, I witnessed the destruction of a city that had enchanted both its natives and foreigners."[2]

Similar scenes were played out across central and western Venezuela, along the costal cordillera and the Andes. Sebastián Bueno, the parish priest of the small coastal town of Choroní, was celebrating Mass when "a terrifying earthquake, accompanied by a horrifying subterranean roar appeared about to consume us all; the earth shook so hard that it threw up boulders from its center; it sundered in various places, vomiting streams of water, and knocked down the buildings of this valley, in whose ruins we would have all been buried, if God had not taken care to show us his mercy, permitting this assault to last only three minutes."[3] Fortunately, few people in Choroní were hurt. Other cities and towns were not so lucky. The French soldiers Poudenx and Mayer wrote that the city of "San Felipe was so thoroughly destroyed, that it was difficult to find traces that it had ever existed." More than half of San Felipe's population perished, and the death toll must have included many members of the patriots' operational army stationed there.[4] In the western city of Mérida, the city's bishop and most of its leading clergy were killed when the cathedral collapsed. "Mérida no longer exists," wrote a survivor named Francisco de Yepes, "and half of its inhabitants are buried in the ruins."[5] The destruction also extended to the coastal port cities of La Guaira and Puerto Cabello, the interior cities of Barquisimeto and San Felipe, and a host of smaller communities. In a few short minutes, the earthquake killed ten thousand people in Caracas and La Guaira, and possibly twenty thousand more people across Venezuela. In the following weeks, aftershocks continued to shake the country. On April 4, the country suffered an aftershock almost as large as the original earthquake. Díaz remembered that "those were eight hours in which we tasted all the bitterness of the death that we saw at our feet." This aftershock "completed the destruction of those things which had escaped the former."[6]

According to modern geologic research, the Holy Thursday earthquake appears to have been produced by a displacement between the Caribbean and the South American tectonic plates, which meet in Venezuela. The shocks probably traveled along the Morón and Boconó faults, moving east to west along the coastal cordillera from Caracas to Puerto Cabello, and then southwest down to the Venezuelan Andes. The most seriously damaged cities were all situated close to these fault lines. The earthquake had three major foci. The first was in Caracas, its port city of La Guaira, and the surrounding coastal region. The second was roughly three hundred kilometers to the west, around the patriot strongholds of Barquisimeto and San Felipe. The third was the Andean city of Mérida, in southwestern Venezuela. Curiously, as Humboldt later noted, the lowland cities of "La Victoria, Maracay, and Valencia, scarcely suffered at all, despite their proximity to the capital." Some seismologists and geologists argue that the Holy Thursday earthquake was a single seismic event with three foci; others argue that the event in Mérida was separate from the one that struck central and western Venezuela; still others argue that there were three separate but almost simultaneous events. They also disagree on the scale of these events, with estimates ranging from six to eight on the Richter scale.[7] While the geologic specifics may be contested, one central fact is clear: patriot cities bore the brunt of the shock, while the royalist cities escaped virtually unscathed. The royalist strongholds of Maracaibo and Coro did experience a "very violent and long shock" but suffered "no disaster whatsoever."[8] Similarly, the royalist city of Angostura in the east was also spared.

The patriots could ill afford this catastrophe. In the colonial period, disaster-stricken cities in Spanish America could count on administrative and logistical support from the empire. The empire had also built a political framework that survived the most catastrophic earthquakes, such as the one that struck Lima in 1746. As Charles Walker has observed, the colonial government "responded effectively to the immediate needs of the population, [then] their attention turned to preventing social protest and to rebuilding."[9] Walker's comparative study of disaster relief in late colonial Latin America found that disasters revealed fractures in colonial domination—"horizontal" fractures between the elites and the lower classes, and an increasing "vertical" division within the upper classes.[10] The Spanish colonial government had contained these fractures. The government of republican Venezuela could not.

Venezuela's independence had aggravated existing vertical and horizontal fissures in Venezuelan society and produced new ones. The Holy Thursday earthquake struck at a critical moment in the political history of Latin America. Venezuela was the first Spanish colony in the New World to declare independence from Spain. Independence in Venezuela was not, however, the product of a widespread, grassroots movement. The road to independence began in 1808, when French troops invaded Spain and deposed King Ferdinand VII. Napoleon installed his brother Joseph Bonaparte on the Spanish throne, but Spain's colonies did not recognize Joseph as their legitimate ruler. At first, many colonies pledged allegiance to a Spanish government in the city of Cádiz, which ruled in the name of the deposed Ferdinand VII. In some colonies, however, local elites established juntas of their own, to govern in Ferdinand's name until he could be restored to the throne. At first, Venezuela followed this essentially conservative pattern. On Holy Thursday of 1810, a group of the local elite deposed the Spanish captain general and replaced him with a Junta Conservadora de los Derechos de Ferdinand VII (Committee to Defend the Rights of Ferdinand VII). The following year, a more radical creole faction gained control of the Caracas junta. This faction included the aged revolutionary Francisco de Miranda, recently returned from European exile, and a young creole named Simón Bolívar. On July 5, 1811, Venezuela declared full independence from Spain and established a congress to govern the new republic.

From the moment it was established, Venezuela's First Republic was beset with internal divisions, which partly reflected the country's racial structure—in which a minority of whites dominated a much larger non-white population. A decade earlier, the French traveler François Depons had estimated that whites (creoles and Spaniards) accounted for 20 percent of the population, slaves of African descent for 30 percent, "effranchised slaves, or their descendants" another 40 percent, and Indians the remaining 10 percent. Depons's categories likely simplified a more complex reality. Many of the "Africans" and "Indians" in his count were likely people of combined African, European, and indigenous parentage. In Venezuela, both pure and mixed-race people of African descent were known as *pardos*, while those of mixed European and Indian descent were known as mestizos.[11] To succeed, the white leaders of the republic needed the support—or at very least the tolerance—of the nonwhite population, especially the pardo majority. For the pardos, independence was a mixed blessing. For example, the constitution abolished many facets of legalized racial and occupational discrimination. But it replaced those older forms of discrimination with new ones. It limited suffrage to propertied Venezuelan creoles; it abolished the slave trade but allowed for the continuation of slavery. While some pardos chose to side with the republic, others chose to rebel. Small insurrections of pardos broke out across the colony, and in July and August of 1811 a major pardo uprising broke out in the city of Valencia. Patriot troops suppressed this revolt with great difficulty. In addition to these struggles over race and class, divisions emerged within the ruling white elite. Independence sparked a resurgence of regionalism. The leaders of the western provinces of Maracaibo, Coro, and the eastern province of Guyana declared their loyalty to Spain, as a way of regaining autonomy from Caracas. In both regions, the royalists began to raise armies to threaten patriot forces. The constitution of December 1811 also declared freedom of worship. This generated resistance from the Catholic Church, particularly from the archbishop of Caracas, Narciso Coll y Prat. He maintained a facade of reluctant cooperation with the new republic, while at the same time secretly supporting royalist movements across the country.[12] Nonetheless, before the Holy Thursday earthquake, the government had been able to manage the complex domestic situation—albeit tenuously—and to fend off the royalist incursions from the provinces. The earthquake upset this delicate balance and precipitated the republic's collapse five months later.

Historical accounts of the First Republic's collapse commonly overstate the disaster's psychic impact on the Venezuela's inhabitants, while understating its material impacts. One common claim—both in contemporary documents and in later scholarship—is that the disaster unleashed a religious (and by implication antirepublican) frenzy among the (supposedly) superstitious masses, who saw it as divine punishment visited upon Venezuela for having declared independence from Spain. For example, a recent article on the earthquake argues that "the superstition and the religious fanaticism inspired by the earthquake tipped the balance in favor of the Spanish government. . . . Later tremors kept alive the fanaticism and superstitious fears that weakened the patriot cause."[13] This picture is a caricature of a much more complex reality. By blaming the collapse of the republic on the superstitious masses, it perpetuates a pernicious stereotype about popular politics and avoids asking hard questions about the republic's significant limitations. The earthquake *did* unleash an outpouring of religious fervor among many Venezuelans. Royalist and patriot elites alike tried to politicize this religious outpouring, but a close look at the surviving documentary evidence suggests that they failed.

Rather, the earthquake propelled many members of Venezuela's "masses" to the royalist camp for more earthly, less ethereal, reasons. First, it broke the military standoff between royalist and patriot forces in western Venezuela, leading to a string of royalist victories that brought them popular support. Second, the government—already under considerable financial and political strain—could not mount adequate relief efforts. In the months after the earthquake, Venezuela's economy ground to a virtual standstill, and starvation became rampant. Third, the earthquake led directly to the suspension of Venezuela's Congress and precipitated the country's slide into dictatorship under Francisco de Miranda. This, in turn, tore apart the fragile republican coalition. As it became apparent that the patriot government could no longer effectively govern, many Venezuelans joined the royalist side. Under those conditions, popular defection to the royalists was more likely motivated by pragmatic concerns for self-preservation, rather than by blind superstition.[14]

God, Nature, and the Politics of Divine Wrath

Even as the dust was settling on Holy Thursday, royalist and patriot leaders alike sought to control the public discourse on the catastrophe—to establish a dominant interpretation. Broadly speaking, the royalist leadership argued that the earthquake was divine punishment for Venezuela's religious and political apostasy. They called for Venezuela's populace to repent and return to the fold of church and crown. In contrast, the patriots publicly contended that the earthquake was simply a natural catastrophe, with no broader divine or political significance. It was not, in this interpretation, divine punishment for anything. Venezuela's political elites—on both sides—conducted a vigorous public debate on these issues in the country's official publications, its newspapers, and in its pulpits. It is more difficult to know what ordinary Venezuelans made of the catastrophe. Many of them *did* see the disaster as divine punishment, but they did *not* politicize it in the way that the royalist elites had hoped. The earthquake produced a widespread popular outpouring of grief and repentance, cast in religious terms. But this did not translate into overt political protest or resistance. Most often, popular responses to the Holy Thursday earthquake followed the patterns of response of the colonial era. Divine punishment was interpreted primarily as response to sin—both individual and communal—and not as a response to Venezuela's political situation.

The royalists found signs of divine anger everywhere they looked. Shortly after the shaking ceased, priests in Caracas preached extemporaneous sermons that claimed the earthquake was divine punishment meted out to Venezuela for having rebelled against Ferdinand VII. The royalist José Domingo Díaz reported that when the Trinidad church collapsed, a stone from one of its pillars rolled across the plaza and knocked down the gallows where the bodies of executed royalists had been hung the previous July. The only pillar of the church that remained standing was the one that bore the Spanish royal coat of arms.[15] Royalists repeated these and other stories to mount a propaganda campaign harping on the theme of divine punishment. In the royalist stronghold of Guayana, officials circulated an edict that argued that the earthquake had been a "punishment from Heaven sent to the infidel citizens of Caracas."[16] Outside observers also noted that this interpretation of the disaster posed a serious political threat to patriot government. The earthquake "was a death blow to Miranda, and his followers," wrote a British naval officer from La Guaira, "if the adherents of Ferdinand the Seventh do not lose time in taking advantage of the effect which this calamitous visitation has had on the minds of the populace. [The earthquake] gave a degree of solemnity to the calamity which was truly awful, and inspired very generally an Idea that it was a Judgment of the Almighty upon them, manifesting his displeasure at their defection from Loyalty to their Sovereign."[17]

Patriot responses to the earthquake were more varied. Some sought a more positive interpretation of divine punishment, while others dismissed the notion of divine punishment altogether. The journalist José Domingo Díaz found one patriot leader, don Rafael de León, walking through the ruined city "with the happiest face I had ever seen . . . congratulating everyone 'because God had so clearly shown his will by destroying even the houses that had been built by the Spaniards.'" Díaz's account is also the only source for the widely repeated account of Simón Bolívar's movements immediately after the earthquake. Díaz claims to have found Bolívar climbing on top of some ruins near the Plaza of San Jacinto, trying to assess the damage. "He saw me and said to me the following impious and extravagant words: 'If nature opposes us we will struggle against her and force her to obey.'"[18] While Díaz intended this as a criticism of Bolívar, Venezuelan nationalists later enshrined this phrase as the "Mensaje de San Jacinto."[19] It would be easy to dismiss Diaz's account as apocryphal, since he was a bitter enemy of the patriots. Yet patriot writings published in the weeks following the earthquake suggest that his accounts of Bolívar and de Léon were consistent with prevailing patriot interpretations of the earthquake. De Léon's almost comically optimistic interpretation was echoed by a passage in the patriot newspaper the *Gazeta de Caracas*, which noted that earthquakes were phenomena "that undoubtedly contribute to the beautification of nature."[20] Similarly, Bolívar's claim that the earthquake was an act of nature rather than an act of God also reflected prevailing patriot interpretations of the disaster in the following months.

Through April, May, and June of 1812, the leaders of patriot government and the Catholic Church argued over the earthquake's meaning, both publicly and privately. Both sides were concerned with swaying popular opinion. At first, the government tried to popularize completely naturalistic explanations. On April 4, for example, the government requested asked Archbishop Coll y Prat to write a pastoral letter that would criticize "superstition" and argue instead that the earthquake was a "common effect in the order of nature." The following day, government leaders asked him to order his parish priests not to blame the earthquake on the political situation.[21] He chose to avoid a direct confrontation with the government but also refused to write the pastoral letter. He questioned the patriots' arguments. "I know quite well that rain, hail, lighting, and earthquakes are effects of natural causes," wrote Coll y Prat, "but I am also aware . . . that the Supreme Author of nature who governs, directs, and moves his agents, uses them to punish vices." He did not directly criticize the political system but pointed to the rampant partisanship, impiety, and libertinage that plagued the republic. He compared Caracas unfavorably to the biblical cities of Sodom and Gomorrah, which God had destroyed for their sins. He did offer to write a pastoral letter that would ask his priests to call for a return to public order and tranquillity, and to have their parishes perform acts of penitence.[22] These suggestions appear not to have satisfied the government. It was only three months later, in June of 1812, that the archbishop finally submitted a pastoral letter on the earthquake for official approval. The letter reiterated his earlier position: while the earthquake was not punishment for having rebelled against Spain, it *was* punishment for the widespread immorality that he saw in the republic. He closed by saying that "religion is the soul of all states. Be true Catholics and all will be perfect and settled." But true virtues "can neither be learned nor practised outside the Apostolic, Roman, Catholic Church." So implicitly, but not very subtly, Coll y Prat was arguing that the earthquake had been caused in part by the republic's decision to allow freedom of worship.[23] Francisco de Miranda and the other patriot leaders disagreed about how to deal with Coll y Prat's refusal to submit an acceptable pastoral letter. Miranda, by then dictator of the republic, ordered the pastoral letter to be suppressed because it was "antipolitical."[24]

Aside from their debates with the church, the patriots also began a publicity campaign to show that the earthquakes could not possibly be connected to the political system. For example, a broadsheet published on April 13 noted that Caracas had suffered earthquakes when the country was under the "tyrant" king, as had Lima, Acapulco, and Guatemala. It concluded that earthquakes carried no political agenda and were just "effects of nature." The patriot *Gazeta de Caracas* reprinted an official report of a 1641 earthquake that had caused proportionally similar damages to Caracas, even though the city's citizens had then described themselves as "most loyal vassals" of the king. The cabildo (town council) of Caracas criticized those who characterized the earthquake as divine punishment for political sins, because "these effects of natural causes happen in all countries of the world, in republics as in monarchies, in Christian, non-Christian, infidel, and protestant countries."[25]

The patriots also tried to sidestep the issue of divine wrath by drawing a distinction between religion and superstition. This way, they hoped that their criticisms of "divine wrath" would not be seen as a public attack against the Catholic Church. They described religion as a "civic virtue," while it was "superstition, fanaticism, and ignorance [that] attribute the natural effects of creation to political opinions." Other patriot publications allowed that the earthquake might have had a divine origin but argued that God's actions were not in any way connected to Venezuela's politics. An official broadsheet described the patriots as "religious" and "Christian" and argued that "earthquakes are not made to punish vices, but to test our constancy, and to remind us that there is a supreme being who can destroy in an instant all that exists in creation." Other patriot writings from this time take a slightly different position, arguing simply that "God rewards and punishes in his kingdom, and we in ours."[26] Still other documents argued that the earthquake was not divine punishment, but rather a divine test of republican virtue: "God . . . wishes to try your firmness, and to make you worthy of the Liberty which you have gained over your tyrants. That Liberty is a supreme felicity, which cannot be meritted, enjoyed, or preserved without the Heroism of Virtue, Patience in Calamities. . . . [I]f you are dismayed in the holy work which you have commenced against the ambitious, you will again be slaves and unworthy to be free."[27]

Most ordinary Venezuelans, however, do not appear to have interpreted the earthquake in purely naturalistic terms. Instead, following colonial patterns, they interpreted it in religious terms. One priest noted prosaically that "these inhabitants, as Catholics, have no other consolation than attending the sacraments of penitence and communion." In Caracas, the "stunned and tearful" survivors flocked to the plazas, fell to their knees, and begged for divine forgiveness. In La Guaira, an English sea captain found a "most awful and afflicting scene": "hundreds of suffering inhabitants were seen mixed with heaps of ruins, and many of them still yet alive with their heads out, imploring assistance from their fellow citizens, who, instead of affording them aid, were throwing themselves prostrate before images, beating their breasts, and imploring for themselves the protection of their saints."[28] These reports are more than simply exaggerations of foreign observers. Internal reports sent by parish priests to Narciso Coll y Prat, the archbishop of Caracas, speak of similar popular responses. A priest in Puerto Cabello, Joseph Felix Roscio, reported that after the earthquake he went to the town plaza, where the people had congregated and "exhorted them to repent, as the only means to placate the wrath of God irritated by our sins. Your lordship would be pleased to see how the people crowded to the confessionals to purify their consciences."

For several days after the disaster, Roscio heard confessions from three in the morning until twelve at night.[29] Similar scenes were played out across the afflicted regions, as priests quickly set up makeshift chapels and confessionals in tents to deal with the widespread popular demand for religious consolation. There is a significant silence in these reports—none of these letters from parish priests to the archbishop connect the earthquake to politics in any way.

While ordinary Venezuelans might have sought spiritual consolation, most of them did not—as royalists hoped and patriots feared—interpret the disaster as divine punishment for their politics. After the earthquake, according to one British account, some survivors sought "to make atonement for their past bad conduct, married the women with whom they had cohabited for many years previous; and even instances have occurred of men of property espousing their slaves, with whom they had illicit intercourse. In fact, every thing was forgotten but a regard to the salvation of their souls."[30] Such behavior suggests that these Venezuelans interpreted divine wrath as punishment for individual sins, rather than collective ones. The turn to the confessional also suggests that most survivors interpreted divine punishment in individual terms.

Other Venezuelans responded to the disaster in a completely secular, pragmatic manner. While some prayed, others looted the ruins and the victims. As in accounts of other disasters in colonial Latin America, the descriptions of the looters are frequently racialized. George Robertson, from England but then in Valencia, reported that the city of San Felipe "was plundered by the Sambos [a derogatory term for people of African descent] immediately after the earthquake." In Caracas, according to the British major George Dawson Flinter, "Negroes were to be seen entering the houses that were still standing . . . carrying off every thing that they could lay hands on; and it has been related to me . . . that those who were buried up to the necks in the ruins . . . had the earrings dragged out of their ears."[31] Both are hearsay accounts reported to foreigners, whose accounts in turn often highlighted the supposed barbarity of nonwhites. Nonetheless, in much of Europe and Latin America, postdisaster looting was common, and there is no reason to suppose that behaviors in Venezuela were any different. Given the racial structure of the population, it is likely that many of the looters were nonwhites. In any case, the accounts of looting reported here suggest that not all ordinary Venezuelans were paralyzed or overwhelmed with superstition.

The popular responses to the Holy Thursday earthquake and its after-shocks reveal the strength of colonial cultural structures in revolution-ary Venezuela. Only a handful of Venezuelans appear to have interpreted the event in purely naturalistic terms. Simón Bolívar's proclamation in the Plaza San Jacinto still represented a minority opinion rather than the mainstream of popular thought. Many ordinary Venezuelans still turned to God and the church for succor in times of crisis. Through their actions—their confessions, their public penitence, and their marriages—they showed that they did not accept the purely naturalistic interpreta-tions advanced by the patriots. On the other hand, these same people seem not to have accepted the prevailing royalist interpretation that the earthquake was punishment for Venezuela's purported political sins. While the disaster produced immediate and widespread popular reli-gious mobilization, this did not translate into the direct popular political action that the royalists had hoped for and the patriots had feared.

The Political Crisis:
Republican Government and Disaster Management

The earthquake produced a vicious circle of material and ideological cri-ses. It produced critical shortages of capital, food, weapons, and soldiers. These shortages made it difficult for the republic to manage the disaster from within and to fend off the royalist challenge from without. This in turn contributed to a domestic and international crisis of confidence in the republic, causing many Venezuelans to abandon the patriot cause and making it difficult for the government to get aid from abroad. In response to these challenges, political power in the republic became increasingly concentrated—and increasingly vulnerable. It was these crises, rather than popular superstition, that ultimately shifted popular support back to the royalist side.

The earthquake was a catastrophe for the patriot military forces and a boon to the royalists. Many patriot troops stationed in Caracas—including sappers, artillerymen, and "a regiment of troops of the line"—were killed when the San Carlos barracks collapsed.[32] In western Venezuela, the earth-quake broke a critical military standoff. Before the earthquake, a force of some twelve hundred well-disciplined and well-armed patriot troops stationed in Barquisimeto had blocked the advance of a royalist invasion from Coro. The force of roughly five hundred royalists, led by Domingo de Monteverde, had been forced to stop in nearby Siqusique, because they had run short of food, ammunition, and weapons. When the earthquake struck, Barquisimeto was "completely destroyed along with the majority of its citizens, and its garrison was entombed in the barracks." More than two-thirds of the patriot troops at Barquisimeto died in the earthquake. Monteverde's royalist troops, stationed on the open plains or in tents, were almost completely unharmed. Following the earthquake, Monteverde sent an advance guard of two hundred troops to Barquisimeto, which they occupied on April 2 without firing a shot. They pulled an arsenal of badly needed weapons and supplies from the ruined patriot garrison, including "four bronze cannons, three of steel, twelve cases of musket balls, over two thousand cartridges, six hundred cannonballs and grapeshot, powder, tents, and other tools." This gave them the supplies that they desperately needed to continue their advance on the patriot capital of Valencia.[33] In the coming weeks, other cities and provinces in western Venezuela quickly succumbed to the advancing royalist armies. Early in May, royalist forces captured Carora, gaining "three hundred muskets, 12 small guns, and a great quantity of ammunition, without H. M.'s arms having sustained the least injury." The ruined city of Mérida surrendered to a royalist army from undamaged Maracaibo.[34] By mid-May, six weeks after the earthquake, most of western Venezuela was under royalist control.

In eastern Venezuela, the patriot army in Guayana also suffered a serious blow on Holy Thursday—even though the earthquake had barely been felt in the area. On that morning, royalist forces mounted a surprise attack on a patriot army advancing toward the city of Angostura. One-third of the patriot force was killed or wounded, six hundred were taken prisoner, and they reportedly lost "thirty armed vessels," and almost all of their weapons and ammunition. They retreated in disorder over land, leaving the royalists in control of the Orinoco River.[35] Later accounts of this event sought to connect it with the earthquake. José Domingo Díaz wrote that "both sides believed that [the earthquake] . . . was divine punishment for the crime of rebellion." According to Díaz, soldiers in the patriot army were "overtaken by terror and despondency" by the earthquake, while the morale of the royalist forces was given a corresponding boost.[36] In this battle, however, the element of surprise likely had a greater impact on the battle's outcome than did the earthquake.

The royalists' military successes—made possible in large part by the earthquake—helped tip volatile popular sentiment in their favor. As

Monteverde's newly energized and rearmed royalist forces in western Venezuela gained control of Barquisimeto and neighboring settlements, their inhabitants quickly pledged allegiance to King Ferdinand VII. Robert Lowry, the U.S. consul at La Guaira, observed that Monteverde's royalist army "had been joined by a considerable portion of the inhabitants of the interior, among whom the superstitious idea principally excited by the priesthood, that the e[arth]quake was a chastisement of Heaven for abandoning the cause of Ferdinand the Seventh, has pretty generally spread itself."[37] Monteverde himself, however, attributed this popular change of heart primarily to his military success. "The enthusiasm of my troops," wrote Monteverde, "and the cowardice that the enemy has shown . . . ensure the good success of what has been undertaken, and to this is added the great shock which the earthquake of the 26th has caused to the citizens of these towns." Monteverde's assessment is insightful—popular support followed primarily from military success. But it was primarily the material shocks of the earthquake—rather than the spiritual ones—that had helped shift popular opinion to the royalists.[38]

In addition to its military defeats, the patriot government was also faced with the immense challenge of delivering disaster relief in the areas it still controlled. The resources of Venezuela's republican government were already badly stretched in fighting the royalists. In the days following the earthquake, the government ordered everyone except rescue workers out of Caracas, to prevent outbreaks of cholera and other diseases and to prevent injuries from the further collapse of buildings. Municipal governments and the Catholic Church conducted most of the disaster relief. In Caracas and La Guaira, survivors set up tent cities on the plains on the outskirts of the cities. The municipal government of Caracas organized teams to clear rubble from the roadways and rivers to allow shipments of food to enter the city and to ensure that the survivors had adequate drinking water. Another major challenge was retrieving and disposing of the victims' bodies. Workers in Caracas "have been digging out the bodies ever since [the earthquake], and burning them. It is shocking to see, at the close of the day, heads, arms, and legs, that have been left unburnt, as the fire dies away, and the stench is terrible." In La Guaira, bodies at first were dumped in the sea. When the seas became too heavy to row out safely, workers began to burn corpses forty at a time. As in Caracas, the stench from the bodies was often overwhelming. In early April the government authorized the cabildo of Caracas to recruit workers from the refugee camps and the areas around Caracas to help with the task.[39] Still, such official relief efforts met only a small part of the population's needs.

The international political situation made it virtually impossible for Venezuela's government to seek aid from abroad. The republic could expect no help from Spain, and most other European countries were embroiled in the Napoleonic wars. As the threat of famine grew through April and May of 1812, the Venezuelan government approached the U.S. government for disaster relief. The Venezuelan representative in the United States, Telésforo de Orea, asked the U.S. secretary of state, James Monroe, to relax the U.S. embargo against trade with South America to allow food shipments through. The U.S. Congress refused, fearing that speculators might take advantage. Nevertheless, it did appropriate fifty thousand dollars to supply aid to Venezuela and chartered six ships to send flour, corn, and other food to Venezuela. The aid came far too late: the first ship did not arrive in Venezuela until early June. Furthermore, most of the supplies remained stuck in La Guaira because of shortages of labor and transportation to ship it to the rest of the country. Back in the United States, de Orea also sought official diplomatic recognition for the Venezuelan republic. Although the U.S. Congress was sympathetic to the republican cause, it decided to withhold recognition to see whether the republic would survive. Its vulnerability was becoming more apparent with each passing day.[40]

Famine and misery spread though the shrinking area under patriot control. "Never was any country in a more deplorable state than this at that period," observed U.S. envoy Alexander Scott. When the patriot armies retreated into the coastal mountain range, they lost access to the herds of cattle on the *llanos*—the grasslands of central Venezuela—which were a key source of food for Caracas. Scott complained that "not a pound of meat could be procured" in Caracas or La Guaira. Caracas got what food it could from Barlovento, the agricultural region to the east of the city. A British observer worried that "the resources of the country were almost totally exhausted, the absence of provisions is threatening to turn into starvation." Later that month the journalist José Domingo Díaz saw hunger "in all its forms for the first time, in a soil which appeared exempt from it by nature." In the besieged patriot areas, the population began to feed on what weeds (*verdolaga*) they could collect. Dysentery became rampant.[41]

The earthquake also aggravated a growing fiscal and agricultural crises that had begun the year before. In the years 1811–1812, Venezuela accumulated a trade deficit of almost 575,000 pesos. Even before the earthquake, the government began issuing paper money to make up for the shortfall in revenues. Its only source of hard currency was foreign trade. But the earthquake destroyed much of the productive infrastructure on Venezuela's coffee, sugar, and cacao plantations, whose exports gave Venezuela most of its hard currency. In response, the government began to print more paper money, which led to further inflation. By early June, the value of the paper money had depreciated by almost a third. It had only "imaginary" value, in the words of José Domingo Díaz. Besides the property losses, which the U.S. consul Alexander Scott later estimated to be around four million dollars, the earthquake provoked capital flight from Venezuela. Because of the earthquake, "all foreigners, and every person having the means, are leaving the place for the islands and elsewhere." One observer estimated that "three fourths of the wealth of Caraccas are lost."[42] In a single gloomy letter, the patriot lawyer and soldier Francisco Paúl summarized Venezuela's catastrophic economic situation. He noted that commerce was paralyzed—some business owners had been taken from their businesses and pressed into military service, while others were confined to prison "simply because of their origin and nature." In short, concluded Paúl, "there are no businessmen and, as a result, there is no business." The regions still under patriot control could not produce enough food, the liberation of the slaves had led to the collapse of commercial agriculture, and the government's failure to meet its contracts meant that few foreign ships would be willing to trade with Venezuela.[43] The country's domestic and commercial agriculture were almost completely paralyzed.

The earthquake also contributed directly to the collapse of congressional government and the emergence of a dictatorship in Venezuela. Many members of Congress had been killed in the earthquake, and others were too busy working on the rescue efforts to attend sessions. The few members of Congress who did attend expressed concern about how to cope with the recovery efforts, dealing with the potential problems that "malice, aided by superstition, could use to profit from the recent calamity." On April 3, the remaining members of Congress, "convinced . . . that the natural and political circumstances in which Venezuela finds itself, demand measures that are incompatible with the calm and meditation of better times," modified the constitution. The new constitution temporarily granted dictatorial powers to a three-person Executive, "so that in the current circumstances it can attend to the salvation of the country." This was meant to be a temporary measure, and they planned to reconvene the full Congress on the 5th of July, the first anniversary of the declaration of independence.[44] But the three-person Executive proved no more capable than the full Congress at managing disaster relief and waging war. By the end of April, it had appointed the controversial Francisco de Miranda head of the army and granted him sweeping powers. Nonetheless, Monteverde's royalist troops kept moving forward through the demoralized patriot cities. He recaptured the patriot capital Valencia on May 3. In desperation, on May 18 the Executive officially named Miranda dictator of Venezuela. This decision split the patriot ranks. The landed creole elite were deeply suspicious of Miranda's radical republicanism. Many patriots did not trust Miranda and obeyed him only with great reluctance.[45]

Faced with crises on all sides, Miranda's government began to unravel. Miranda's patriot army was still larger and better trained than that of Monteverde's royalist forces, but it was completely demoralized. Miranda was unwilling to attack the royalist army because of the "despondency and discontent" so clearly evident in his own forces. Increasingly desperate, on June 19 Miranda imposed martial law. The law allowed Miranda to conscript all free citizens (including pardos) and a thousand slaves. This declaration provoked an insurrection of pardos and slaves in Barlovento on June 24, the day of San Juan Bautista, patron saint of blacks in Venezuela. The insurrection in Barlovento cut Caracas from its remaining source of food. On July 5, the critical patriot garrison at Puerto Cabello betrayed its leader, Simón Bolívar, and defected to the royalists. Faced with a destroyed capital, a demoralized army, a starving citizenry, and an impending race war, Miranda capitulated to Monteverde on the 25th of July. Venezuela's first republic had collapsed. Reflecting on the state of Venezuela in the following months, Alexander Scott concluded that "the earthquake and its fatal consequences, the civil war and its unfortunate termination, the merciless reign of the conquerors, . . . the destruction of the Estates, and [the] misery of the inhabitants, have reduced the country to a state from which it will not emerge for years."[46]

Holy Thursday and the Collapse of the First Republic

For the royalists, Monteverde's victory proved that the earthquake had been divine punishment for rebellion. On October 15, Archbishop Coll y Prat published the pastoral letter on the earthquake that had been banned by the patriots. He called for a public fast and public acts of penitence. On

October 19, "the image of Nuestra Señora del Rosario, ancient patroness of earthquakes in this capital, was carried from the chapel of Santo
Domingo to that of San Pedro, followed by sermons in the plaza mayor."
The fast was observed from the 21st to the 24th, and from the 19th to
the 30th the church offered the sacrament of penitence to anyone who
presented themselves. On October 30, the patroness of earthquakes was
returned to the chapel of Santo Domingo. Waiting at the altar were all
the royalist high military command and the leadership of the church. This
included the victorious general Domingo de Monteverde who, as a reward
for his victory, had been appointed captain general of Venezuela and president of the Royal Audiencia of Caracas. It also included the triumphant
but somewhat chastened Coll y Prat, whom Monteverde and the royalists
had criticized for not having mounted a more active opposition to the
patriots. By honoring the patroness of earthquakes, Monteverde and Coll
y Prat reaffirmed the unity of church and state and the rule of Ferdinand
VII in the troubled province.[47]

Not everyone, however, drew the same conclusions about the meanings of the earthquake. Exiled in Cartagena, six hundred miles to the west
of Caracas, Simón Bolívar reflected on the collapse of the republican government. He argued that the deaths caused by the earthquake, and the
"general consternation" that it caused, "were only of secondary importance among the causes which led to the annihilation of our liberty and
independence. Political errors committed by the government had a more
direct influence on the catastrophe."[48] Bolívar sketched out these lessons
in greater detail in his *Manifiesto de Cartagena*, published in December of
1812. He described the earthquake as "the immediate cause of Venezuela's
ruin" but continued that "this event could have happened without producing such fatal results had Caracas been governed at that time, by a
single authority."[49] A centralized government, argued Bolívar, could have
responded to the disaster—and to other threats—much more quickly
and effectively. The lessons of the earthquake formed the cornerstone of
Bolívar's philosophy of government during the long wars of independence
that followed.

While the Holy Thursday earthquake did not alone cause the collapse of the First Republic, it changed the course of the collapse. Even
without the earthquake, it is unlikely that the First Republic could have
survived over the long term. Manuel Lucena Samoral has shown convincingly that the republic faced severe economic problems that would have

been difficult to overcome. The republic would also have probably faced repeated insurrections from the pardo majority and from the *llaneros*— mestizos from Venezuela's vast grasslands—who did, in fact, help topple the Second Republic in 1814. But had the earthquake not destroyed the patriot garrisons in Caracas and Barquisimeto, they could have counted on more troops and weapons to meet the royalist armies. The patriot army at Barquisimeto would likely have fended off—and possibly even defeated— Monteverde's smaller and poorly armed royalist contingent. These military victories, in turn, might have won the patriots continued popular support. They might have been able to use the reserve army stationed in Caracas to regain control of eastern Venezuela and the Orinoco. Without the earthquake, the Venezuelan Congress would likely have remained in charge of the republic. Miranda would never have had the opportunity to become dictator and the patriots would not have become so internally divided. A more stable republic might also have received diplomatic recognition, foreign aid, and even troops. French mercenaries arrived in Venezuela in June and July of 1812, and a few years later British mercenaries reinforced the patriot armies and contributed to their ultimate victory. Even if the patriot government had lost in the end, a stronger government could have sued for peace and signed an armistice on more equitable terms. Francisco de Miranda might have returned to England to continue drumming up British support for Latin American independence, instead of ending his days in a Spanish prison. Simón Bolívar might have remained just another footnote in history, a minor creole leader in a failed attempt at independence. Had the colony eventually achieved independence—as seems likely—it would have begun its life as a republic with more of its productive infrastructure intact, instead of languishing in poverty and ruin for a half century.

More broadly, the story of the Holy Thursday earthquake sheds light on how societies in Latin America responded to disaster during the age of Independence—a long "middle period" that lasted from the mid-eighteenth century to the mid-nineteenth century. In spite of the political and social upheaval that accompanied the First Republic, the response to disaster followed well-established colonial patterns. People turned to their faith and the Catholic Church for spiritual consolation. Purely naturalistic interpretations of natural disaster—which had been much in vogue in Europe for at least a century—did not have deep roots in colonial society. The debates over divine punishment among the royalist and patriot elite suggest that the modern/traditional divide was not absolute. Even Archbishop Coll y Prat allowed that nature followed laws (albeit ones designed by God), while many patriot publications conceded that the disaster may have been divine punishment. Conversely, the repeated elite condemnations of popular "superstition" show how poorly they understood the lives and interests of Venezuela's majority. At a popular level, the failure of both patriots and royalists alike to make any significant political capital out of the catastrophe shows just how alienated most ordinary Venezuelans were from elite interests on both sides.

From a political perspective, the Holy Thursday earthquake was a dramatic test of a new form of government in Latin America and gave the new republics a foretaste of the domestic and international challenges that they were to face in the years to come. When the disaster struck, the Venezuelan republic was doubly isolated. It could not draw upon the resources of the Spanish empire for disaster relief, as cities across Latin America had done when disaster struck in the colonial period. But since the republic had not been recognized by most of the world's major powers, it could not count upon the international community for relief either. This might not have mattered so much if the republic had enjoyed more solid support from its own citizens. But the earthquake highlighted the republic's vulnerability on many fronts. It could not effectively meet the population's immediate needs, nor could it do much in the way of preventing social protest or rebuilding. The disaster may have tipped popular opinion toward the royalists, but this shift was not motivated primarily by superstition. Rather, it was motivated by the republic's failure to deal swiftly and adequately with military, economic, and political crises—all of which were aggravated by the earthquake. The collapse of the First Republic showed Bolívar and other patriot leaders that they needed to build their new republics on more solid political foundations.

The Legacies of Holy Thursday

The royalist victory proved fleeting, but the earthquake's long-term physical and economic consequences endured. Much of Venezuela's physical and economic infrastructure was in ruins. Over the next seven years, the destruction caused by the earthquakes was compounded by brutal warfare. In 1813, the patriots reconquered much of their lost territory, including Caracas, and established the Second Republic. That republican experiment also failed, and royalists regained control of Caracas in 1814. In 1816, while the colony was in royalist hands, the archbishop and the Ayuntamiento petitioned King Ferdinand VII for financial support for reconstruction. They noted that most of the colony remained in ruins and that its economy was too poor to fund the work of reconstruction on its own. Caracas was in such poor condition that in 1817 the Spanish authorities even considered moving the city to a different location. By 1820, Caracas's population had fallen to half the size it had been a decade before. In the end, then, the Spanish empire was no longer able to manage natural disasters and contain social fissures as it had in the late colonial period. No doubt, this failure helped the patriots regain control of the nation and its ruined capital in 1821. For much of the nineteenth century, successive governments tried—with only limited success—to rebuild Venezuela's devastated cities and infrastructure.[50]

Venezuela's recovery began after independence was finally consolidated in the early 1820s. Even so, however, ruins continued to dominate the landscapes of Venezuela's major cities. Upon arriving in La Guaira in the mid-1820s, for example, William Duane from the United States noted that "the effects of the earthquake of the 26th of March 1812 are visible at every step." One half of the city's houses were still in ruins. "The dissonance of the cracked bells [in La Guaira's churches] reminds the inhabitants three or four times [daily] of the calamity. . . . Whole squares are still in ruins, little having been done but to clear the streets of rubbish." Caracas was in somewhat better shape. From a distance the view of Caracas was dominated by its famous red roofs, but upon closer inspection Duane found that "one fifth of the city was still in ruins. . . . In this quarter, little has been done but to disencumber the streets of rubbish, which has been thrown within the cracked and tottering walls of the roofless buildings." The British diplomat Sir Robert Ker Porter found the city in much the same shape several years later.[51] As late as the 1850s, ruined churches, monasteries, and houses still dotted the landscapes of Caracas, and only two bridges provided access to the city. It was not until President Antonio Guzmán Blanco began a program of urban renewal in Caracas during the 1870s and 1880s that the final physical traces of the earthquake in Caracas were erased.[52]

Although the Holy Thursday earthquake's physical traces are gone, it has gained an increasingly important cultural and political significance. In 1831 Richard Vowell, a former British volunteer in the Venezuelan Lancers, published a novel entitled *The Earthquake of Caraccas*, as part of a trilogy on Venezuelan independence. Much of the novel is pure invention, although Vowell did fight for the patriot armies in Venezuela from late 1817 to 1819 and so witnessed the damage that the earthquake had caused.[53] More significantly, the earthquake—and in particular Bolívar's "mensaje de San Jacinto"—became an iconic moment in the national founding myth of Venezuela. This process began in the early twentieth century, around the time of the centennial of independence. In the 1920s, the Venezuelan artist Tito Salas depicted Bolívar's proclamation in a painting for Bolívar's newly restored birthplace. As part of the celebrations of Caracas's 400th anniversary in 1967, Bolívar's words were carved onto a monumental wall on the Plaza San Jacinto in foot-high letters, underneath the shields and flags of all the countries he helped liberate. In a 1967 article celebrating the plaza's restoration, the historian—and later president—Rafael Caldera described the earthquake as "the moment that split the history of Venezuela in two."[54] In fact, it did nothing of the kind. If anything, the Holy Thursday earthquake showed the patriots just how fragile the republican project was, and how much work lay ahead of them before they could succeed.

✢ NOTES ✢

1. Samuel L. Mitchill, "The Leading Facts Relative to the Earthquakes Which Desolated Venezuela, in South America, in the Months of March and April, 1812," *Transactions of the Literary and Philosophical Society of New York* 1 (1815): 42; Alexander von Humboldt, *Personal Narrative of Travels to the Equinoctial Regions of the New Continent: During the Years 1799–1804*, 1st ed. (London: Longman, Hurst, Rees, Orme, Brown, and Green, 1819), bk. 5, 14; José Domingo Díaz, *Recuerdos sobre la rebelión de Caracas* (Caracas: Academia Nacional de la Historia, 1961), 100.

2. Drouet, in Mitchill, "Leading Facts," 309–10; Díaz, *Rebelión de Caracas*, 98.

3. Sebastián Bueno to Archbishop Narciso Coll y Pratt, Choroní, March 28, 1812, no. 682, Colección Laureano Valenilla, Papeles del Arzobispado en relación con el terremoto de 1812, Archivo de la Academia Nacional de Historia de Venezuela, Caracas (hereafter cited as ANHV).

4. H. Poudenx and F. Mayer, *Memoria para contribuir a la historia de la revolución de la capitanía general de Caracas desde la abdicación de Carlos IV hasta el mes de agosto de 1814* (Paris, 1815; repr. in *Tres testigos europeos de la Primera República*, ed. Ramón Escovar Salom [Caracas: Ediciones de la Presidencia de la República, 1974], 131). Urquinaona estimated San Felipe's population to be 75,000 people. This is excessively large for the period, and is probably just a typographical error. The true population was probably closer to 7,500. In 1806 Depons estimated San Felipe's population to be 6,800. See Pedro Urquinaona y Pardo, *Memorias de Urqinaona (Comisionado de la regencia Española para la pacificación del Nuevo Reino de Granada)* (1820; repr. Madrid: Editorial América, 1917), 90; and F. Depons, *Travels in Parts of South America during the Years 1801, 1802, 1803, and 1804* (London: Phillips, 1806), 126–27.

5. Francisco de Yepes to Juana, March 31, 1812, in *Epistolario de la Primera República*, vol. 2 (Caracas: Academia Nacional de la Historia, 1960), 444–45.

6. Humboldt, *Personal Narrative*, 21; Mitchill, "Leading Facts," 310; Díaz, *Rebelión de Caracas*, 102. Humboldt gives the date of this second large shock as April 5, but all other sources point to the 4th.

7. Humboldt, *Personal Narrative*, 17–22. For an accessible overview of earthquakes in Venezuela, see Carlos Schubert, *Los terremotos en Venezuela y su origen* (Caracas: Cuadernos Lagoven, 1983). The differing scientific interpretations of Holy Thursday's seismic events are concisely summarized in Jaime Laffaille and Carlos Ferrer, "El terremoto del jueves santo en Mérida: Año 1812," *Revista Geográfica Venezolana* 44, no. 1 (2003): 107–23.

8. Hodgson to the Earl of Liverpool, April 23, 1812, fol. 149, War Department In-Letters and Papers: 1. Of the French Wars Period; b. West Indies and South America; vi. Curaçao: Governor's Dispatches, January–August, 1812, War Office of the United Kingdom (hereafter cited as WO) 1/111, Public Record Office, Kew, England (now the National Archives of the United Kingdom; hereafter cited as PRO).

9. Charles F. Walker, "Shaking the Unstable Empire: The Lima, Quito, and Arequipa Earthquakes, 1746, 1783, and 1797," in *Dreadful Visitations: Confronting Natural Catastrophe in the Age of Enlightenment*, ed. Alessa Johns (New York: Routledge, 1999), 138.

10. Walker, "Shaking the Unstable Empire," 127.

11. Depons, *Travels in South America*, 30.

12. For succinct overviews of the First Republic, see Jaime E. Rodríguez O., *The Independence of Spanish America* (Cambridge: Cambridge University Press, 1998), 109–19; John Lynch, *The Spanish-American Revolutions, 1808–1826* (New York: Norton, 1973), 18–198. On Miranda's role in the First Republic,

see Karen L. Racine, *Francisco de Miranda: A Transatlantic Life in the Age of Revolution* (Wilmington: Scholarly Resources, 2003), 211–41.

13. Laffaille and Ferrer, "Terremoto," 109.

14. John V. Lombardi's account of the First Republic in *Venezuela: The Search for Order, the Dream of Progress* does not mention the earthquake at all (New York: Oxford University Press, 1982), 127–30. Two accounts that mention it in passing are Guillermo Morón's *A History of Venezuela* (New York: Roy, 1963), 109; J. L. Salcedo-Bastardo's *Historia fundamental de Venezuela*, 10th ed. (Caracas: Universidad Central de Venezuela, 1993), 243–44. John Lynch describes the earthquake as an "external shock" in *Spanish American Revolutions*, 198. Caracciolo Parra-Pérez's magisterial *Historia de la Primera República de Venezuela* (1939; repr. Caracas: Biblioteca Ayacucho, 1992) characterizes the earthquake as a secondary cause of the republic's decline. See especially chapter 10.

15. Díaz, *Rebelión de Caracas*, 99–100; Poudenx and Mayer, *Historia de la revolución*, 132.

16. Letter of May 29, 1812, quoted in Report by the Interim Governor of the Province of Guayana, October 20, 1812, fols. 408–9, tras. 5.4.22, Independencia y República, 1808–1814, Archivo General de la Nación, Caracas, 421–24.

17. Forrest to Stirling, March 30, 1812, fol. 72/139, in William Spence Robertson, *The Life of Miranda* (New York: Cooper Square, 1969), 2, 146–47.

18. Díaz, *Rebelión de Caracas*, 98–99.

19. Rafael Caldera, "El mensaje de San Jacinto," *Revista de la Sociedad Bolivariana de Venezuela* 27, no. 92 (1967): 480–82.

20. "Terremoto del año de 1641," *Gazeta de Caracas*, April 25, 1812, 6n2.

21. Urquinaona y Pardo, *Memorias*, 91–92; Antonio Muñoz Tébar to Narciso Coll y Prat, April 4, 1812, Valencia; Antonio Muñoz Tébar to Narciso Coll y Prat, April 5, 1812, Valencia, both reprinted in Gabriel Muñoz, *Monteverde: cuatro años de historia patria* (Caracas: Academia Nacional de la Historia, 1987), 1:106–8; José Gil Fortul, *Historia constitucional de Venezuela*, 5th ed., vol. 4 (Caracas: Sales, 1964), 292–94.

22. Narciso Coll y Prat to Antonio Muñoz Tébar, Caracas (Ñaraluí), April 10, 1812, reprinted in Muñoz, *Monteverde*, 108–9.

23. Narciso Coll y Prat to Secretary of State, Caracas (Ñaraulí), June 1, 1812, reprinted in Muñoz, *Monteverde*, 113–21.

24. Urquinaona y Pardo, *Memorias*, 98–105; Muñoz, *Monteverde*, 102; Díaz, *Rebelión de Caracas*, 105.

25. "Terremoto del año de 1641," *Gazeta de Caracas*; Concejo Municipal del Distrito Federal, *Actas del Cabildo, 1812–1814* (Caracas: Tipografía Vargas, 1972), 2:76.

26. "A los militares del estado de Caracas," broadsheet reprinted in Escovar Salom, *Tres testigos*, 224–25; "Carta de un ciudadano, a un amigo suyo," *Gazeta de Caracas*, April 25, 1812.

27. Hall of Representatives to the Sovereign People of Caracas, April 9, 1812, WO 1/111, PRO.

28. Various Authors to Archbishop Narciso Colly y Prat, Papeles del Arzobispado, ANHV; Díaz, *Rebelión de Caracas*, 99: Poudenx and Mayer, *Historia de la revolución*, 132; *Times* (London), May 29, 1812.

29. Joseph Felix Roscio to Narciso Coll y Prat, March 30, 1812, Papeles del Arzobispado, ANHV.

30. George Dawson Flinter, *A History of the Revolution of Caracas* (London: Allman, 1819), 34–35.

31. George Robertson, "Abstracted from a Letter from George Robertson, Esq., dated Valentea, April 17, 1812," *Gentleman's Magazine* 82 (August 1812): 110; Flinter, *Revolution of Caracas*, 33.

32. On the deployment of troops in Caracas, see Humboldt, *Personal Narrative*, bk. 5, 14; Poudenx and Mayer, *Historia de la revolución*, 130–1; Díaz, *Rebelión de Caracas*, 98.

33. Domingo de Monteverde to the Governor of Coro, March 29, 1812, Carora, in Muñoz, *Monteverde* 1:91–94; Urquinaona y Pardo, *Memorias*, 89, 90, 106; Luis Iribarren-Celis, "La destrucción de Barquisimeto por el terremoto de 1812 como una de las causas que determinaron la caida de la Primera República," *Boletín de la Academia Nacional de la Historia* 45, no. 117 (1962): 37–41.

34. Cevallos to Governor of Curaçao, May 17, 1812, WO 1/111, PRO.

35. Parra-Pérez, *Historia*, 421; Francisco de Mijares to the Governor of Curaçao, May 15, 1812, WO 1/111, PRO.

36. Díaz, *Rebelión de Caracas*, 101.

37. Robert K. Lowry to James Monroe, June 5, 1812, La Guaira, in *Diplomatic Correspondence of the United States concerning the Independence of the Latin-American Nations*, vol. 2, ed. William R. Manning (New York: Oxford University Press, 1925), 1158.

38. Domingo de Monteverde to the Governor of Coro, March 29, 1812, Carora, in Muñoz, *Monteverde*, 1:92.

39. Poudenx and Mayer, *Historia de la revolución*, 132; Mitchill, "Leading Facts," 310–12; Concejo Municipal, *Actas del Cabildo*, 2:75; "Earthquake in Venezuela," *Weekly Register* (Baltimore), April 25, 1812; Enrique Bernardo Nuñez, "26 de Marzo de 1812," *Crónica de Caracas*, January–March 1957, 552–56.

40. See the correspondence between Telésforo de Orea and James Monroe, reprinted in Cristóbal L. Mendoza, "Las primeras relaciones diplomáticas de Venezuela con los Estados Unidos," *Boletín de la Academia Nacional de la Historia* 27 (October–December 1944): 346–72. See also Harold A. Bierck, Jr., "The First Instance of U.S. Foreign Aid: Venezuelan Relief in 1812," *Inter-American Economic Affairs* 9, no. 1 (1955): 47–59.

41. Scott to Monroe, November 16, 1812, Caracas, in Manning, *Diplomatic Correspondence*, 1159–63; Caracciolo Parra-Pérez, ed. *Documentos de cancillerías europeas sobre independencia venezolana* (Caracas: Academia Nacional de la Historia, 1962), 2:530–31; Díaz, *Rebelión de Caracas*, 105–6.

42. Parra-Pérez, ed., *Documentos de cancillerías europeas*, 2:530–31; Díaz, *Rebelión de Caracas*, 105–6; Mitchill, "Leading Facts," 312; Manuel Lucena Samoral, "Incidencia del comercio exterior en la caída de la primera república de Venezuela," in *Primer Congreso Internacional de Historia Económica y Social de la Cuenca del Caribe, 1763–1898* (San Juan: Centro de Estudios Avanzados de Puerto Rico y el Caribe, 1992), 411–53. See also his *Características del comercio exterior de la provincia de Caracas durante el sexenio revolucionario (1807–1812)* (Madrid: IEF, 1990).

43. Francisco Paúl to General Miranda, July 7, 1812, in *Epistolario*, 64–67.

44. El Poder Ejecutivo de la Unión a los Estados Unidos de Venezuela, April 5, 1812, Valencia, doc. 14, carpeta 1, gaveta 1, archivo 5, Colleción Arístides Rojas, ANHV; *Libro de actas del Supremo Congreso de Venezuela, 1811–1812* (Caracas: Academia Nacional de Historia, 1959), 392–99; Parra-Pérez, *Historia*, 2:259; Fortul, *Historia constitucional*, 290.

45. Racine, *Francisco de Miranda*, 232–37.

46. José Francisco Heredia, *Memorias del regente Heredia* (Caracas: Academia Nacional de la Historia, 1986), 64; Scott to Monroe, November 16, 1812, Caracas, in Manning, *Diplomatic Correspondence*, 1159–63.

47. "Penitencia pública," *Gazeta de Caracas*, November 8, 1812.

48. Simón Bolívar to the Sovereign Congress of New Granada, November 27, 1812, in *Selected Writings of Bolívar*, ed. Vicente Lecuna and Harold A. Bierck, Jr. (New York: Colonial, 1951), 1:15–17.

49. Simón Bolívar, "Memorial to the Citizens of New Granada by a Citizen of Caracas, December 15, 1812," in Lecuna and Bierck, *Selected Writings of Bolívar*, 18–26.

50. Tomás Polanco Alcántara, *Historia de Caracas* (Caracas: Academia Nacional de la Historia, 1995), 36–37.

51. William Duane, *Notes on Colombia Taken in the Years 1822–3* (Philadelphia: Carey & Lea, 1827), 22–23, 3–37. See also Walter Dupouy, "Tres aspectos de Caracas en el diario de Sir Robert Ker Porter," *Boletín de la Academia Nacional de la Historia* 50, no. 199 (1967): 411–16.

52. Ermila Troconis de Veracoechea, *Caracas* (Caracas: Grijalbo, 1993), 181–92; Polanco Alcántara, *Historia de Caracas*, 53–71.

53. Richard Longfield Vowell, *The Earthquake at Caraccas*, vol. 2 of *Campaigns and Cruises, in Venezuela and New Grenada, and in the Pacific Ocean, from 1817 to 1830* (London: Longman, 1831).

54. Caldera, "Mensaje de San Jacinto," 480.

CHAPTER THREE

Social and Political Fault Lines
The Valparaíso Earthquake of 1906

SAMUEL J. MARTLAND

✣ ON AUGUST 16, 1906, A LITTLE BEFORE 8:00 P.M., "THE WELL-KNOWN merchant don Manuel González," his wife Consuela Quesada de González, and their children Amparo, Maria, Felicia, Angela, Manuel, and Carmela, were at home in their posh apartment, the second floor of a house in the middle of Valparaíso's Almendral neighborhood.[1] In their published pictures, they wear the suits and dresses of the well-off. Two or more maids were working in the apartment.

When the first of the earthquake's two main shocks struck at 7:55 p.m., the González family ran downstairs and outside. They got to the sidewalk just in time for everyone, "including the servants," to be crushed by the falling wall of the "solid" building that had almost been completed next door on the corner of Jaime and Victoria streets. Their own house seems not to have collapsed: their upstairs neighbors, the Mery family, got out safely, although they had to step over the victims and the debris on their way. Rescuers got the mother, the two surviving children, and the bodies of the other Gonzálezes out shortly after the earthquake. They took the living members of the family to an emergency infirmary in a nearby convent. Carmela lived two days. Consuelo and Manuel survived. The 1906 book that recounts the story does not say whether the servants survived, or even mention them until they are crushed.[2]

Like the Gonzálezes, many of Valparaíso's residents, especially well-to-do ones, were at home when the earthquake struck. Others were in bars, but the theaters had not opened yet and most other businesses were closed. The first shock sent everyone running into the streets. Many died there as a second shock, at 8:06 p.m., sent more buildings crashing to the ground. Those who survived found themselves in chilly, damp darkness. The electricity had gone out, and the gaslights had lasted just long enough to ignite some of the ruins. The fires provided the only heat and light in the city that night.[3]

Other towns, from neighboring Viña del Mar to more distant Casablanca and Quillota, suffered significant damage and casualties. The same damage to the railroad that kept food from reaching Valparaíso kept imports from reaching Santiago through its only convenient port, and kept the central valley's produce from reaching the sea. By August 24, food was reportedly running short a thousand miles to the north in desert Tarapacá, because the earthquake had cut off supplies usually sent by sea from Valparaíso.[4] However, the quake was most deadly and most destructive in the crowded port city, where about three thousand died.[5]

The story of the González family and their servants suggests some key issues of the aftermath and context. During the building boom of the previous decades, Valparaíso's builders and officials had apparently thought it impossible to prepare for earthquakes; they must have known about the great Valparaíso quakes of 1575, 1647, 1730, and 1822, as well as many others in Chile and neighboring countries. The profits from Chile's nitrate boom and the related boom in imports through Valparaíso, combined with an embrace of new technology, had produced fire safety regulations and the beginnings of a sewer system, but not antiseismic building codes. Ill-designed cornices and heavy outer walls killed or injured many people, including those in the González household. The Almendral, Valparaíso's most prestigious neighborhood, suffered disproportionately because it stood on a sandy landfill built to extend the flat part of the city for the convenience of the prosperous.

Valparaíso had not prepared for an earthquake, but it had built up extensive state and private capacity to deal with crises. Experience with lesser disasters, volunteer firefighting and related community and government activity made it possible to organize an effective response very quickly. Indeed, the social prestige of volunteer firefighting probably helped create the willingness to volunteer that helped the city survive after the earthquake. The city had no disaster plan, but doctors, nuns, and so on set up impromptu medical posts in whatever safe place they could. Priests crisscrossed the city, helping the living and absolving the dying.[6] Victims and their neighbors ran helter-skelter, and the lucky ones found help.

The earthquake illuminated notions of order and class in early twentieth-century Chile. Surely someone knew the González servants' names and what happened to them and many other poor citizens, but newspaper accounts of the devastation focused on the affluent. The poor appeared mostly as generalized objects of sympathy or as the implicit, unspoken source of the potential civil unrest and crime that spooked the city's officials. Their fears may not have been ungrounded. Inmates tried to escape from the ruins of the prison, and there was a little looting; moreover, recent years had seen violent riots and strikes in Valparaíso and elsewhere in Chile. However, either strict security measures or a shortage of potential criminals kept the weeks after the earthquake peaceful.

Finally, the earthquake, and the reconstruction that followed, illuminated the economic and political position of Valparaíso in Chile and the world—a strong position that helped attract resources for rebuilding. For much of the nineteenth century, Valparaíso dominated the trade and finance of the Pacific coast of South America. In 1906 it was still a major international commercial and banking center, with many European residents. It also handled most imports and exports for Chile's inland capital, Santiago, and the populous central valley that stretched to the south of the capital.

For all its importance, Valparaíso was fairly isolated. Only one railroad and two or three improved roads led out of it. (One reason officials feared civil unrest was that earthquake damage cut the city off from its usual food supplies.) There were not enough deepwater piers, so much cargo and many passengers came ashore in large rowboats. On the north and west the city faced the ocean, on the south and east, small mountains. The sliver of flat land between the waves and the hills held the city's most valuable buildings, from mansions and theaters to factories and warehouses, with some tenements mixed in. The steep hills held a variety of residential neighborhoods. Well-to-do Germans and Britons lived on Alegre Hill and Concepción Hill, while poor and working-class Chileans inhabited most

Valparaíso, showing earthquake destruction. The lightly shaded blocks
were destroyed by the earthquake, and the darker blocks burned. Playa
Ancha is on the hills in the northwest corner. The Puerto is along the
waterfront just east of Playa Ancha. Concepción Hill divides the Puerto
from the Almendral, which is the large, flat, mostly destroyed area
in the eastern part of the city. Barón Hill is in the northeast corner.
The railroad runs along the waterfront to Viña del Mar, off the map
to the northeast; the road to Santiago climbs a ravine to the southeast
(RODRÍGUEZ ROZAS AND GAJARDO CRUZAT, "PLANO DE VALPARAÍSO,"
CATÁSTROFE, BETWEEN 130 AND 131).

of the others. At the west end of the city, the hills of Playa Ancha held a
growing neighborhood with some middle-class homes; in the east, Baron
Hill's population included many railroad and factory workers. Even on the
relatively flat-topped hills of Playa Ancha and Barón, many sidewalks had
stairs or rose far above the streets; on the rougher hills in between, some
streets turned into staircases, narrowed to alleys, or became dirt paths.
Houses clung to the hillsides. Elite porteños (port folk, as residents were
called) tended to think of the hills as precarious—physically, economically, and socially—and were nonplussed when they suffered less than the
flat areas.

Immediate Reactions and Relief Efforts

Huddled in parks, plazas, and streets, the people of Valparaíso improvised shelters, wondered, and worried through the night. Some hunted for relatives or rescued neighbors. Some members of the generally excellent volunteer fire department tried to put out the fires, and others dug for survivors, but the quake had decimated the department and the fires burned for three days.[7] Broken water pipes and the most fires ever seen in the city would have overpowered even the full-strength department. In the Plaza de la Victoria, Intendant Enrique Larraín Alcalde, the chief national government official in Valparaíso, was improvising, too. In the first hour, he sent about 250 marines from ships in the bay to patrol the city. He also assigned doctors to two major medical posts and sent a mounted messenger to Santiago, but soldiers, sailors, and police dominate the official actions of the first hours.[8] If he assigned anyone that night to dig victims out of the ruins, or communicated with the fire department, the city's major newspaper, *El Mercurio*, did not think it worth mentioning. Neither Valparaíso nor Chile nor even the fire department had any particular plan for responding to major disasters. On his own, Larraín responded to the earthquake as though it were a riot. Whether or not this was the best plan, the fact that he was able to do it demonstrated the state's capacity to make and carry out plans.

In the first days, Larraín bypassed many preexisting offices and government functions and set up a provisional military government using the people who happened to come to hand. The morning after the quake, Larraín met with the manager of the water company, arranged "contracts for the construction of sheds" for the homeless, appointed two food supply committees, and asked the national government for military engineers to demolish dangerous ruins.[9] The municipal government was legally autonomous, but the national government had ultimate authority and greater resources. Mayor Enrique Bermúdez, the municipal government, and local institutions helped, rather than led. Larraín even made a Santiago city councilor, who simply happened to be in town, head of one food committee. Other special committees of local and national government officials, military officers, clergy, and wealthy citizens tackled other key problems. Navy captain Luis Gómez Carreño, whom Larraín made military commander of the city the day after the quake, had walked in from Viña del Mar on his own initiative. In keeping with this impromptu organization, contemporary comment focused on individuals, not on systems or institutions.

Larraín thought about health, food, and dangerous buildings, but, above all, he thought about security and order. By noon on August 17, the police, the marines, and two companies of regular infantry were guarding Valparaíso. Not satisfied with the regular forces at hand, Larraín armed "many private citizens and firefighters" and even allowed the French and Italian consuls to form security units, the latter with fifty men.[10] The next day, he recalled two warships and sent steamers to northern cities to bring more troops.[11]

At first glance, the preoccupation with guards and security seems beyond all proportion to the number of potential criminals in or near Valparaíso, even a Valparaíso broken open into a looter's paradise. The context, however, suggests that Larraín and the rest feared not just habitual criminals but a general uprising. The large number of stores, mansions, factories, warehouses, and offices in ruins or ablaze in the hour after the earthquake may have stirred memories of another day of fires. In April 1903, striking port workers had clashed with strikebreakers and troops on the Valparaíso waterfront. Between thirty-two and one hundred people died in the confrontation, and strikers burned the Compañía Sudamericana de Vapores's waterfront office building.[12] In fact, strikes, political protests, and sometimes violent social conflicts were common in Chile in the years around the quake. In 1905, for example, a protest over rising food prices had sparked "red week," "an orgy of looting and burning" and violence in Chile's capital, Santiago, suppressed at the cost of about 200 lives by "the city's twelve [volunteer] fire companies and some 300 upper-class 'white guards,' armed by the government with rifles." (In Santiago, as in Valparaíso, the volunteer firefighters included many young men from elite families.) Then, "in Antofagasta in 1906, [Chilean] marines exacted a further toll in lives during a railwayman's strike."[13]

With these events in their minds, the authorities in Valparaíso organized forces to defend property and the social order. On August 18, Larraín Alcalde proclaimed a 6 p.m. to 7 a.m. curfew, promised severe punishment for crimes against people or property, and ordered the survivors to obey the police.[14] The decree, published "by proclamation [*bando*]," may have been read aloud in the streets; there would be no newspaper until the next day, and a substantial minority of porteños could not read.[15] Shortly thereafter, Gómez promised swift punishment to "instigators of disorder or people who do not obey instructions immediately," thieves, and other criminals. On August 20, Gómez added breaking the water mains to the list; his decree implies that people were breaking water mains to avoid going to the public faucets.[16]

A few people did loot and burn, at least according to the military authorities. Gómez's firing squads shot some of them in public and displayed their bodies as a warning to others. On August 19 or 20, thousands of refugees camped on Avenida Brazil (a major avenue and tree-lined promenade) could see "the bodies of some of those so punished, one of them attached to a post on which could be read the following sign: 'for theft.'" Lesser criminals were beaten, presumably in public. On August 20, *El Mercurio* credited summary punishments with keeping looting so small and so brief "that it's not even worth paying attention to."[17] The paper also claimed that "San Francisco shows that only absolute discipline and . . . central control can completely handle" the aftermath of a major earthquake.[18] The English iron merchant and amateur poet Henry Swinglehurst wrote that "Gomez . . . stood for the common good, / Like a fortress of tempered steel." Swinglehurst cast Gomez as the city's champion, fighting a vague but implicitly terrifying adversary:

Like a hero sprung from the head of Jove,
He rushed at the foeman's throat;
Before and behind, and around he strove,
But straight to the heart he smote.[19]

All these sources represent prosperous porteños. Poorer residents, the likely targets of such repression, may not have been as fearful at first or as appreciative after.

Whether because the executions deterred it, or because people weren't inclined to do it, there were no riots, no revolution. There was still some crime, and the military tribunal meted out harsh, fast punishments. Agustin Rojas received 150 lashes on August 24, and another 150 the next day, "for assaulting a police sergeant and Sr. Manuel Acevedo, wounding the latter with a knife."[20] The collapse of the city's prison may have encouraged summary corporal and capital punishment, which continued for some time. Bartolo Rubio Araya, only seventeen, got 200 lashes for trying to steal cash from "the Girls' High School." Afterward he turned to arson. He was shot on Barón Hill, in front of one of several buildings he allegedly tried to burn. For the edification of the passersby, the troops left his body there for several hours with a sign: "A bandit and an arsonist."[21]

The motive for looting is straightforward, although patrolling sol-diers must have used assumptions about clothing, class, and accents to sort looters from people salvaging their own possessions and may sometimes have erred. Arson was a typical part of urban uprisings at the time, and the authorities may have feared that property owners without earthquake insurance would burn the ruins of their homes to collect fire insurance.[22] Were Rubio Araya and the other arsonists hoping to spark revolution, try-ing to collect insurance, or simply deranged? Perhaps Rubio Araya fell in the last category, as he had reportedly been in juvenile prison for poison-ing his mother.[23] On August 24, several residents of Polanco Hill, next to Barón, insisted that "straw soaked in paraffin has been found in several houses" and demanded a guard of twenty soldiers instead of the two they currently had. Neither the letter writers nor the newspaper offered any motives for burning rather poor houses there, except that the hill was "one of the most populous after Baron Hill" and most of its houses had survived the earthquake.[24] Rubio Araya's arrest on nearby Baron Hill, combined with recent memories of torched buildings and streetcars in Valparaíso and Santiago, may have burned fear into people's minds.

While the authorities were most preoccupied with order, they also addressed the people's other needs. From medical care to food, the emer-gency authorities seem to have cared for Valparaíso's inhabitants thor-oughly, and perhaps more fairly than usual, despite their suspicious, authoritarian attitude toward the ordinary people. The authorities tried to feed those porteños who could not feed themselves. Larraín and Gómez tried to impose their notion of fair commerce (on merchants who may not have agreed) with ceilings on the price of food and other necessities.[25] Individual citizens built tents and shanties in every open space, groups of new neighbors cooperated to make the camps livable, and both the emer-gency authorities and the municipal government stepped in to regulate the camps after the first few days. The national government even evacuated many porteños to reduce crowding and to stretch the food supply.

Surrounded by ocean and rugged hills, Valparaíso depended on far-away food sources. Everything from flour for the pasta factories and indus-trial bakeries to animals for slaughter, even fresh produce, came some distance by train or cart. The earthquake cut the railroad between Viña del Mar and the next town inland, Quilpué, isolating the city from most suppliers. At first, Larraín and Gómez expected the railroad to be closed for over a month, but they found a month's supply of food in stores and warehouses. They repeatedly and publicly insisted that there was enough food and that they were giving it free to everyone.[26] In its tiny August 19 issue, the first after the quake, *El Mercurio* reported that there was plenty of food for everyone but encouraged those who could get their food privately to leave the free public supplies for the needy.[27] Considering that rising food prices had sparked the 1905 riots in Santiago, the authorities and the journalistic representatives of the elite probably felt acute pressure to reassure the people that no one would go hungry.

Many Chilean cities, companies, and individuals sent aid to Valparaíso. Foreign donors helped both their own resident nationals and Chilean victims, even though the Chilean government said Chile had enough resources to handle the crisis.[28] A committee of resident Peruvians distributed aid from Peru, apparently food and clothing for poor porteños.[29] Chilean and Argentine bishops collected money for aid from their clergy and parishioners.[30]

Even when the railroad opened after only a week and a half, Valparaíso still faced food problems. Perhaps no one would starve, but distribution was difficult, and the usual staple foods scarce. The railroad could run only to the eastern end of the city because the waterfront tracks to the rest of the city were destroyed. Rubble still blocked many streets. The public markets lay in ruins, as did many stores. The local bakeries could not reopen until inspected for fire hazards created by earthquake damage. When they did reopen, Gómez sent soldiers to supervise the distribution of bread.[31] He apparently feared that porteños would fight over the scarce loaves. On the same day, local fishers planned to sell their catch retail on the dock.[32] Although *El Mercurio* cast this as a way for customers to "obtain the fish as cheaply as possible," the fishers probably also got a better price than they would have selling wholesale, even if the markets and distribution infrastructure had still been in place. The shortage of bread and other fresh foods gave some poor porteños a first taste of pricey, processed foods. Relief supplies from local department stores, many probably imported, subverted culinary class distinctions. The national illustrated magazine *Zig-Zag* claimed that such food was "too fine for working-class consumers" who got it.[33]

Not every outsider came to help. A week and a half after the earthquake *El Mercurio* (and its largely independent Santiago edition) complained of many "idle, curious people" coming to see the destruction just for fun. The editorial argued that the "strange and bloody farce" of "indifferent

. . . correctly dressed, well-fed" gawkers roaming the city would hurt local morale and objected to any of the city's food going to "useless mouths." Pointing out that Valparaíso was under martial law, the paper called on the commander to allow into the city only those bringing aid, those on government business, and those seeking close relatives.[34] For this newspaper, idlers of any class were unwelcome in the stricken city.

Rodríguez and Gajardo's December 1906 book *Catástrofe* claims that porteños responded to the earthquake without class conflict or class distinction. The authors partly mean the absence of riots, anarchist plots, general strikes, and the like. They also appreciate the maintenance of class distinctions. For example, they tell of a maid salvaging her bed and giving it to her employer as though it were a voluntary act of generosity on the part of the maid, and they clearly approved.[35] Rodríguez and Gajardo also note that "many very distinguished families" spent the first night as refugees in the Plaza Victoria, the city's most central square and an aristocratic promenade.[36] The authors imply a social paradox in which *even the rich* were homeless. The focus on the upper classes throughout the book suggests that the authors thought they mattered most, although the fact that the destruction targeted the city's wealthiest neighborhoods may account for some of the focus. The authors, like some other commentators, mention that the rich had been indulging in too much luxury and that the quake might cure that, but they do not cast the quake as a punishment.[37]

In the hours after the earthquake, thousands of homeless porteños looked for shelter. According to Rodríguez and Gajardo, "many families, especially those with sick members or small children" took shelter in stranded trolley cars. They do not explain whether those families just got lucky or whether some common street consensus reserved the ready-made shelters for the most vulnerable.[38] Others found shelter in convents and other religious institutions, or in ships in the harbor. Most, however, salvaged food, bedding, and other supplies from the ruins of their homes and built shelters where they could.

Within days, the authorities began evacuating the homeless with the aid of newspaper publicity. On August 20, the steamer *Puno* sailed for the southern port of Talcahuano; those who could not pay sailed free in third class.[39] The next day, August 21, in an attempt to reduce the crowding in the camps, the ministers of marine and interior decided to arrange for free passage to other parts of Chile for all who wanted to leave and could not

Valparaiso
Terremoto del 16 de Agosto de 1906
Avenida del Brasil

Postcard of a streetcar serving as a house. Note the carefully stacked salvaged bricks at right (SAMUEL J. MARTLAND'S COLLECTION).

pay.[40] Many ships left in the next few days. The authorities even provided free launches to take destitute evacuees from the shore to their ships.[41] On August 25, after repairing the line to Santiago, the state railroad offered free passage to Santiago to anyone who wanted to leave Valparaíso.[42] Many cities and towns around Chile offered to receive refugees. The town of Angol, for example, offered to put up eight hundred people.[43] Amid widespread generosity, some offers had limits. The Santiago City Council offered "lodging for thirty families of good social class." The city councilor who telegraphed the offer used the word "*tú*," which implied friendship with Gómez Carreño. *El Mercurio* printed the telegram without comment but perhaps implied that those with proper social credentials should talk to Gómez Carreño.[44] Foreign governments also got into the act. The Ecuadorian consulate, operating from an address on the undamaged Cerro Alegre, offered free sea passage to Ecuadorians wishing to leave Chile.[45] Once the crisis was past, some local employers complained that too many people had evacuated, leaving them with a labor shortage.

Many porteños stayed, however, filling Valparaíso's squares, parks, and two wide avenues. Many would still be living in theoretically temporary homes and camps in April 1907. On August 19, 1906, *El Mercurio* began to call for better sanitary organization in the camps, with designated latrines and garbage dumps.[46] On August 21, determinedly upbeat about the disaster, the paper claimed that "[t]he camps . . . are becoming less like shelters for the homeless and more like cheerful bivouacs."[47] Indeed, the many published pictures of the camps show elaborate tents and shanties, cook stoves, and remarkably well-dressed refugees. In late September, Mayor Bermúdez explored a special fire service for the camps.[48] Even the Italian consul set up a temporary consulate in one of the camps.[49] The well-to-do homeless bought what they could not salvage. By August 25, banks, stores, and restaurants were open and clothing companies had enough orders to hire extra "seamstresses." A small but prominent newspaper notice advertised that "Jerman Bruhn carries out carpentry jobs and offers his services for making tents, sheds, shanties, etc."[50] Anyone thinking of paying someone to build their camp shack had money and expected to be in the camp for some time.

A few lucky (and probably affluent) people who lost their homes were able to move into other houses. Ads in the August 25 *El Mercurio* offered at least three houses for sale or rent, claiming that they were undamaged. The enterprising Bruhn offered a factory building for rent.[51] A cartoon in *Zig-Zag* satirizes the plight of porteño tenants and landlords. It shows two adjacent houses, one of three stories and one of one. In the quake, the third floor apartment of the one falls onto the other. The hapless tenant and her children, still in residence, face the owners of both buildings, each trying to collect the rent.[52] The cartoon is whimsical, and the landlords are anti-Semitic caricatures, but the caricatures go along with other anti-Semitic complaints about landlords, and there must have been confusion and disputes about living spaces.[53] On August 23, an ad hoc panel of prominent porteño engineers, appointed by the mayor, set out to inspect the city's buildings to see which ones people could move back into.[54] Most people were not so lucky, however, and with the inevitable delays in getting money, materials, workers, and permits, constructing enough new houses, rooms, and apartments took quite some time. Meanwhile, rents doubled.[55]

Cleanup brought its own disputes. A few weeks after the earthquake, *La Unión* complained that soldiers and officers were not giving owners receipts for reusable building materials salvaged from the ruins by the government cleanup crews.[56] Rubble still smoldered in some areas in late September, obstructing reconstruction and giving off annoying smoke besides.[57] Faced with over 130 blocks of rubble to clear with finite workers, money, and equipment, the authorities and private builders had probably set to work on the unburned areas and left the smoldering rubble to burn itself out. Demolishing precarious walls and other dangerous ruins was more pressing for public safety and perhaps less dangerous to workers.

Huge mounds of newly imported building materials clogged waterfront streets by late November.[58] In early December, *La Unión* reported that the state railroad had cut its rates for shipping wood and other building materials to encourage rebuilding. The newspaper called on the government to go further and eliminate import duties on building materials, arguing that without rapid reconstruction rents would stay high and workers would stay homeless.[59] By early December Mayor Bermúdez had removed some of the camps from public spaces, but he had left others in place because of the ongoing housing shortage. To prevent epidemics among the people in the tents and sheds, the mayor ordered his director of Municipal Works to install sewers in the camps and decided that the city would use drinking water to wash out the city's streambeds, where much of the human waste had ended up.[60]

The earthquake and the camps came into being in the midst of an ongoing debate among Valparaíso's newspapers, authorities, pundits, workers' organizations, and so on about the conditions under which the bulk of the population lived. The debate, of course, extended far beyond Valparaíso to other cities throughout the industrial and industrializing world, from Santiago to Chicago. Whether they blamed rapacious landlords, ill-bred poor people, or some other evil, many political actors regarded creating sanitary urban workers' housing as a key issue for both public health and social progress. In Valparaíso, the temporary camps became part of this larger debate. Participants spoke of hygiene, health, and workers and sometimes explicitly explained the ties between the general housing question and the camps. An inherited housing shortage made it especially difficult to move earthquake victims, especially poor people, out of the camps and into real housing. The earthquake destruction, in turn, complicated the government's ongoing efforts to eliminate the most unsanitary tenements. The camps kept the issue of housing in the newspapers, leading commentators to demand change as fast, if not faster, than before the earthquake, even though there were fewer means by which to achieve it.

On April 9, 1907, Mayor Bermúdez threatened inhabitants of certain camps with eviction and a hefty "daily $20-peso fine" unless they moved within fourteen days.[61] (*El Mercurio* had complained that these particular camps, on the Avenida de las Delicias, were particularly ugly.)[62] The mayor said that subsequent orders would eliminate unsanitary tent camps from the city. He argued that eight months was plenty of time to find a new home but promised to let camp residents put up their shacks somewhere else. He presented the order as part of his response to poor housing conditions; the other parts were a plan for building sanitary housing, which both he and Intendant Larraín were waiting for the national government to fund, and a plan to condemn certain small rented rooms under an 1893 ordinance. Larraín, less optimistic about people's chances of finding new homes, said that closing down unsanitary *conventillos* (tenements built around courtyards) would be difficult because the earthquake had left "an absolute lack of places for these people to live."[63] Most of the Almendral had yet to be rebuilt; rubble and ruins were all over.[64] Around the same time, workers' mutual and protective societies advertised several meetings about abusive landlords.[65]

Repairing and Reopening the City

Business went on as normally as possible after the earthquake. The helpful and the opportunistic coexisted, probably often in the same person. The Chilean writer August D'Halmar described a vendor hawking tortillas in the streets the morning after the disaster.[66] Street vendors, generally not the newspapers' or authorities' favorite merchants, must have found it easy to sell profitably in the camps. Some barbershops, restaurants, and other small businesses reopened in the camps. On August 25, newspaper ads announced that various stores and businesses were open at their usual address or in temporary premises. Some, such as the Grand Oyster Hall and Jonathan Swinglehurst's iron yard, advertised their usual services, now in more demand than ever. Others ran special ads to appeal to disaster victims. "Burmeister & Co. offer their stock of kitchen articles, crockery, crystal, etc., at the price in effect before the catastrophe, with a ten percent discount. Cash only." John R. Beaver Engineering Co. advertised "Portable Cottages, American-style Wooden Chalets, Metal Structures for tall buildings, Steel Sheds." The ad noted that the buildings were "easy to assemble." One ad listed such useful items as preserves, liqueurs, ropes, and china dishes, but added in much larger type: "and, for the nerves, Presidente brand port and . . . beer."[67]

Businesses needed workers to reopen. Starting on August 22, an ad from the Casa Pra called in its "clerks and seamstresses" and said it wanted to put all of them back to work if possible.[68] On August 25, the clothing firms of Ponciano Sanz y Co. and Nieto Hermanos urged their old employees and others to come and pick up homework. They also informed their employees that they could now bring in old piecework from before the earthquake for payment.[69]

State agencies needed extra workers because of the quake and took steps to get them. In its second issue after the earthquake, *El Mercurio* called on the authorities to put all able-bodied men to work, particularly from "the working class," who would clear the rubble from the streets.[70] As early as August 19, the government gave better food to "those who work on tasks in the general interest," probably meaning cleanup and other related tasks.[71] On August 22, the state railroad announced it was hiring workers to repair the line. To encourage men to sign up, it reminded them that the authorities would feed able-bodied men only if they worked.[72] Authorities began to draft unoccupied men for emergency cleanup duties, which included salvaging materials from collapsed buildings, within a few days of the quake. Railroad workers, for example, needed identity cards so as not to be detained on the street. There were disputes. In early September, *La Unión* charged that soldiers on guard duty were setting themselves up as petty bullies, tearing up workers' identity cards and drafting them for public works. The paper claimed that this illegal abuse was chasing many workers out of Valparaíso.[73]

Two extreme examples show the extent to which some businesses helped reconstruction—and received good press in return. Several pawn shops tried to get workers back to work by giving back pawned tools and clothes to workers for free if they could show their pawn tickets. Some tickets might have been lost in the earthquake, but the shops seem to have been trying to contribute to the welfare of the workers and the rebuilding of the city at the same time.[74] For the rich, the Penco Sugar Refinery Company declared an extra 20 percent dividend. The company, whose factory some 250 miles south of Valparaíso was undamaged, said that the extra cash in the hands of its stockholders, "almost all porteños," would help rebuild their city.[75] Maybe the directors hoped to rally support for the sugar tariff, which President Montt was said to be considering removing as a quake relief measure. Maybe they just hoped the stockholders would keep them in their jobs.

Praise and Patriotism

Valparaíso's orderly, resilient reaction to the earthquake fed local, national, and even racial pride. On August 20, for example, even as *El Mercurio* published a list of duties and tasks for Gómez Carreño, Larraín Alcalde, and other officials, the paper said they had so far acted with "patriotism and self-denial" in protecting lives and property and providing the necessities of life for porteños.[76] *Zig-Zag* praised porteños's "good humor" and courage.[77] Money bought some comforts, but the rich were not the only ones to keep "good humor: Within a few days, the city's popular musicians [perhaps the improvising satirists known as *payadores*] were singing a ballad that lamented the disaster but consigned it to the past."[78] *La Unión* called the city's rapid response—it said cleanup began on the third day, rebuilding in a week, and trolley service in eight days—"an energetic refutation of the charge of indolence and laziness made against the Latin race."[79] For good measure, it called porteños "a people born for the fertile life of work."[80] Several weeks later, the bishop who presided at the group funeral for the victims devoted more of his eulogy to the many concrete virtues shown by porteños in the aftermath, and to his personal affection and admiration for Valparaíso, than to the possibility that abstract sins might have angered God.[81]

Some observers stretched patriotic pride to cover not only their reactions but the world's interest and even world-class rubble. One accorded the ruins of the Iglesia de la Merced "all the grandeur and majesty of those that draw the travelers of all nations to Rome."[82] On the surface, newspaper reports of foreign aid and of condolences from overseas expressed gratitude. However, they also implied patriotic pride that so many people around the world cared about Chile and Valparaíso. That pride was more open in articles about foreign visitors, such as correspondents from Buenos Aires's two leading newspapers and the U.S. secretary of state Elihu Root.[83]

Destruction of Structures and Places

On August 18, Intendant Larraín told the minister of the interior in Santiago that Valparaíso had been "almost completely destroyed."[84] Larraín used a restricted definition of Valparaíso, because many important hill neighborhoods, including the large ones on Cerro Baron, Cerro Alegre, Cerro Concepción, and Playa Ancha, had relatively light damage thanks to their rocky ground.[85] Baron alone had over 10,000 residents by 1910, in a city of fewer than 170,000.[86] One Santiago newspaper article said two-thirds of Valparaíso was destroyed, while another said two-thirds of the *plan* (the flat part of the city, consisting of the Almendral and the Puerto).[87] The more restricted notion that equated Valparaíso with the plan shaped rebuilding strategies.

Although the earthquake struck both rich and poor, it turned common assumptions about class in Valparaíso on their heads. The greatest destruction came to the Almendral, which was almost entirely a district of expensive buildings—churches, mansions, tenements, theaters, stores, factories—with well-off owners. The Puerto, the city's financial and mercantile district, lost many inhabitants and a significant number of its buildings. The city's hills, mostly inhabited by the poor, suffered much less destruction than the flat parts of the city.[88] This no doubt surprised many elite porteños, who for decades had thought of the hills as the epitome of shoddy construction, bad hygiene, and general urban danger.

The type of building destroyed likewise defied common assumptions. *El Mercurio*'s first description of the destruction included a litany of prominent buildings destroyed. The landmark Teatro de la Victoria became a spectacular pile of rubble. Rodríguez and Gajardo said that the theater's "construction was so solid that many would have believed themselves perfectly . . . safe from earthquakes, inside it, under its enormous walls" and made similar comments about other "solid" buildings that had collapsed.[89] The destruction of so many expensive homes and businesses probably surprised many porteños, but it made good engineering sense. To an early twentieth-century Chilean, a "solid" building was a hybrid structure of masonry walls and wooden floors and internal partitions. Neither the wooden parts nor the masonry parts could stand on their own, but the two were usually not tightly connected to each other; in particular, the firewalls and chimneys got less support where they extended above the roof and internal walls. Civil engineer Hormidas Henríquez blamed poorly connected hybrid structures for the failure of many buildings, pointing out that many "external or fire-break walls are lying on the ground intact."[90] The government's director of public works blamed *bad* brickwork, but Henríquez saw the fact that many brick buildings had collapsed not only in Valparaíso's quake but also in San Francisco's (April 1906) as evidence that *any* brickwork was dangerous in earthquakes.

Valparaíso's "solid" buildings crumbled by the score, while on many hills the wooden houses and even shacks mostly survived. Most of the "solid" buildings were on flat land, scarce and expensive in Valparaíso. The English parishioners of Valparaíso's Anglican church put up a plaque thanking God that none of them had died, but, more to the point, they mostly lived on the bedrock of Alegre and Concepción Hills. Most of the flat land, especially in the Almendral, was either sandy soil or landfill. Neither carries buildings well in earthquakes. Expensive features—multiple stories, arches, balconies, and large rooms—weakened "solid" buildings and made them more dangerous when they collapsed. In short, everything that made a building expensive in Valparaíso also made it more dangerous in an earthquake. The rich residents of the Almendral suffered so heavily because they had been able to afford the latest earthquake death trap.

Rebuilding

On August 23, 24, and 25, *El Mercurio* ran a large notice of an interview with Captain Arturo Middleton, the "distinguished naval officer who predicted the earthquake . . . six days in advance."[91] The gist of the notice was that "Middleton, head of the Meteorological Office . . . [has] informed us that there was not the least probability of" another major earthquake. Middleton had become a bit of a celebrity for his prediction of an earthquake for August 16 based on astronomical calculations. Many commentators later noted that no one had paid much attention to the prediction before the earthquake. As Rodríguez and Gajardo stated, previous predictions of disaster had been wrong too often to be trusted.[92] Middleton's prediction was an ironic coincidence, but a coincidence nonetheless. A U.S. geologist who, in June 1906, told the San Francisco *Bulletin* that the series of earthquakes leading up to San Francisco would probably continue far to the south, was on firmer scientific ground, but if his prediction had reached Valparaíso no one remembered it.[93] In any case, neither prediction could have saved the city's buildings, even if Middleton's lucky guess could have saved lives.

It is not especially surprising that porteños ignored the short-term forecasts and the two-month spate of frequent tremors that preceded the quake (the study of which contributed to Chilean seismology afterward).[94] It is somewhat surprising that government officials, engineers, builders, newspapers, and others involved in decades of creating and regulating

Valparaíso had not foreseen the danger of earthquakes or had seen no way of reducing it. Porteños were hardly fatalists. After the quake porteños and Chileans sought scientific, rather than religious, explanations, just as they had generally eschewed religious explanations for nineteenth-century events. Their press had urged active measures against some kinds of disaster for decades. Their city government had acted against some disasters and been scolded for not acting against others. Decades of disaster preparation, as noted earlier, had prepared porteños to help the victims and rebuild the city. A quake had destroyed much of the city in 1822, and some porteños had noted that light wooden houses resisted shaking better.[95] Still, nothing had prepared buildings to withstand the earthquake.

More than any other danger, porteños had prepared for fire. Conflagrations that burned many city blocks in the 1840s and 1850s brought the first building codes and inspired the creation of the leading voluntary society, the volunteer fire department. For over half a century, the city's fears and safety regulations focused on fires, industrial explosions, and related hazards, urged on by a chorus of elite donations, sensational editorials, heated city council debates, and accusations against slumlords. By 1906, fire regulations and firefighting had mostly eliminated their main target: fires that spread through many buildings.

In contrast, Valparaíso's few earthquake rules focused on isolated deaths and ignored the possibility that an earthquake might bring down many whole buildings. In spite of its name, the 1873 "Ordinance to Guard against Fires and Earthquakes" contained only one earthquake-safety requirement: a ban on heavy, protruding cornices and other ornaments that might fall on passersby in an earthquake, inspired by two small earthquakes that year.[96] The ban on cornices, minor beside the huge firewalls, was nevertheless among the main official mentions of earthquake safety in the six decades before the earthquake. The councilors and other government officials must have known of Valparaíso's earlier major earthquakes, and at least one contemporary porteño wrote that brick buildings were known to be dangerous in earthquakes, but the ordinance's title refers not to *terremotos* (major earthquakes) but to *temblores* (minor earthquakes).[97] Was a major earthquake too big to prepare for?

Some fire regulations even made earthquakes more dangerous. Since 1858, fire ordinances had required thick masonry firewalls (forty centimeters after 1873) between adjacent buildings but said nothing about internal frames to hold them up. In the debate on the 1873 ordinance, City

Councilor Lorenzo Justiniano argued that such firewalls would crush people in an earthquake. Justiniano convinced his colleagues to allow hollow iron firewalls, which he thought less likely to fall.[98] Under normal conditions, firewalls may have slowed the spread of some fires, although such walls often failed to contain fires in other cities, but they proved dangerous even before the quake.[99] A shoddy firewall killed a volunteer firefighter on April 19, 1906.[100] Mayor Bermúdez told the fire department that many older buildings "only have a masonry wall above the roof, meant to make it look like there is a solid wall" below. Bermúdez warned that even the complete brick firewalls of "modern buildings" could fall once the wooden frame burned up.[101] In the earthquake, falling firewalls crushed many people, like the González family mentioned earlier, and the wood fueled massive fires that claimed some intact buildings.

In another area, flooding, Valparaíso had made less progress, but journalists and politicians agreed that floods should be prevented. Because they flowed from hills deforested in the previous century, the streams dried in summer to trickles insufficient to remove the sewage and trash illegally dumped there. They rose rapidly in each rain and often overflowed into the streets of the plan, bringing accumulated filth with them. Pundits and politicians had called for putting the streams underground since the 1820s and had worked seriously on the matter since the 1870s.[102] The city council was discussing yet another plan for drainage and sanitation in the weeks before the earthquake.[103] A year before the earthquake, *Zig-Zag* had denounced repeated urban floods, not as natural events but as the result of deplorable human (in)action. It called Valparaíso's municipal government a "[model] of disorganization and bad service" for viewing floods with a passivity that the magazine thought suitable for uncivilized people, and demanded major government projects to eliminate the floods and prevent waterborne epidemics.[104] Through late November 1906, the magazine did not lay similar blame for the earthquake. Neither did most other people, apparently, even though the press resumed its habitual criticism of public officials for poor street cleaning and the like.[105] The minister of Foreign Relations called the quake "the blow which nature has dealt us," effectively absolving humans from blame.[106] Civil engineer Hormidas Henríquez referred to earthquake safety rules already in effect in some other countries, but as a suggestion for future reference, not as a condemnation of past actions.[107]

Chile was not the only country unprepared for earthquakes. In 1909, the "geologist and general geographer" G. K. Gilbert claimed that although "the proposition that it should be the policy of the inhabitants of an earth-quake district to recognize the danger and make provision for it appears self-evident," California business interests had not only ignored but even tried to suppress talk of the likelihood of earthquakes, which they feared would drive away investors. Gilbert, who advocated antiseismic build-ing codes, wrote that Californian newspapers and others tried to spin the 1906 San Francisco disaster as a conflagration "and so far as possible the fact is ignored that the conflagration was caused, and its extinguishment prevented, by . . . the earthquake."[108] Such a cover-up did not happen in Chile. Press, government, and business did not immediately mention that they should have been ready for an earthquake, but they admitted that the earthquake had caused the damage—except in arguments with insurance companies, which tried not to pay fire claims on the grounds that they were really earthquake claims.[109] *La Unión* claimed that U.S. courts had made companies pay for San Francisco fires, which suggests similar tactics in San Francisco.

Porteños and others produced suggestions for rebuilding the Almen-dral while the rubble was still smoldering. Decades of debate about city planning, street widths, and so on had prepared the city's leaders and resi-dents to decide what to do with a burned-out neighborhood. Various pro-posals included some form of expropriation and redrawing of the street map in the Almendral, where there were almost no buildings left stand-ing and planners saw a chance to plan a crowded city from a blank slate. On August 21, *El Mercurio* passed along the suggestion of expropriating the entire destroyed area as a way to prevent the mortgagors from going bankrupt.[110] One of the most extreme ideas called for replacing most of the Almendral with an artificial harbor.[111] *Zig-Zag*, a bit less drastic, imag-ined the hills gentrified with fancy houses, a bustling commercial district below, and a harbor protected by a substantial breakwater.[112] Proponents of rebuilding schemes rarely lost sight of Valparaíso's economic and politi-cal position in Chile and on the trade routes.

Even after the earthquake, the reconstruction law passed by congress had more to say about drainage and flooding than about earthquake safety. In 1910 the Chilean architect Ricardo Larraín Bravo complained that, unlike other countries that had suffered severe earthquakes in the past few decades, Chile had not named any commissions to study the damage and to recommend regulations to reduce future danger.[113] Chile did estab-lish the Servicio Sismológico Nacional in 1908, but the service seems to have focused on studying the earthquakes themselves, not their effects on buildings or possible safety measures.[114] The 1907 *Informes de la Comision de Estudios del Terremoto del 16 de Agosto de 1906* may also have focused on seismology rather than construction.[115] Even if the planners of 1906 said little about safer buildings, they said a great deal about the opportunity to fix other problems, such as narrow streets, poor drainage, and uneven grades. Ironically, rebuilding plans included additional landfill to improve drainage in the Almendral.

Landowners opposed the general expropriation of the Almendral.[116] They seem to have appealed to the central government to restrain the city council while still securing central government funding for minor realignment of streets and major rebuilding. The president and minister of the interior approved just such a moderate plan and convinced congress to pass it. The law created a special reconstruction commission, part city officials but mostly presidential appointees, to make detailed plans and manage the rebuilding.[117] The commission lasted at least six years. It improved the Almendral's infrastructure, as advertised. In so doing, it took on the ability to regulate the mundane details of business and daily life that the Valparaíso municipal government had cultivated over the previous six decades. The central government was just beginning to experiment with safety regulations and similar rules. Valparaíso gave it an entrance into a previously municipal sphere. The reconstruction of Valparaíso was an in-between stage for the central government. The reconstruction commission was a creature of the national government, but its powers were strictly local. Restricted as it was to the Almendral, it was not a regional government for greater Valparaíso. Still less did it involve the national government in nationwide rules for city planning or anything else. However, in the following decades the national government did expand into those areas, partly using experience and examples gained in Valparaíso. In the meantime, although the municipal government did not lose explicit powers, it did lose the initiative in planning Valparaíso's development. The reconstruction commission, not the city government, had the most exciting sphere of activity. Moreover, from 1910 to 1917, the municipal share of the reconstruction costs ate up much of the city's revenue, and the central government took control of tax collection to be sure the city paid the bills.[118]

Anthony Oliver-Smith writes of a "perspective . . . that views hazards as basic elements of environments and as constructed features of human systems rather than as extreme and unpredictable events." He adds that "if a society cannot withstand without major damage and disruption a predictable feature of its environment, that society has not developed in a sustainable way."[19] Valparaíso's building regulations failed that test, having carefully prepared for other hazards, but not for the earthquakes that centuries of experience in Chilean cities should have made obvious. However, its society—people, institutions, government—came close to passing.

Before 1906, Valparaíso and Chile had made no specific preparations for a great earthquake, either for dealing with a disaster area or for preventing damage to begin with. Decades of work in firefighting and the development of national and municipal regulatory capacity, policing, and civic institutions, however, had created a robust society able to handle the devastation of the earthquake. City and country had fairly strong, effective governments that were able to survive the disaster and respond to it, but that response depended on the quick thinking of capable individuals, rather than on any kind of disaster plan. Those officials, Enrique Larraín Alcalde chief among them, concocted ad hoc administrative and relief agencies based on their experience in government. Their closest analogy, the large urban strikes and protests of the previous few years, led them—and many of their affluent constituents—to focus especially strongly on security and public order. The supply of experienced administrators, merchants, military logisticians, doctors, and so on helped them to feed, house, water, drain, cure, and clean the city as well, but security dominated their actions.

Although Valparaíso's nineteenth-century leaders had enacted rules for fire safety in buildings and tried to minimize floods in the city, they had done almost nothing to ensure that buildings would survive an earthquake. Indeed, some of their fire protection rules may have made those buildings more likely to fall down. When the predictable earthquake came, vast swaths of buildings obligingly collapsed. In the aftermath, some people proposed safer ways to build. This fit well with a city usually eager to dominate its difficult natural environment. The reconstruction law, however, focused on traffic and drainage and did little to prepare for a future quake. In building law, at least, Chile was content to remain unprepared for another twenty-five years, until a 1928 earthquake in Talca inspired national antiseismic building rules in 1931.[120]

✤ NOTES ✤

1. The Gonzálezes' story appears in Alfredo Rodríguez Rozas and Carlos Gajardo Cruzat, *La catástrofe del 16 de agosto de 1906 en la República de Chile* (Santiago: Barcelona, 1906), 80–82. This book is available in pdf form on Memoria Chilena, www.memoriachilena.cl, operated by the Dirección de Bibliotecas, Archivos y Museos, Santiago, Chile (accessed March 8, 2006).

2. Rodríguez and Gajardo, *Catástrofe*, 80–81.

3. This paragraph is based on Rodríguez and Gajardo, *Catástrofe*, 41–52; "La relación del terremoto," *El Mercurio*, August 20, 1906; and Antonio Acevedo Hernández, "Cuando Valparaíso agonizó: el terremoto de 1906, en Valparaíso y el Pueblo," in *Memorial de Valparaíso*, ed. Alfonso Calderón (Valparaíso: Ediciones Universitarias de Valparaíso, 1986), 324–26.

4. "Escasez de víveres en Tarapacá," *El Mercurio*, August 14, 1906.

5. On August 20, *El Mercurio* claimed at least 3,000 were dead ("La relación del terremoto"). In December 1906, Rodríguez and Gajardo listed 615 *identified* victims in Valparaíso; the burial committee counted about 1,500 bodies (*Catástrofe*, 169–74, 219). Four years later, Juan de D. Ugarte Yávar indicated 3,000 for Valparaíso alone (*Valparaíso: 1536–1910; Recopilación histórica, comercial y social* [Valparaíso: Minerva, 1910], 128).

6. Rodríguez and Gajardo, *Catástrofe*, 50.

7. "Los incendios," *El Mercurio*, August 19, 1906.

8. Rodríguez and Gajardo, *Catástrofe*, 178.

9. Ibid., quotation, 179; details in rest of paragraph, 179–80.

10. Ibid., 179–80; "Consulado de Italia," *Zig-Zag*, October 14, 1906. (The issues of *Zig-Zag* cited in this chapter have no page numbers.)

11. Enrique Larraín Alcalde, Valparaíso, to Minister of Interior, Santiago, August 18, 1906, in Rodríguez and Gajardo, *Catástrofe*, 182. Larraín said he still needed reinforcements. His phrasing is ambiguous, so he may have meant to send some troops to help Santiago if it was also destroyed, but either way he feared serious disorder.

12. Simon Collier and William F. Sater, *A History of Chile, 1808–1994* (Cambridge: Cambridge University Press, 1996); Simon Collier, "From Independence to the War of the Pacific," in *Chile since Independence*, ed. Leslie Bethel (Cambridge: Cambridge University Press, 1993), 63.

13. Collier and Sater, *History of Chile*, 196.

14. The full text of the decree is in "Ordenes de la autoridad," *El Mercurio*, August 19, 1906.

15. Collier, "From Independence," 61.

16. Rodríguez and Gajardo, *Catástrofe*, quotation, 198; 199.

17. "El orden público," *El Mercurio*, August 20, 1906.

18. "Lo que queda por hacer," *El Mercurio*, August 19, 1906.

19. Henry E. Swinglehurst, "An Englishman to a Chilean: Capitan Luis Gómez Carreño (after the Valparaíso Earthquake, 16th August, 1906)," *Valparaíso Songs* (London: Dargan, 1911), 51–52. Similar sentiments endure today. In 2001, an elderly porteña, whom I met while exploring the "street" of winding stairs in front of her house, volunteered that her relatives had lived in the Almendral in 1906 and that Gómez had saved them, their property, and their city.

20. "Azotes," *El Mercurio*, August 14, 1906.

21. "Fusilamiento," *El Mercurio*, August 17, 1906.

22. Captain Leonard D. Wildman of the U.S. Army Signal Corps reported that a firefighter had reported this phenomenon to him in San Francisco "on the morning of the earthquake"; Wildman, Fort Mason, California, to Military Secretary, Dept. of California, n.p., April 27, 1906, in *The Virtual Museum of the City of San Francisco*, www.sfmuseum.org/1906.2/arson.html (accessed December 4, 2007). I do not know whether there really was insurance arson in San Francisco, or whether anyone in Valparaíso had heard the reports by August 17, but, by December 8, Valparaíso newspapers and officials were paying close attention to insurance precedents from San Francisco; "Los seguros," *La Unión*, December 8, 1906.

23. "Fusilamiento," *El Mercurio*, 2.

24. "Un denuncio grave," *El Mercurio*, August 16, 1906.

25. "El aprovisionamiento," *El Mercurio*, August 19, 1906.

26. Larraín Alcalde, Valparaíso, to Minister of Interior, Santiago, August 18, 1906, in Rodríguez and Gajardo, *Catástrofe*, 182–83; Enrique Larraín Alcalde, August [19?], 1906, Proclamation, in Rodríguez and Gajardo, *Catástrofe*, 184; Gómez Carreño, Orden del Día, August [18?], 1906, in Rodríguez and Gajardo, *Catástrofe*, 199.

27. "Aprovisionamiento," *El Mercurio*.

28. "Noticias de Santiago" and "Ofrecimiento de ausilios," *El Mercurio*, August 23, 1906.

29. "Los socorros peruanos," *Zig-Zag*, October 21, 1906.

30. Rodríguez and Gajardo, *Catástrofe*, 106, 307.

31. "Órdenes de la Plaza," *El Mercurio*, August 26, 1906.

32. "Pescado barato," *El Mercurio*, August 26, 1906.

33. "Escenas de la vida en Valparaíso," *Zig-Zag*, September 16, 1906.

34. "Valparaíso y los turistas," *El Mercurio*, August 24, 1906.

35. Rodríguez and Gajardo, *Catástrofe*, 55.

36. Ibid., 66, 70.

37. Ibid., 78.

38. Ibid., 61, 93.

39. "Para la jente que quiera salir," *El Mercurio*, August 20, 1906.

40. "Detalles de la catástrofe," *El Mercurio*, August 21, 1906.

41. "Lanchas para el público," *El Mercurio*, August 24, 1906.

42. "Última hora," *El Mercurio*, August 24, 1906.

43. "Local para los damnificados en Angol," *El Mercurio*, August 26, 1906.

44. Carlos Edwards M., Santiago, to Luis Gómez Carreño, Valparaíso, reprinted as "Albergues en Santiago," *El Mercurio*, August 26, 1906.

45. "Consulado Jeneral del Ecuador," *El Mercurio*, August 24, 1906.

46. "Lo que queda," *El Mercurio*.

47. "La vida en Valparaíso," *El Mercurio*, August 20, 1906.

48. Enrique Bermúdez, Valparaíso, to Superintendente del Cuerpo de Bomberos, Valparaíso, September 26, 1906, volume mislabeled Año 1905 but actually containing 1906–1907, Cuerpo de Bomberos de Valparaíso, Archivo.

49. "Consulado de Italia," *Zig-Zag*, October 14, 1906.

50. Advertisement, *El Mercurio*, August 25, 1906. The microfilm is blurred; the last name may be Bruhn or Brunn.

51. Ibid.

52. "Cuestión litijiosa," *Zig-Zag*, September 9, 1906.

53. María Ximena Urbina C., "El terremoto de 1906: cambios y permanencias el el habitar porteño," *Archivium* 7, no. 8 (2007): 333.

54. "Reunión de ingenieros," *El Mercurio*, August 24, 1906.

55. Urbina, "Terremoto de 1906," 332–33.

56. "Las cédulas personales. el derecho de propiedad," *La Unión*, September 6, 1906.

57. Bermúdez to Superintendente, Cuerpo de Bomberos de Valparaíso, Archivo.

58. "En el Malecón de Valparaíso," *Zig-Zag*, November 25, 1906.

59. "Para construir más y más barato," *La Unión*, December 7, 1906.

60. "La higiene de la ciudad," *La Unión*, December 7, 1906.

61. "Las carpas de la Avenida del Brasil," *El Mercurio*, April 10, 1907.

62. "Una visita a la ciudad," *El Mercurio*, April 8, 1907.

63. "Habitaciones para obreros," *El Mercurio*, April 10, 1907.

64. "Una visita," *El Mercurio*.

65. Ads in various editions of *El Mercurio*, April 6–11, 1907.

66. Augusto D'Halmar, "Valparaíso en su elemento," in *Recuerdos olvidados* (a collection of D'Halmar's newspaper columns from 1939–1940), prologue by Alfonso Calderón (Santiago: Nascimento, 1975), 310. D'Halmar was twenty-six in 1906.

67. Advertisements, *El Mercurio*, August 25, 1906.

68. Ibid., August 22, 1906.

69. Ibid., August 25, 1906.

70. "Los deberes del momento," *El Mercurio*, August 20, 1906.

71. "Comida a los trabajadores," *El Mercurio*, August 19, 1906.

72. "Los ferrocarriles del estado," *El Mercurio*, August 22, 1906.

73. "Las cédulas personales," *La Unión*.

74. "A los trabajadores," *El Mercurio*, August 24, 1906.

75. "Digno de imitarse," *El Mercurio*, August 25, 1906. The Compañía de Refinería de Azúcar de Penco was in Penco, near Concepción.

76. "Los deberes del momento," *El Mercurio*.

77. "Escenas de la vida," *Zig-Zag*.

78. Acevedo Hernández, "Cuando Valparaíso agonizó," in Calderón, *Memorial*, 324–26.

79. "Después de la catástrofe," *La Unión*, August 29, 1906.

80. Just as this chapter was going to press, Pablo Páez G. argued convincingly that the local and national elites seized upon the disaster as an opportunity for creative destruction. "La oportunidad de la destrucción en la urbanística moderna: planes y proyectos para la reconstrucción de Valparaíso tras el terremoto de 1906" (master's thesis, Instituto de Estudios Urbanos y Territoriales, Pontificia Universidad Católica de Chile, Santiago de Chile, 2008).

81. Ramón Ángel Jara, "Oración Fúnebre," *La Unión*, October 2, 1906.

82. Anonymous "well-known writer," quoted in Rodríguez and Gajardo, *Catástrofe*, 84–85.

83. "A ver la catástrofe," *El Mercurio*, August 24, 1906; "Mr. Root en Valparaíso," *Zig-Zag*, September 9, 1906.

84. Larraín Alcalde, Valparaíso, to Minister of Interior, Santiago, August 18, 1906, in Rodríguez and Gajardo, *Catástrofe*, 181.

85. Rodríguez and Gajardo describe the state of the hills in *Catástrofe*, 93–94, 102, 150–64. Other reports are scattered through the early newspapers.

86. Ugarte Yávar, *Valparaíso*, 28.

87. "De Santiago," *La Unión*, August 30, 1906.

88. See Urbina, "Terremoto de 1906," 328–32.

89. Rodríguez and Gajardo, *Catástrofe*, 67, 80, 92.

90. Hormidas Henríquez, "El terremoto de Valparaíso considerado bajo su aspecto reconstructivo," in Rodríguez and Gajardo, *Catástrofe*, 351.

91. "No más terremoto," *El Mercurio*, August 25, 1906.

92. Rodríguez and Gajardo, *Catástrofe*, 40.

93. Grove K. Gilbert, "Earthquake Forecasts," *Science* 29, no. 734 (January 22, 1909): 129.

94. Luis Zegers, "El terremoto del 16 de agosto," *Anales de la Universidad, Memorias Científicas i Literarias*, vol. 119 (Santiago de Chile, 1906), quoted in Diana Comte et al., "The 1985 Central Chile Earthquake: A Repeat of Previous Great Earthquakes in the Region?" *Science* 233, no. 4762 (July 25, 1986): 451.

95. Urbina, "Terremoto de 1906," 328; Vicente Mesina H. "Algunos testimonios escritos, tres dibujos y un plano: el aspecto del centro de Valparaíso hasta poco antes del terremoto de 1822," *Archivium* 7, no. 8 (2007): 278.

96. "Proyecto de Ordenanza para precaver los incendios i temblores," ordinance passed by the city council November 6, 1873, and annotated by the Council of State December 24, 1873, filed with Echaurren to Minister, November 8, 1873, vol. 660; Archivo Nacional Histórico (ANH), Santiago, Chile, Ministerio del Interior (hereafter ANHI); Carlos Escobar, Valparaíso, Intendancy Engineer, to Intendant, Valparaíso, March 18, 1874, reports on damages from quakes of May 15 and July 7, 1873, vol. 678, ANHI.

97. Recaredo S. Tornero, *Chile ilustrado: guía descriptiva del territorio de Chile, de las capitales de provincia, i de los puertos principales* (Valparaíso: Librerias i Ajencias del Mercurio, 1872), 126.

98. City Council Minutes for August 22, 1873, in Valparaíso, Chile, *Documentos municipales i administrativos de Valparaíso* (Valparaíso: Imprenta del Progresso, 1875–1908), 1:328.

99. Sara A. Wermeil, *The Fireproof Building: Technology and Public Safety in the Nineteenth-Century American City*, Studies in Industry and Society, ed. Philip B. Scranton (Baltimore: Johns Hopkins University Press, 2000), 75–84.

100. C. H. C. Armstrong, Comandante, to Superintendente de Bomberos, Valparaíso, July 12, 1906, volume mislabeled Año 1905, Cuerpo de Bomberos de Valparaíso, Archivo.

101. Enrique Bermúdez, Valparaíso, to Superintendente de Bomberos, Valparaíso, May 26, 1906, volume mislabeled Año 1905, Cuerpo de Bomberos de Valparaíso, Archivo.

102. Cabildo, Valparaíso, to Minister of Interior, Santiago, December 19, 1828, vol. 86, ANHI, 93; Report for May 1, 1870–May 1, 1871, in the form of a letter, Francisco Echáurren, Intendant, Valparaíso, to Minister, Santiago, May 22, 1871, vol. 608, ANHI.

103. "El saneamiento de Valparaíso," *El Mercurio*, August 8 and 10, 1906.

104. *Zig-Zag*, August 6, 1905.

105. "El barrido," *La Unión*, August 30, 1906.

106. Santiago Aldunate Bascuñán, speech, Santiago, quoted in Rodríguez and Gajardo, *Catástrofe*, 333.

107. Henríquez, "Aspecto reconstructivo," in Rodríguez and Gajardo, *Catástrofe*, 353.

108. Gilbert, "Earthquake Forecasts," 135, 138.

109. "Los seguros," *La Unión*.

110. "Ideas acerca de los remedios para la situación," *El Mercurio*, August 21, 1906.

111. "Nuevo puerto de Valparaíso," *La Unión*, August 30, 1906.

112. "De las ruinas," *Zig-Zag*, September 9, 1906.

113. Ricardo Larraín Bravo, *La higiene aplicada en las construcciones* (Santiago: Cervantes, 1910), 3:1618.

114. Servicio Sismológico Nacional (Chile) Web site, http://ssn.dgf.uchile.cl/home/sismohisto.html (accessed June 8, 2006).

115. Hans Steffen, *Informes de la Comision de Estudios del Terremoto del 16 de Agosto de 1906* (Santiago: Universo, 1907).

116. Ugarte Yávar, *Valparaíso*, 53.

117. "Trabajos que se ordenan ejecutar para reparar los daños causados a la ciudad de Valparaíso por el terremoto de agosto de 1906," December 6, 1906, Ley 1, 887, Chile. *Leyes promulgados en Chile: desde 1810 hasta 1 de junio de 1913* (Santiago: Imprenta Lit. i Encuadernación Barcelona, 1912–18), 4:138.

118. I show the role of nineteenth-century municipal activity and the earthquake reconstruction in the development of state power in Chile in "Reconstructing the City, Constructing the State: Government in Valparaíso after the Earthquake of 1906," *Hispanic American Historical Review* 87, no. 2 (May 2007): 221–54.

119. Anthony Oliver-Smith, "Anthropological Research on Hazards and Disasters," *Annual Review of Anthropology* 25 (1996): 304.

120. Rodrigo Flores Álvarez, "Ingeniería sísmica en Chile," lecture delivered to the Academia de Ciencias, Santiago, Chile, August 1999; Empresas RFA, www.rfa.cl/confert.htm (accessed June 8, 2006).

CHAPTER FOUR

The "Superstition of Adobe" and the Certainty of Concrete

Shelter and Power after the
1944 San Juan Earthquake in Argentina

MARK ALAN HEALEY

✢ "ONE'S FIRST IMPRESSION IS OF GRAPES EVERYWHERE," A NORTH
American visitor wrote after a 1942 visit to the Argentine wine belt, "and
everything—houses, fences, stores, factories, even the provincial capital—
built of adobe brick."[1] Over six decades, a new elite of immigrant entrepreneurs and old notables had transformed this thinly occupied desert terrain
into a dense patchwork of vineyards, making San Juan and the neighboring province of Mendoza the home of the fifth-largest wine industry in
the world. But this modern landscape was forged from archaic elements
and marked by persistent social conflict, with its commanding institutions
built of mud. Dominated by the wineries, this was a place of great wealth
and deep inequality, many doctors and terrible health, in short, as one
local social critic put it, a land of "rooted vines and uprooted men."[2]

As the home of most of the province's wineries and nearly half of
its population, the capital city embodied the vitality and contradictions
of the wine boom, the prosperity and the dispossession, from the dusty
elegance of traditional houses downtown to the gritty sprawl of outlying
factories and shacks. This was where the winery elite had consolidated its

rule—and where that rule had met its most enduring challenge. Three times *cantonismo*, a local populist movement, had won the governorship and launched a broad range of reforms aimed at weakening the grip of the wineries and democratizing the province. Each time, the winery elite had managed to have cantonistas removed from office by force, but then proved incapable of doing much more, holding on to power only through intimidation, assassination, and widespread fraud. Finally, after years of instability, the Catholic branch of local conservatives won the governorship in 1942 with promises to finally overcome the challenge of cantonismo by modernizing the province. Although they too had won power by fraud, they dreamed of a counterreform that would finally win them legitimacy.

The centerpiece of their program was a transformation of the capital city. They hired two leading urbanists who proposed a battery of measures, including parks, a ring highway, and a monumental government complex. To improve housing, they called for the city's first building code. But their concerns about housing were not with its cost, quality, size, or materials. Despite a major earthquake fifty years earlier, even "the seismic problem" was "not technically crucial for San Juan at this time." Instead, their focus was on restoring traditional appearance by requiring all new buildings to have white walls and red tile roofs. This, then, was the city of San Juan on January 15, 1944, a fragile and unequal place ruled by a discredited elite more interested in securing their own power and an imagined tradition than in adapting to the social and physical challenges of modernity.[3]

That evening, Buenos Aires builder Luis Romero was about to return home after a four-day trip to survey local construction. San Juan boasted several recent showpiece projects, nearly all of them in reinforced concrete—despite the demands for white walls and red tile roofs. The new buildings included the town hall, a cinema, a hotel, a car dealership, a few private homes, and the flagship headquarters building of the largest winery owner. Impressed by the achievements of his colleagues and the work still before them in remaking this flat city of adobe, Romero had begun writing an article for a professional magazine, and now he was relaxing with new friends in a café downtown just off the main plaza.

As the band started in on its first tango, the ground suddenly began to move. Romero and his friends scrambled out onto the patio, barely escaping the falling building, and then later had to use a metal bar to smash through to the street. Stepping over downed electrical lines and piles of rubble, Romero and his friends made it to the main plaza and turned back to see an "immense pyre" of flames where the café had stood. As Romero recalled, "the block the café was on, and the next, and the next, and every block as far as we could see were nothing but ruins."[4] After spending the night at the main plaza, in the center of a desperate rescue effort, Romero and a few others slowly made their way to the train station in the early morning in hopes of leaving. "On every street corner during the long walk" they saw wounded bodies on the ground and relatives keeping watch over their dead "with small oil lamps and prayers that, out in the open air, took on a strange and moving solemnity."[5]

In less than a minute, an earthquake registering 7.4 on the Richter scale had brought the city to the ground. Every major civic building collapsed: the government house, the courts, the police station, the new city hall, and all but one of the score of churches. In the days after the quake, newspapers spoke of the percentage of buildings destroyed, but for Romero these numbers were "arbitrary." Except for a handful of "modern constructions in steel or reinforced concrete," there were no more buildings in San Juan. Almost all of them "had disappeared," and, in his view, "anything still standing should be demolished as soon as possible because it doesn't offer the least possibility of safety." The city had to be rebuilt, but first it had to be rethought—beginning with how its buildings were made.[6]

Structures and Transformation

Coming at an unsettled moment in Argentine history, the disaster brought the poverty and inequality of much of the interior into national view and sparked ambitious proposals for transformation. The worst natural disaster in Argentine history, it left an estimated ten thousand dead and one hundred thousand homeless.

The ruins were a clear indictment of the previous order. "There can be no doubt that the absence of foresight has been the root cause of the destruction of San Juan," one geologist stated flatly.[7] "Bad faith has been made evident," one architect declared.[8] Poor construction with no controls had guaranteed that buildings would collapse. "The authorities were utterly unconcerned with this problem," a local judge wrote, "and the consequences of this lack of planning and willful negligence is apparent to all."[9] Standing in front of the ruins of the three-year-old city hall, one

local observed that many local "buildings should more precisely be called
. . . papered-over graves."[10]

The tragedy was also a spark for the new order to come. Only six
months before, a military coup had overthrown a fraudulently elected
civilian government, promising to restore order, virtue, and "social justice." The earthquake was its first major opportunity to deliver on those
promises. The day after the earthquake, the recently appointed labor secretary, Colonel Juan Domingo Perón, launched an aid campaign for victims. Proving a signal success, this campaign and the massive provision
of relief made Perón a hero, won credibility for the military, and set his
emerging political project in motion. This was widely seen as a defining
moment, a new social compact, which an opposition paper later compared
to the writing of the national constitution.[11]

Perón portrayed the social crisis faced by survivors after the earthquake as an intensification of the social crisis faced by the popular classes
every day. "On a social plane, most Argentines are comparable to the
homeless" of San Juan, as he later argued, and aid to victims in San Juan
was the first step toward aid to the poor nationally. Indeed, recognizing
the *sanjuaninos'* right to aid and shelter would be the first step to recognizing a broader set of social rights for all Argentines.[12] The city was to
be rebuilt as a model for Argentina as a nation, evidence of the technical
capacity and social vision of the military regime.

"Earthquakes are not disasters in themselves," as Mexican seismolo-
gist Cinna Lomnitz has reminded us; "structures make them so."[13] The
history of natural disasters is a history of constructed vulnerabilities. It is
only human presence, and the failure of human constructions, that make a
seismic event into a natural disaster. In a literal sense, Lomnitz was speaking of structures as physical buildings, and these will indeed be at the center of this essay. But he was also alluding to structures in a broader sense, as
relations of social power. He was arguing against the common view which,
in describing an event as a natural disaster, attributes its cause exclusively
to the workings of the natural world. As Lomnitz emphasized, part of the
responsibility can also be found in social structures, such as the economic
forces that place certain groups in harm's way. If these structures often
remain invisible, supposedly natural and therefore unquestionable, a major
disaster can also serve to bring them fully into view, and into question.

Structures produce disasters, and this essay will examine disputes
over how to build houses after the quake. Far from a narrowly technical

concern, this will be shown as central to rethinking both politics and place
in this period. Of course, debates over structural principles and building
materials are never wholly innocent of politics. But at moments of disaster
and rebuilding, they can become foundational issues. For the city to be
safe, how should it build its houses? And what other structures—social
structures—might also need to be rethought?

Within days of the quake, two distinct visions of how to rebuild San
Juan emerged. On the one hand, architects and state officials proposed
rebuilding the city in a radically new way, on a different site, as a model for
the nation. On the other, local elites and engineers defended rebuilding
on the same site but with new materials, restoration rather than renewal.
The struggle between these two visions over the first six months after the
quake would set the course for rebuilding; this essay will therefore concentrate on this opening moment in depth before turning at the close to
a more compressed account of how those visions played out. This essay
deliberately highlights the cultural and material complexities of rebuilding, and the political obstacles they produced, to explain the paradoxical
outcome of the earthquake. Out of the response to the disaster emerged
Peronism, one of the most powerful political movements in modern Latin
America. But while Peronism certainly did remake the social and even the
physical landscape of Argentina in profound ways, it ultimately produced
a far less dramatic transformation in the place it had begun, the province
of San Juan.

"Movers"

Surveying the rubble, many thought back to the last major earthquake in
1894. While far less deadly, the earlier temblor had nonetheless leveled
many buildings and damaged nearly all. Coming early in the wine boom,
when the city was just beginning to expand, the disaster prompted leading geologists in Argentina to openly debate where that expansion should
take place. With every home in San Juan "an open grave, a constant danger," the director of the provincial mining school recommended that the
city follow the example of neighboring Mendoza, which had been completely destroyed by an 1861 quake and successfully rebuilt on new and
supposedly more solid ground. San Juan too should be rebuilt "on a new
basis" and a different site, one less threatened by floods and earthquakes,
with wide streets and solidly made homes. The city was small, with little

modern infrastructure to replace, and the governor endorsed the proposal, although he lacked a clear means to fund it.

Not all geologists agreed. A distinguished professor from Córdoba argued against a move, claiming it would take the city away from one fault line but closer to another. Instead, he recommended rebuilding on the same site but in a new manner, with wider streets, better materials, and a prohibition on the high facades that had collapsed into the streets. Grateful for this argument and wary of debt, the legislature rejected the move and then went on to also reject any changes in housing construction. The city was rebuilt on the same narrow streets in the same way.

"Never was there a more opportune time to move the city," an assistant to the mining school director observed fifty years later, and if the state had acted then, "no imaginative effort is necessary to grasp what the city of San Juan would be now."[14] With the city destroyed, however, two competing visions emerged, with striking parallels to 1894: reconstruction on a new site with new building techniques versus new building techniques alone.

The first proposal came from the national government. The extent of the destruction, the illegitimacy of local elites, and the possibilities for dramatic success all led military officials to bring rebuilding under national control. Within a week, Perón had discarded the prequake master plan and recruited a new team of architects with bold ideas. The president endorsed the team and their approach, but put the team and the overall rebuilding effort under Minister of Public Works Juan Pistarini.

Modernist architects had long criticized the densely packed buildings, tiny lots, narrow streets, and absence of greenery of cities like San Juan, proposing instead cities "completely different from those . . . we are used to contemplating and enduring."[15] Now several of these flaws had proven deadly, and any rebuilding would clearly have to address them, by widening streets, enlarging and regularizing lots, and providing far more parks and trees along the streets. In practical terms, this would mean expropriating part of virtually every property in the city, a daunting prospect that was further compounded by the shoddiness of local records.

Rather than breathe new life into old errors, the architects proposed a break: the city in ruins should be abandoned. San Juan should be rebuilt on a new site and in a new form, thoroughly rethought on every scale, from the layout of homes to the structure of the city to its relationship to the surrounding countryside. Indeed, as the architects noted, "the construction problem in San Juan is the problem of the entire region. All the towns must be rebuilt and this is a unique opportunity to do it in unbeatable form: the next quake will find garden cities and towns of houses that will never collapse again."[16]

The new city would rise on firmer ground a few kilometers to the southwest, with broad streets, shaded canals, and durable homes for all. There was a clear geologic argument for this move: the city was built on unsettled alluvial soil ten meters below the level of the surrounding river, while sites only a few kilometers west or southwest rested on bedrock well above the river. But in advocating the move, architects did not stress geology. This was partly because they did not yet have detailed data to support their position. More importantly, though, they wanted to make an active case based on the virtues of the city they could build, rather than offer a passive case based on the quality of the soil.

The social and ecological benefits of the new city, and the precedent it would set, were far more important (and conclusive) than the geology. By moving the city, the architects hoped to outflank an entrenched system of property relations and produce a demonstration effect for all other Argentine cities. As the architects' professional journal declared in support a few weeks later, "We should speak not of rebuilding, but rather of a new city. . . . a large-scale 'test' of what will have to be done later in every city in the country."[17]

Dramatic action was required: instead of expropriating the thousands of small parcels covered with ruins, the architects recommended that the state expropriate a single large parcel just outside them. According to the architects, the freedom from the constraints of existing property, infrastructure, and interests would allow the design of a city that was more humane, equitable, and enduring. The new city would have decent housing for all, not just the third who owned property. But the propertied would not be left behind. When the layout of the new city was finalized, they would be able to "swap" their lots in the old city for those in the new, avoiding a welter of complicated expropriation proceedings. Once the swap was finally complete, the state would own all the property in the old city and could proceed to clear the rubble, restore the monuments, and turn the ruined area into a great park.[18]

The architects maintained that property in the new city would be even more valuable and secure than in the old. Reasonable as this argument might be, it could not remove the threat the move still posed to property as such. After all, those with capital owned property not only for shelter but also as a sign and guarantee of their social power. The swift and uniform construction of a new city threatened to deal a terrible blow to this power, making clear that property owners would not have the same power over the new city.

Rethinking the physical place of the city went along with reconsidering its economic and political place within the province. Along with moving the city, architects proposed to diversify the local economy and create new villages against smaller cooperative wineries, weakening the hold of large wineries. As architects refined their plan between January and May, it became more and more evident that regardless of efforts to assuage local fears, their proposal for a new site already was a proposal for remaking the region, or at least for remaking local economic and political power.

Here then, architects proposed to undertake a radical modernist experiment, building an entirely new San Juan on a new site. Given the intensity with which the military regime was calling for a new beginning nationally, the architects' proposal was particularly attractive to the government. But there was a catch: official proclamations of unanimity barely concealed deep rivalries within the regime. While some state officials, particularly Perón, would see this as an opportunity to get a broad transformation underway, others would instead favor a less ambitious course, more favorable to the local elite, in the hopes of winning time and support to launch that transformation across the nation and not simply in one province.

This division within the military allowed for a relatively open struggle between the "keepers" and the "movers," those who wanted to keep San Juan where it was and those who saw a new site as crucial. For the first group, fidelity to the former order was the key objective, while, for the second, it was precisely the thing to be avoided at all costs. The struggle between them would play out from January to June 1944, in the pages of the national, regional, and eventually the local papers—once they starting publishing again in March.

"Keepers"

The proposal to move the city met the resistance of the propertied in San Juan as soon as it became public.[19] The local elite had different priorities for the future, as they had made evident the day after the earthquake, when a group of winery owners made three extraordinary demands of the interior minister: the state should compensate them for their losses, repair their wineries at no expense, and conscript men to rebuild the city as a whole, beginning with their properties. They wanted fifty thousand conscripts for the task, at a time when there were only thirty-five thousand men in the entire army.[20] While these demands were not met, and indeed provided further evidence to support military critiques of the previous social order, their very boldness helped to ensure this group would remain spokesperson for an important part of the community. By the middle of February, this same group would become the main defenders of rebuilding the city on the same site—and use this argument to once again demand compensation for their losses.[21]

Not all of the local elite were initially opposed to rethinking the city. One of the handfuls of local architects immediately wrote foreign colleagues for information about postearthquake reconstruction elsewhere. Every one of his forty buildings was standing, but he still believed the city would have to be rebuilt in a different way, and most likely at a new location.[22] A more public statement came from provincial judge Pablo Ramella, who published his ideas for rebuilding in a national paper eight days after the quake. An imaginative legal thinker, Ramella was close to the conservative leadership but also a committed Catholic reformer and a sharp critic of the province's social failings. His article, the first specific proposal from a local leader, agreed with the architects on several key points. Like them, he saw the tragedy as an opportunity: a force of nature had overcome "the unjustified resistance to the master plan" developed by the conservatives, and their counterreform could now go forward. The existing plan could be the basis of a restored city, built under expert supervision, with antiseismic construction, wider streets, and larger and more regular house lots. This last point was crucial: although the city should be rebuilt in the same place, Ramella stressed that lots would need to be redrawn, to prevent future collapses, ensure greater access to light and air, and allow for more gardens. Like the architects, he proposed a kind of swap, with the state expropriating every lot and then giving owners a voucher to purchase a redrawn lot in the same area of the city. Although this meant every owner would not be able to rebuild on his previous site—indeed, if lots increased in size, some could not rebuild within the previous city limits at all—Ramella argued that safety and health demanded it.[23]

Ramella's vision was distinctly reformist, particularly in its critique of the past, respect for expertise, and willingness to reshape property relations. But it also contained the core of a conservative counterproposal: instead of reimagining the city, just make the buildings stronger.

This latter strand of thinking would soon prevail. In early February, the local association of engineers and architects came out against the move for "geological, economic, and historic reasons," and then the local elite formed a Commission for Restoration of the Province to lobby for rebuilding in situ.[24] Led by the province's wealthiest winemaker, the Commission for Restoration included a broad selection of the political and economic elite—though no one from labor, the left, or the cantonistas—under the overall dominance of the Catholic conservatives. Even though the new site was only a few kilometers away and on much firmer ground, the move was a threat to owners of property and a blow against memories of community. Distorting or ignoring official arguments, the Commission for Restoration built on the widespread sense of dispossession to insist that the city could be rebuilt only on its prior site. Any problems could be resolved by widening the streets and requiring all new buildings to be antiseismic, they argued, and there was thus no need to rethink the larger economy of the province or to consider rebuilding elsewhere. All the government needed to do was compensate the wealthy, require antiseismic building, set new street widths, and get out of the way.[25]

Recruiting backers from a narrow but crucial segment of local civil society, they made their case to Minister of Public Works Pistarini at a February 14 meeting. While Pistarini supported the move, he also felt he could not impose a solution yet, so he opted to let the debate continue while focusing his attention on emergency housing. There was local support for the move, but with military officials divided in their opinions and reluctant to mobilize supporters, these groups remained weak. By contrast, the commission swiftly unified a fractious elite and isolated advocates of the move, bringing together a range of allies from the archbishop to the Rotary Club, and even winning over Colonel Sosa Molina, the nationally appointed head of the provincial government.[26]

While there was a minority within the Commission for Restoration who wanted, like Ramella, to resurrect the prequake master plan and undertake a controlled reform, they deferred to the narrower views of the majority. Ramella immediately lined up behind the commission in an article the day after the meeting with Pistarini. He condemned delays,

denounced those who "wish to wipe away everything existing," and rejected
aggressive proposals for reform, "lest the ideal city impede building the
real city."[27] In short order, he was calling the property swap a violation
of rights—forgetting that he had proposed the same thing himself—and
falsely asserting that the proposed new site was more than fifty kilometers
away. Claiming that architects and officials "want to complicate something
that is not complicated at all," he came to argue that rebuilding required
only widening the streets and passing a "severe building code."[28]

When the two main local newspapers returned in March, both supported rebuilding on the old site. One defended a minimal approach, while
the other spoke of the need for reform, but both mocked architects as
foolish dreamers and agreed with the supposedly pragmatic Commission
for Restoration.[29] "One need not be an architect to build a city," as one
editorial maintained; "on the contrary, it would be better not to be one."[30]
Nationally, however, the press took a broader range of views, including
several major dailies that argued in favor of the move.

This debate was about power as much as location. Wherever the new
city rose, moreover, it had to withstand earthquakes, so the debate over
where to rebuild was also over how to rebuild. Here, similarly, state planners and modernist architects spoke of a city of new kinds of houses for all.
This was a far harder claim for the local elite to combat. They could argue
against the move from history and tradition, playing on deeply rooted feelings of belonging to bring much of the province to their side. In its first
public declaration, the Commission for Restoration stated that "every corner of this present city spiritually and effectively evokes a history written
and lived over nearly four centuries, which cannot be destroyed without
harming respectable feelings."[31] This argument had its effects, winning
them broader support than at first. Against modern housing, however,
they had fewer rhetorical weapons to wield. The sense of attachment to
the ruined city could be marshaled in favor of rebuilding on the same
site, but not in favor of rebuilding the same homes. The memory of collapse was too fresh. To secure their position they had to imagine a cred-
ible future for the city, and this clearly meant rethinking the way houses
were built.

Thus, after ignoring the housing problem for years, the winery elite
would now stress that a simple technical solution was at hand. When the
architects argued for a broad rethinking, they pushed for a narrow retool-
ing. At the center of their argument was the attack on adobe.

Adobe

Why did the 1944 earthquake level San Juan? "It would seem as if the experience of earlier quakes did not survive in the memory of the population," one geologist remarked, as "there is the deep-rooted belief that adobe buildings are the most resistant to earthquakes."[32] This belief extended even to the national newspaper of record, which claimed in its first reports the night of the catastrophe that adobe was "the most appropriate material in areas subject to seismic movements."[33] On the morning after, nearly every adobe building had been reduced to rubble or damaged beyond repair.

"This adobe superstition has been destroyed by the earthquake," Judge Pablo Ramella wrote.[34] Several weeks later, a commission of geologists and engineers reported that "the earthquake caused destruction out of all proportion to its intensity . . . due to the terrible quality of most of the buildings, made out of adobe." Indeed, the commission declared adobe "the worst imaginable material for seismic zones."[35] Considering "strategic necessity, building aesthetics, and security against earthquakes," one military officer declared, "adobe must disappear."[36]

Nearly every building in the province had been made from mud and straw, from the cathedral down to the most modest shack, as the North American visitor had noted. But they had not been built in the same way. Larger and more important structures, and urban dwellings in general, were built from adobe bricks: their massive load-bearing walls were composed of solid sun-dried blocks joined together by mud mortar and covered with an outer layer of lime plaster. The thick walls and the heavy roofs perched atop them enabled little heat to pass through, which was crucial in this desert climate, keeping houses cool in the day and warm at night. There were more or less refined versions of this, with the better homes hiding their earthen walls behind elegant masonry facades, but the basic structure was the same. All partook of a cultural value assigned to buildings offering rooted, solid, and firm protection against an often harsh and threatening outside.

By contrast, out in the countryside, or on the poorer fringes of the city, most homes had been built from *quincha*, an indigenous technique refined during Spanish colonial rule. Here the load was carried by a frame rather than by the walls. Quincha homes consisted of a wooden frame made from logs or trunks, covered by thin walls of intertwined canes or twigs smeared with a mixture of mud, straw, and animal excrement. The roof was made in a similar way to the walls. Rather than presenting a massive wall to the outside world, quincha offered a thin screen, often rough, irregular, and apparently unsanitary. Precisely because it was light, quincha was held to offer little shelter, and because it was simple and inexpensive, it was often portrayed as a sign of primitiveness and penury. Local elites had long drawn sharp contrasts between the solid and the frail, the finished and the rough, the cultured and the barbaric, making a rancho of quincha the very image of rural backwardness. Replacing such homes with something more solid and sanitary had been a long-standing rhetorical aim for reform-minded elites and a common material objective for many striving workers.

Even if nearly all of San Juan had been built of adobe, then, certain forms of adobe had been regarded as degraded materials from which no legitimate shelter could be made. Critiques of quincha were largely unconcerned with technical matters of construction; they drew on science only insofar as quincha was regarded as an unsanitary breeding ground for disease. More importantly, strong denunciations of quincha did not lead to programs for its replacement and yielded precious little in terms of specific initiatives in housing or public health. Rather than spurring efforts at reform, this discourse primarily served to draw a sharp line between city and country and to justify continued exclusion of the supposedly ignorant and unworthy poor. But the discourse was solidly established, in the end more solidly than the houses it regarded as signs of virtue. And after those supposedly solid constructions of the city came down in the earthquake, this familiar line of argument was deployed to new ends.

Looking at the rubble, many locals would repudiate practices they had long accepted as natural and join Ramella in condemning "this adobe superstition." Over the following months, this visceral reaction would be reinforced by a series of expert analyses of building collapses, focused largely on the first type of adobe construction, the heavier houses with load-bearing walls that predominated within city limits.

The failure of these adobe houses, visiting experts concluded, was due to the weaknesses of the material and the lack of structural reinforcement, irregular layout, and high heavy roofs in most buildings. The basic problem was that adobe withstood compression well but tension or lateral force hardly at all. This meant that these houses were extremely deformable: one part of a structure would resist any given force quite well, while another would gave way almost immediately. This weakness was compounded by the absence of any reinforcement or ties holding the whole together. Most houses were sprawling, irregular affairs, built a few rooms at a time, organized around long hallways and interior patios. The more spread-out the floor plan, the more likely it became that the building would break apart in a quake. The high ceilings and heavy roofs that shielded locals from the intense climate also played a role. The higher center of gravity meant houses were more likely to move, and, with the roof merely resting unsecured on the walls, any shifting was likely to knock the roof off and bring the walls down. Pulled apart in quakes, walls broke free and simply collapsed. In response to this movement and fragmentation, experts recommended fixity and unity: future homes should be more compact, symmetrical, and structurally rigid. Above all, they should not be made of adobe.

There was one striking counterpoint to this analysis, although it was largely ignored at the time. Those quincha shacks long regarded as backward, which "even when new . . . give a feeling of immediate collapse and maximum insecurity," had turned out to be far more secure than the homes of their betters. "None of these houses was knocked down by the quake," one geologist noted, thanks to their flexible construction, light roof, and low center of gravity.[37] But the lesson was lost on locals: only solidity could offer a project for the future, and solid building in adobe was flawed, so adobe had to be discarded.

Even the repudiation of the past drew powerfully on precedent. The technical reasons for the failure of adobe were not complicated, but newspapers did not report them in detail, focusing instead on discrediting the material itself. Similarly, many locals moved quickly from the technical analysis of structural failure to a broader campaign to ban adobe as a building material entirely. Ignoring the possible virtues of quincha, they instead revived the familiar campaign against it, now expanding it to a campaign against all structures in adobe.[38] While the campaign against adobe quickly won broad support in San Juan, particularly among the elite, the temporary closure of the local newspapers meant that its arguments were most fully spelled out in regional newspapers, above all the Mendoza daily *Los Andes*, the only paper circulating in San Juan at the time.[39] Because the neighboring provincial capital was built in a similar way on comparable soil, the professional association of architects and engineers there took the earthquake as a call to action: "Popular belief has always held that adobe constructions, because of their greater 'elasticity,' were more adequate for resisting seismic motion. Because it is so widespread and deeply rooted . . . this belief must be destroyed with an intense and prolonged campaign. New construction, without exception, whatever its location, must be made in keeping with what anti-seismic expertise suggests."[40]

"We live in a city of mud," *Los Andes* declared, constantly threatened by failings of hygiene and safety.[41] Just as the government defended citizens against disease, so here "the State should rise up with all its force to defend the lives of its inhabitants in their habitations."[42] In the past, the paper had sporadically undertaken "enlightened" campaigns against quincha shacks, viewing vernacular housing as a measure of popular backwardness and an infectious threat to the social order. But now the newspaper shifted the blame, portraying adobe as the measure of the indifference of the government and the injustice of the social order. Abolishing it would be the first step toward building a new nation: "The future Argentina will not be forged in adobe ranches . . . but in dignified and safe homes, where mothers are not ashamed of their misery but can display the strength of their children in a clean frame."[43] The call for dignity marked a crucial shift. While dignity had always been at the center of ideas about housing, in the past it had been portrayed as an individual conquest, gained by saving and striving, but now it would be created by broad state intervention. A month after the earthquake, all new adobe construction was banned in the city of Mendoza.[44]

The critique of adobe could become the vehicle for a particularly powerful repudiation of the past. It was easy to make adobe exemplify the fragile, unjust, and inadequate arrangements that had anchored local social life prior to the earthquake. The failure of the state to ensure the safety of its citizens in their homes was emblematic of many broader failings. Conversely, the resilience of new houses would be the proof of a new social compact. This was the line of argument advanced in the Mendoza campaign and also embraced by various groups in San Juan.

At the same time, this repudiation could easily be used to avoid a serious reckoning with the past. By blaming the tragedy on a building material, local elites could turn attention away from questions of power. Rather than presenting adobe as emblematic of a broader pattern of corruption and shortsightedness, they could isolate it as a single fatal flaw, easily remedied by technical means.

Concrete

From early on, the "movers" made surprisingly little reference to the possible geologic advantages of a new site, while the "keepers" asserted with odd confidence—given their lack of any specific knowledge and the near-total destruction of the city—that the current location was ideal. Both groups agreed on the need for geologic studies, and, in the months after the disaster, several geologists came to assess the causes and impact of the earthquake and suggest how to protect against future recurrences.

The most prominent group was sent by a quasi-governmental body best known for funding studies to promote industrialization.[45] They were charged with two tasks: determining where the soil was suitable for construction and surveying mineral deposits to see if a cement industry could be established in the province.[46] Given this double mission, it was hardly a surprise when they concluded that moving the city was unnecessary, but the use of new construction techniques involving concrete was essential.[47]

Still, other geologists with less obvious agendas reached similar conclusions. They were not arguing that soil conditions were irrelevant—on the contrary, each of the geologists pointed out that similar structures on different terrain behaved quite differently, and some noted the particularly unstable nature of the alluvial soil the city had been built on.[48] They were arguing instead that the limited knowledge of local soils, and the even more limited knowledge of the behavior of those soils during seismic motion, made it impossible to predict with much precision where it was safest to build. Those areas that clearly did seem safe in geologic terms, moreover, were unacceptable for other reasons—lack of water, inability to support vegetation, or physical isolation.[49] For the geologists, improved structures were more likely to save lives than improved locations and therefore, as one wrote, they left "the problem of the future of the city of San Juan to the engineers, especially those who specialize in the design and construction of reinforced concrete."[50]

Rebuilding on the old site was perfectly safe, local elites would now argue, provided all houses were antiseismic. Some also recognized the need for a few minor adjustments to streets and property lots. All stressed this was not a social issue, just a narrow technical matter. After years of ignoring earthquakes and technical knowledge, they now embraced it as a complete solution.

According to this argument, only two things were needed to make the city safe: expertise and concrete. Having denounced "this superstition of adobe," local judge Ramella insisted that all future construction be entrusted to experts, "not builders with no technical knowledge or homeowners themselves."[51] Outside experts agreed, like the geologist who flatly declared that "it is within the power of builders, architects and engineers, to erase earthquakes from the list of human scourges, if they wish it."[52] The irregular and disorderly shacks and mansions in adobe would give way to regular and ordered construction in reinforced concrete. Advocates of concrete had a clear model in mind, according to one local engineer: stiff, symmetrical boxes rigidly guarded against the threats of nature.[53]

The dream of a concrete city was appealing for several reasons. First, reinforced concrete was a sign of modernity. The concrete industry in Argentina was relatively new but quite dynamic, the fifth largest in the world.[54] Here as elsewhere, the industry had been a consistent backer of cutting-edge architecture. All the new infrastructure built by an expanding state—roads, bridges, tunnels, and dams—was also made of concrete, strengthening the association with modernity.

Second, concrete could also be tied to tradition. While there was some light wood-frame construction in Argentina, most building was heavy load-bearing construction (in masonry or adobe), and that was what constituted local notions of a proper house. Indeed, in the local language of construction, to say something was made with "material" meant that it was made with stone or brick. Concrete could easily supplant masonry in this role, while building in wood or steel required different designs and techniques, and produced quite different results. Reinforced concrete could thus speak to historically well-established ideas of home while also signaling a dramatic break with local history.

Finally, reinforced concrete seemed especially appropriate for anti-seismic design, as pioneered in Japan and publicized by the influential writings of North American engineers. The central question was "flexibility versus rigidity," and, as a North American engineer had put it, "the utmost practicable structural rigidity is desirable."[55] While the technical reasoning behind this argument was lost on most locals, solidity and stiffness had a clear visceral appeal and also fit well with the other cultural virtues of concrete.[56]

All three lines of argument—modernity, solidity, and antiseismic strength—converged on a vision of a future city of free-standing boxes of

concrete. Powerful as this vision was, it did contain some striking para-
doxes and contradictions. Most obviously, this concrete vision, with its
powerful symbolic links to the modernist project, was here being deployed
precisely to oppose modernism. A technique closely identified with the
comprehensive rethinking of structure and the city was being used to
block such a rethinking. Beyond the tactical brilliance of this move, however, and the ways in which it enabled a fundamentally backwards-looking
project to offer a future, concrete still posed a range of broader challenges
locals were unwilling to confront.

Rebuilding everything in concrete was actually a more radical idea
than its proponents seemed to realize. Achieving even a narrowly technical solution would demand a major social transformation: establishing
mandatory antiseismic standards might seem at first like a simple technical
question, one architect observed, but "their full implementation in a city
constitutes not just a sum of individual matters but a truly collective problem."[57] In the previous examples local advocates were drawing on, in Japan
and the United States, the expense of antiseismic techniques in reinforced
concrete meant they were largely reserved to major multistory buildings,
while the vast majority of construction, particularly residential building,
continued to employ other materials, especially wood. Here, by contrast,
local leaders were proposing that an entire city, from the largest structure
to the smallest, be fashioned from reinforced concrete. This was the first
time such an ambitious project had been attempted.

Concrete marked an expensive change for local construction, which
until now had obtained most of its primary materials for next to nothing. Only reinforced concrete would work as claimed, as concrete without
steel reinforcement would be nearly as vulnerable to tension and shear
forces as adobe, but Argentina produced no steel of its own. Clearly, as the
geologists recognized, concrete would prove "too expensive . . . for the
modest inhabitants of these areas."[58] Without subsidies, simply requiring new construction to be in concrete would guarantee little: a rigor-
ously enforced ban on adobe would leave most of the province homeless,
while a flexibly observed ban would simply ensure that most building took
place outside the city, or outside the law. This obstacle could force broader
rethinking: one outside architect presented the need for the state to sub-
sidize antiseismic construction as the starting point for justifying a far
more comprehensive state role in housing overall.[59] But local advocates of
concrete made no mention of subsidies for the poor.

There was also the question of expertise. For decades, local elites had ignored and disdained the technical authority they now claimed to embrace: as one geologist noted, the collapsed buildings showed a constant drive "to save on the costs of materials and the fees of qualified experts."[60] After the quake, members of the Commission for Restoration listened only to the experts who agreed with them, and the local press mocked any who disagreed as absurd dreamers unworthy of any respect. None of this was a particularly promising start for the kind of strong, independent authority that would be required to supervise a vast construction project. In a province that had never had a building code, making every building antiseismic would not be a simple task. Designs needed to be vetted; concrete itself needed to be tested; every aspect of building needed to be controlled. This was a major change in governance, for the state itself and the experts it would employ. It was unlikely that the sixty engineers and half-dozen architects in San Juan would be enough to carry it out. It was also a major change in construction technique, which would require training or importing large numbers of workers in a sector now poorly paid and almost entirely unskilled.

Finally, there was the question of concrete supply. San Juan seemed to meet the basic requirements for a cement plant: raw materials were nearby, public or private capital was available, and a market was virtually guaranteed. But one thing was missing: cheap electrical power. The best way to obtain this was by building a hydroelectric dam, which in turn would provide power for many other operations beyond the cement plant, promoting the creation of new industries. Yet to do so meant pursuing exactly the goals local elites were resisting and modernist architects were advocating: industrialization, economic diversification, and extensive public works.

Rebuilding in concrete would set into motion many of the same processes as modernist planning, rendering the local attempt to use concrete to resist planning at least partly self-defeating. The link between modernist planning and reinforced concrete was functional as well as symbolic. Thinking through this, one is left with three possibilities: local advocates did not foresee that opting for concrete would bring about many of the changes they wanted to resist; they thought by opting for concrete they could at least control those changes; or they were not really opting for concrete at all, but rather deploying the idea to defeat the dangerous initiatives of modernists before rebuilding on a more limited basis, more favorable to existing property and power.

The Provisional City

Meanwhile, whatever the long-term direction of rebuilding, the national state faced an unprecedented short-term demand for shelter. Tens of thousands were homeless in San Juan, and, while the state had bought some time by evacuating many survivors and providing tents to those remaining, the need remained stark. What this called for was a crash program to build temporary shelter, a program that offered the state an opportunity to test new methods, strengthen authority, and establish credibility. Once the wounded had been healed, the streets had been cleared, and the all-important grape harvest had begun, state officials turned to this task in earnest.

The state provided three kinds of emergency shelter. First were three thousand small wooden structures offered to landowners in the city and the countryside. While they were little more than huts, they were placed on the recipient's land, enabling survivors to remain near their former home while preparing for rebuilding. Second were four hundred masonry homes, conceived as workers' housing under the conservative government, but completed as relatively luxurious emergency quarters under the military. Third were nearly three thousand emergency homes the military put up in a series of large projects around the perimeter of the former city.

This last type would shelter the most families and have the greatest symbolic impact. There were a dozen projects, ranging in size from a few dozen to several hundred houses, all filled with the same modern variants on the traditional countryside rancho. These designs were the fruit of a decade of small state-funded experiments with rural housing, now implemented on a massive scale. Built with walls and roofs of fibercement cladding on a frame of machined lumber, these were industrialized shelters, better equipped than the previous homes of most locals.[61]

For the military, this was the first step toward a more just, ordered, and industrial future, the opening installment of rebuilding as a whole. Even the Catholic conservative paper saw an egalitarian future in these projects: "There are no social classes anymore . . . and out of the provisional projects a new society will emerge, an aristocracy of the earthquake."[62] While no one claimed they were a permanent solution, the projects were widely seen as a dramatic improvement from the past and a major political achievement for the regime. The government capitalized on this, naming every project after a government minister or hero of the rescue effort and placing two sample houses from San Juan at the entrance to the major exhibit in Buenos Aires celebrating one year of military rule.

Impressive as they were, the emergency projects also had major flaws. Some were technical: the experimental materials were poorly adapted to the local climate, leaving the homes bitterly cold in winter and scorching in summer, and the amount of infrastructure installed, while remarkable enough, was sufficient to provide only a fraction of the homes with direct water, sewer, or electrical service, which would become a major problem over time.

Equally important, however, were the political flaws. The housing was built by the national state but distributed by the provincial administration. To ensure housing for those who most needed it, provincial officials exhorted the wealthy to build their own shelter and initially proposed to charge rent on a sliding scale for government-built housing. But the exhortations came to little, the rent proposal was quashed, and housing was ultimately allocated in a way that reaffirmed previous class divisions. As the projects neared completion, the administration released a daily list with the names, professions, and family size of those receiving housing. These lists revealed that the better-built homes originally intended for workers and the emergency structures in the smaller projects went almost exclusively to the middle and upper classes, while the more austere emergency homes in the two mammoth projects went overwhelmingly to workers.[63] In practice, emergency housing was looking less like a triumph of the egalitarian vision of national officials than an entrenchment of the parochial power of local elites.

Alongside the orderly rows of state-built housing stood the disorderly improvisations of locals. While the broad consensus that adobe had little place in the future city meant, for example, that requests to repair permanent structures in adobe were routinely rejected, the government also knew its projects would not be enough for everyone and thus encouraged anyone who could build their own temporary housing to do so.[64] All adobe mansions were banned, but some adobe shacks seemed unavoidable, at least in the short term. Indeed, the state chose to use experimental materials in emergency housing not only to create a market for them but also, and more importantly, to leave any adobe or reusable material from the ruins to those building their own shelter.

Here was another paradox of the aftermath: the return of adobe at the very moment it was being denounced and outlawed. "Speaking ill of adobe is easy," as one journalist noted; "the hard thing will be replacing it."[65] While awaiting government action, thousands put up quincha shacks, fashioned from scavenged materials, wherever they could: behind their ruined homes, on the edges of public parks, in open fields, and along the roadside. If until recently the rancho had been a "symbol of rural backwardness," a conservative paper noted, now the force of "necessity was restoring its former importance" at the heart of the city proper.[66] To be sure, even the builders of these shacks did not see them as a lasting alternative: most were fragile and unhealthy affairs that offered minimal shelter and were readily abandoned when something better came along.

The unexpected return of the rancho did inspire a few builders and observers to think differently.[67] Several geologists suggested antiseismic construction techniques could be adapted to materials other than concrete, and a few locals attempted to find ways to use adobe in structures that were properly reinforced.[68] After all, adobe remained excellent protection from the climate and, as one writer speculated, "solidly placed in a modest cage of concrete, cement, and steel, would make a safe, healthy, and comfortable fort for the average family."[69] Another local proposed a variation on this technique, halfway between the flexible resilience of quincha and the rigid strength of concrete, using a cane frame to strengthen adobe walls.[70] All these dissenters understood that the problem was less a matter of banning unsafe materials than of designing safe structures. They also understood that, in the absence of sufficient workers and materials, banning adobe completely meant delaying reconstruction "who knows how many years," as one observer prophetically remarked.[71]

But such ideas fit poorly in a professional field increasingly committed to concrete and a political debate organized around blaming the disaster on a building material. Neither adobe nor fibercement was ever seriously considered as the starting point for an alternative approach to antiseismic building. Instead, the authorities would wager the local future on reinforced concrete, without pursuing the subsidies or broader strategies that might make it viable for everyone.

Settlements

Despite the symbolic achievement of emergency housing, the military leadership was soon aware that its first attempt at radically remaking the city had failed. Shortly after making the architects' plan the centerpiece of a June 1944 exhibition marking one year of military rule, authorities discarded it and entrusted rebuilding to a new federal agency, the Reconstruction Council.

The new agency took over just as Perón finally pushed aside his main rivals within the regime, became vice president, and launched a broad project of social reform, with workers at its center. Over the following year, Perón's social project would take off, but rebuilding would stall. Because it was based in San Juan and included representation for locals, the Reconstruction Council had initially seemed like a triumph for the winery elite, but the leadership of the new agency soon made clear that it enjoyed enhanced powers to expropriate and plan, that a move was still on the agenda, and that representation for local elites was strictly ornamental. Despite these powers, the leadership of the agency did not have a clear vision for rebuilding or much political acumen and soon had burned through three teams of architects, advancing toward a plan only in fits and starts.

By the time the agency finally announced a plan for rebuilding on the same site, in July 1945, it was too little, and too late, and served only to galvanize a mass protest in early August 1945. Condemning the military for needlessly complicating rebuilding, protestors demanded immediate action, called for "houses not plans," and refused to be "tenants on their own land."[72] Dominated by the middle and upper classes, as the rhetoric of ownership suggested, the group soon sparked countermobilizations by workers supporting Perón. Significantly, however, while the opposition was equally against the social agenda and rebuilding plans of the regime, supporters were far more enthusiastic about social reforms than about visions for the new city. The opposition eventually managed to force elections and drive Perón briefly from office, only to see him win decisively at the ballot box. But while Perón's candidate for governor won the local election, his narrow margin forced him to ally with conservatives in order to rule. Making a virtue of necessity, he appointed Catholic intellectuals as his advisors and proclaimed the elite's minimal program for rebuilding as official Peronist policy. Launching a frontal attack on the Reconstruction Council at his inauguration, he made a particular point of attacking the "delirium of intellectual pride" of Reconstruction Council experts who had devised a building code locals now found excessive.[73] The governor failed to overthrow the council and fell to palace intrigues within a year, but his rule marked the end of any talk of rethinking the province as part of rebuilding.

Through their sustained resistance, local elites succeeded in blunting the most radical and transformative visions of rebuilding. Their lobbying in 1944 defeated the first plan and drove the Ministry of Public Works from the scene; their protests in 1945 defeated the successor plan and set the terms for the ultimate debate. They failed to defeat Peronism but won a space within it; they failed to defeat the Reconstruction Council but partly bent it to their terms. In turn, the Reconstruction Council adapted itself to the resistance, backing off from controversial actions and welcoming backroom negotiations even as, after 1946, it flooded the city with communiqués, decrees, subsidies, and eventually even buildings. While remaining a national agency, with outsiders in many key posts, it also became a crucial machine for patronage jobs, particularly for the local elite. As early as 1948, a prominent Catholic activist was named chief counsel, and many of his peers followed him into the agency's service. Over the years, the council gradually made itself as enduring as the rubble, an unassailable fact on the ground, the bureaucracy everyone denounced but ultimately had to turn to. Local elites had long proclaimed that a rigorous building code was all that was needed for the city to rise again, then began to protest and complain as soon as the council actually put one in place. But they eventually came around.

Eight years after the disaster, another earthquake struck San Juan. Although it was stronger than the first, with an epicenter southwest of the capital, it left only five dead. Damages were far less for several reasons: many of the weakest structures had already fallen; the buildings in most affected areas were quincha shacks; and, particularly, the strength of antiseismic construction passed the test. Even if less than a third of the city was in antiseismic construction, because building in concrete had proven slower and more expensive than promised, still that was a confirmation of the disputed agency.

Even as Peronism boldly remade Argentine society as a whole, it pursued a conservative course in San Juan. The narrow technical solution prevailed over the broader plans for transformation. And even that technical solution was restricted in its application. After a compromise made in the 1948 code, the Reconstruction Council allowed the countryside to be rebuilt in adobe.[74] Instead of serving to modernize the province as a whole, rebuilding served to deepen the divide between country and city and to further concentrate resources and power in the capital. Despite the growth in union power, grape monoculture only strengthened its hold over the countryside.

San Juan was rebuilt on the same site, a city of concrete fortresses arrayed against future attacks of nature. Outside of the four avenues, where large plots of land could be assembled, a scattering of neighborhoods were built, small-scale versions of the grand plans of 1944, unrelated to each other or to the city as a whole. Inside the four avenues, construction proceeded more slowly. Even when locals were freed of any restrictions on building but the code and given generous subsidies by the Reconstruction Council, they were reluctant to act. The widening of the streets ultimately required fifteen years of legal wrangling and thousands of expropriation cases, just as the architects had warned. For two decades, downtown was a spectral place of ruins punctuated by massive official buildings and scattered private homes. The city rose again more secure but also more fragmented than before.

⁂ NOTES ⁂

1. Carl Taylor, *Rural Life in Argentina* (Baton Rouge: Louisiana State University Press, 1948), 38.

2. Benito Marianetti, *El racimo y su aventura: la cuestión vitivinícola* (Mendoza: Platina, 1965).

3. Benito Carrasco and Ángel Guido, *Plan regulador de San Juan* (San Juan: Gobierno de San Juan, 1942), 7, 8, 65, 70, 10.

4. Luis Romero, "Horas de terror y de ruina," *Revista del CACYA*, February 1944, 193–94.

5. Romero, "Horas de terror," 198.

6. Ibid.

7. Alfredo Castellanos, *Anotaciones preliminares con motivo de una visita a la ciudad de San Juan a propósito del terremoto del 15 de enero de 1944*, mon. 2, tomo 2 (Rosario, Argentina: Universidad Nacional del Litoral, 1944), 27.

8. Eduardo Sacriste, "Arquitectura popular de San Juan," *Revista de Arquitectura* 281 (May 1944): 216.

9. Pablo Ramella, "Legislación de la propiedad en zonas expuestas a movimientos sísmicos," *El Pueblo*, February 4, 1944.

10. "Meditando," *El Censor*, January 25, 1945. The architect of this building was Eduardo Carrizo Vita, former secretary of public works and the main source of information for the urbanists who prepared the master plan.

11. "San Juan," *Los Andes*, January 15, 1946.

12. Perón quoted in César Civita, ed. *Perón, el hombre del destino* (Buenos Aires: Abril Educativa, 1974), 1:247.

13. Cinna Lomnitz, *Fundamentals of Earthquake Prediction* (New York: Wiley, 1994), ix.

14. Juan Siri, "El terremoto de 1894," *La Acción*, January 18, 1945.

15. Fermín Bereterbide and Carlos Muzio, "Contribución al estudio de la reconstrucción de la ciudad de San Juan y poblaciones vecinas," *Revista de Arquitectura* 293 (May 1945): 194.

16. Bereterbide and Muzio, "Contribución," 196.

17. José M. F. Pastor, "San Juan," *Revista de Arquitectura* 277 (January 1944): 4.

18. Bereterbide and Muzio, "Contribución," 194–95.

19. Examples include the "wealthy industrialist and investor Saúl Aubone," quoted in "Varios vecinos opinan que la ciudad no debe cambiar de ubicación," *La Prensa*, January 24, 1944; and the federal judge quoted in "La ciudad no debe ser reconstruida fuera del ejido en que se halla," *La Prensa*, January 28, 1944.

20. "Para la reconstrucción de la ciudad se pide la conscripción de 50,000 obreros," *La Voz del Interior*, January 17, 1944. Another paper spoke of a request for one hundred thousand workers: "Se pide la emisión de un empréstito patriótico de 150,000,000," *El Pueblo*, January 18, 1944.

21. "Para la reconstrucción," *La Voz del Interior*; "Se pide la emisión," *El Pueblo*.

22. Enévaro Rossi, San Juan, to Emil Lorch, Ann Arbor, February 1, 1944, State Department Decimal Files, 835.48/36, U.S. National Archives, Washington, DC.

23. Ramella sketched his initial proposal in three articles: "Reflexiones acerca de la tragedia de San Juan," *El Pueblo*, January 23, 1944; "Problemas jurídicos que suscita la reconstrucción de San Juan," *El Pueblo*, January 29, 1944; and "Legislación de la propiedad," *El Pueblo*.

24. "Por la actual ubicación de la ciudad abógase," *Los Andes*, February 8, 1944.

25. "Se creará una comisión que tratará diversos problemas de San Juan," *Los Andes*, February 13, 1944; "Hubo un cambio de ideas sobre los planes de reconstrucción," *La Nación*, February 17, 1944.

26. For supporters of the move, see "Pedido de la Asociación Amigos de San Juan." *La Prensa*, February 19, 1944; Rubén Sarmiento, "¿Reconstruir o fundar una nueva ciudad de San Juan?" *Los Andes*, March 17, 1944. For opponents, see "Comisión sanjuanina de restauración," *La Prensa*, April 20, 1944.

27. Pablo Ramella, "Idealistas y realistas en la reconstrucción de San Juan." *El Pueblo*, February 15, 1944.

28. Pablo Ramella, "Nuevos problemas jurídicos acerca de la reconstrucción de San Juan," *El Pueblo*, April 14, 1944.

29. "La aspiración común: que la ciudad se reconstruya en el mismo lugar," *La Acción*, March 16, 1944.

30. "El gobernante y el arquitecto," *Tribuna*, April 9, 1944.

31. "Una comisión solicita que no sea cambiada la ubicación de San Juan." *La Prensa*, March 7, 1944.

32. Castellanos, *Anotaciones*, 12, 24.

33. "La ciudad de San Juan," *La Prensa*, January 16, 1944.

34. Ramella, "Reflexiones," *El Pueblo*.

35. "La ubicación de la ciudad de San Juan no debe modificarse," *La Prensa*, April 30, 1944.

36. "Se disertó ayer sobre urbanismo y defensa antiaérea," *Los Andes*, February 26, 1944. The "strategic necessity" the officer had in mind was protection against aerial bombardment.

37. Horacio Harrington, *El sismo de San Juan del 15 de enero de 1944* (Buenos Aires: CPI, 1944), 20–21.

38. For example, "El espejismo del adobe: la edificación de Cuyo," *La Acción*, June 2, 1944.

39. *Los Andes* was also the sponsor of the blackboards at food distribution points downtown that served as the primary information source for most locals until the middle of March.

40. "Propúsose un plan para dar seguridad a las viviendas," *Los Andes*, January 26, 1944.

41. "El estado debe ser el primero en ofrecer el ejemplo en la edificación antisísmica," *Los Andes*, February 14, 1944.

42. "La casa de adobe es una amenaza para la seguridad pública en la zona sísmica," *Los Andes*, February 11, 1944.

43. "Es necesario que el hogar mendocino tenga casa digna y sobretodo, seguro," *Los Andes*, February 12, 1944.

44. "Se prohibió la edificación con adobe en Mendoza," *Los Andes*, February 17, 1944.

45. Founded in 1941 as part of a conservative plan to diversify Argentine exports and acquire imports, the Corporación para la Promoción del Intercambio

(CPI) turned under the impact of the war toward "other activities, such as sponsoring surveys on the Argentine economy and its capacity for industrial development." Gisela Cramer, "Argentine Riddle" *JLAS* 30, no. 3 (October 1998): 435, 448. See, for example, John Hopkins, *La estructura económica y el desarollo industrial de la Argentina* (Buenos Aires: CPI, 1944).

46. "Posibilidades de la producción de cemento," *La Prensa*, February 9, 1944.

47. "Una comisión de técnicos dio a conocer sus conclusiones relacionadas con el sismo," *La Prensa*, May 4, 1944. See also the report itself: Harrington, *Sismo de San Juan*, 28–29.

48. Harrington contrasted the endurance of adobe houses on bedrock less than a kilometer from the epicenter with the collapse of identical houses much farther away but on alluvial soil (*Sismo de San Juan*, 20).

49. In addition to Harrington and Castellanos, see Erwin Kittl, "Sobre la estabilidad del terreno de la ciudad de San Juan y sus alrededores," *Revista Minera, Geología y Mineralogía* 15, no. 4 (1944): 90–96.

50. Castellanos, *Anotaciones*, 28.

51. Ramella, "Reflexiones," *El Pueblo*.

52. Martín Cappelletti, quoted in Juan Kulik, "Fundaciones de los edificios asísmicos," *La Ingenería* 855 (January 1946): 29.

53. "Un estudio geológico del subsuelo requerirá la ciudad a construirse," *La Prensa*, January 25, 1944.

54. Argentina held this position from 1938 until the early 1950s. See Graciela Silvestri, "Cemento" in Jorge Francisco Liernur, ed. *Diccionario Histórico de Arquitectura, Habitat y Urbanismo en la Argentina* (Buenos Aires: Proyecto Editorial, 1996), 76–78.

55. John R. Freeman, *Earthquake Damage and Earthquake Insurance* (New York: McGraw-Hill, 1932), 799.

56. For a discussion of Japanese precedents in technical literature, see Rodolfo Martin, "Nociones de ingenería antisísmica" *Boletín de YPF* (1944): 47–71. The popular press also picked up on this, as in "Deben ser transformadas las viviendas de emergencia empleadas actualmente en San Juan," *Los Andes*, December 14, 1944.

57. Emilio Maisonnave, "Previsiones antisísmicas: necesidad de hacerlas obligatorias en las obras nuevas y en las existentes en nuestras regiones afectadas por los terremotos," in *Contribución a los estudios sísmicos en la República Argentina: el caso de San Juan*, ed. Ermete de Lorenzi (Rosario, Argentina: Universidad Nacional del Litoral, 1944), 96.

58. "Ubicación de la ciudad," *La Prensa*.

59. Maisonnave, "Previsiones antisísmicas," 96–97.

60. Castellanos, *Anotaciones*, 27.

61. The walls and roofs were made from fibercement, a new material introduced only a few years before. *Obra de emergencia en San Juan* (Buenos Aires: Ministerio de Obras Públicas, 1944).

62. Emiliano Lee, "La casa vacía," *Tribuna*, August 21, 1944; see also "Buenos días," *Tribuna*, March 27, 1944.

63. See *Tribuna*, April–May 1944.

64. "Desde hoy harán el racionamiento de la población en San Juan," *La Nación*, February 7, 1944.

65. "El adobe en San Juan," *Tribuna*, December 17, 1944.

66. "San Juan después del terremoto: la reivindicación del rancho." *Tribuna*, March 27, 1944.

67. "Elogio de la quincha," *Tribuna*, April 14, 1944.

68. Harrington, *Sismo de San Juan*; and Martin, "Nociones de ingenería antisísmica."

69. "El adobe," *Tribuna*. A modernist defense of adobe was made by Sacriste, "Arquitectura popular," 216.

70. Francisco Cano, "El adobe como material apto para construcciones antisísmicas," *Revista Sarmiento* 3 (October 1945): 17.

71. Francisco Cano, "Aporte a la solución del problema de la reconstrucción," *Revista Sarmiento* 5 (December 1945): 24–25.

72. "Fue examinado el problema de S. Juan," *La Acción*, August 9, 1945.

73. "El mensaje del nuevo mandatario," *Tribuna*, May 26, 1946.

74. "El consejo de reconstrucción adoptó una importante resolución," *La Reforma*, March 30, 1948.

CHAPTER FIVE

Natural Disaster, Political Earthquake

The 1972 Destruction of Managua
and the Somoza Dynasty

PAUL J. DOSAL

✝ IN THE EARLY MORNING HOURS OF DECEMBER 23, 1972, THE EARTH beneath downtown Managua shook back and forth horizontally, awaking residents from their sleep with a warning that a more powerful earthquake was yet to come. Anastasio (Tachito) Somoza Debayle, commander of the Nicaraguan National Guard and the most powerful member of a three-person governing junta, grabbed his wife, Hope, and ran outside their private residence, where they felt two more powerful jolts. As Tachito described his experience, "the second and third [quakes] oscillated up and down. That third one was the killer. We thought we were pieces of ice in a cocktail shaker."[1]

Tachito, to whom cocktails were not strangers, quickly placed himself in charge of rescue, relief, and reconstruction. The worst of the earthquakes measured only 6.25 on the Richter scale, but it destroyed the picturesque city on the shores of Lake Managua. The capital city, located directly over three faults, had been destroyed twice before, in 1885 and again in 1931. Both times, the Nicaraguan government decided to rebuild the city on the same site. The responsibility for the second reconstruction of Managua on notoriously vulnerable foundations rested primarily on the shoulders of Somoza's father, Anastasio (Tacho) Somoza Garcia, the original commander of the U.S.-trained National Guard. From his military base, Tacho built a unique family dynasty that dominated the Nicaraguan government until 1979.

The 1972 series of quakes leveled the city and produced political aftershocks that brought down the Somoza dynasty six and a half years later. The earthquake literally destroyed the institutions that symbolized and housed the regime's centers of power, including Tachito's personal residence on La Loma, as well as the nearby presidential palace, National Guard headquarters, and the U.S. Embassy. Fires engulfed Managua's commercial district within twenty-four hours. With the water lines severed, firefighters and rescue workers could only watch as Managua crumbled to the ground or burned out of control, producing scenes of devastation comparable to a World War II carpet-bombing raid. Juan Castenera, manager of a communications station in the suburbs of Managua, described the scene as "like the end of the world."[2]

Collapsed three-story reinforced concrete customs house office building
(IMAGE 4, NICARAGUA, 1972, U.S. GEOLOGICAL SURVEY PHOTOGRAPHIC LIBRARY).

Swath of destroyed buildings along fault C. Fault trace is through the center of the photograph. Open fractures that trend north-south in the street pavement are in echelon to the fault. Structure on the right is typical of *tarquezal* (wood and adobe) construction that was extensively damaged (IMAGE 5, NICARAGUA, 1972, U.S. GEOLOGICAL SURVEY PHOTOGRAPHIC LIBRARY).

When the fires finally burned out and the buildings settled into indistinguishable piles of metal and concrete, not much was left of Managua or the institutions that kept the Somozas in power. Managua had once been the picturesque home to nearly 600,000 people, concentrated in an area of thirty-three square kilometers. The capital featured some architectural wonders such as the Moorish-style presidential palace on La Loma hill, the pyramid-shaped Hotel Intercontinental just below it, and a Spanish colonial cathedral near the lakefront. Sadly, the earthquakes completely destroyed or severely damaged more than 80 percent of total buildings. At least 250,000 people lost their homes; 10,000 lost their lives; and 20,000 suffered injuries. Almost the entire commercial district of Managua was destroyed, with the notable exception of the seventeen-story Bank of America building. However, most of downtown Managua's buildings, including the cathedral and all four hospitals, were damaged beyond repair.[3]

Less tragic perhaps, at least in the eyes of Somoza's many critics, was the loss of the institutions that had propped up the Somoza dynasty. Prior to the earthquake, the Somozas had crushed every military challenge to their political domination, thanks in large part to political, military, and economic support from the United States. After the earthquake, the United States expected Somoza to rebuild Managua and restore Nicaraguan democracy. He failed to do either to the satisfaction of the United States. Instead, Somoza pushed the junta aside, reestablished firm dictatorial control, profited from reconstruction assistance, and rejected the United States' efforts to engineer a peaceful transition to a democratically elected government.

Tachito, his top military officers, and U.S. ambassador Turner Shelton survived the initial devastation, but the political and economic aftershocks dealt a fatal blow to all of them. Anastasio Somoza quit drinking several years after the disaster, but he never rehabilitated his relationship with the United States. Ambassador Shelton served until 1975, when the State Department replaced him and applied a new, less friendly policy toward the Somoza regime. By that time, Somoza had become a political liability to the United States, largely because he had abused international reconstruction assistance for the benefit of himself and his allies. As a result, the earthquake had destroyed a city and opened deep fissures in the political, economic, and diplomatic foundations of the Somoza regime. When Sandinista military units led a caravan of jubilant people through the barren lots of downtown Managua to the ruins of the national cathedral on July 19, 1979, they celebrated the end of a bloody political struggle unleashed and intensified by the natural disaster of 1972.

The Use and Abuse of Reconstruction Aid

Roberto Clemente, the Puerto Rican star of the Pittsburgh Pirates, had completed his seventeenth season in the major leagues by recording his three-thousandth hit, a feat that placed him among baseball's all-time leading players. In November 1972, he traveled to Nicaragua as the coach of the Puerto Rican baseball team in the world championships. Three weeks after he returned to Puerto Rico, Clemente was at his home in Río Piedras when he learned of the earthquake that destroyed Managua.

Clemente immediately began to collect food, clothing, and medical supplies for Managua. He went on radio and television to encourage all

Puerto Ricans to take their donations of food, medicines, and supplies to the parking lot of the Hiram Bithorn stadium of San Juan. If they preferred to make a cash donation, he instructed donors to make their checks out to the Roberto Clemente Relief Committee for Nicaragua. Unfortunately for Nicaraguans and all baseball fans, Somoza was not so careful about making sure that all donations reached the victims of the earthquakes. Clemente's first shipment of relief supplies to Managua was nearly confiscated at the Managua airport by National Guard soldiers under the command of Tachito's son, Anastasio Somoza Portocarrero, who had been put in charge of the relief effort at the airport.[4]

Clemente, having heard enough of Somoza's misappropriation of relief supplies, decided that he would personally deliver the fourth planeload of supplies to Managua. He had raised more than a hundred thousand dollars in cash, 210 tons of clothing, and 36 tons of food, and he intended to make sure that these supplies were distributed properly. A chartered plane carrying Clemente and over forty-four thousand pounds of supplies (four thousand pounds over the plane's limit) took off from San Juan airport at 9:21 p.m. on December 31, 1972. It crashed into the Atlantic Ocean two minutes later. Clemente's body was never found.[5]

The reports of Somoza's greed and corruption lured Roberto Clemente to his death and revealed to the world the character of a state so famously corrupt that it is often described as a "kleptocracy." It should have come as no surprise that General Somoza dictated relief operations from El Retiro and that he appointed his son, Anastasio Somoza Portocarrero, known as El Chigüín (the Kid), to take command of collecting and distributing relief supplies from a hanger at the Managua airport. Managuans, with a characteristic sense of humor about such things, referred to the airport warehouse as "Tacho's supermarket."[6]

The natural disaster exposed the government for what it was, a corrupt and authoritarian regime, to the entire world. Nicaraguans had long known of the corrupt practices of Tachito and his father, but their complaints to the international community had not generated any diplomatic support before the earthquake. With foreign assistance pouring into Nicaragua, General Somoza could have dispensed social and economic assistance to the wounded, homeless, and hopeless, making himself into a populist leader in the tradition of his father, who once enjoyed strong support from the working classes. Instead, he saw an opportunity to get richer. Mauricio Solaún, appointed U.S. ambassador to Nicaragua in 1977, found general agreement among Nicaraguans—even among Somoza family members—that the earthquake had revealed the corruption endemic to the Somocista state. He reported, "The devastating Managua earthquake of 1972 was a critical turning point ushering in a ludicrous period of exacerbated kleptocracy, wanton National Guard repression, debauchery of the ruler, corrupt expansion of his [Somoza's] personal business empire and mismanagement scandals in it, and a syndrome of normlessness further delegitimizing the Somocista state."[7]

Two other high-ranking U.S. officials confirmed the accounts of Somoza's misappropriation of international aid following the earthquake. The United States alone contributed over $80 million in low-interest loans and grants in the five years after Managua's destruction. Anthony Lake, director of policy planning in the State Department (1978–1979), learned from contacts in the Nicaraguan business community that Somoza had "unscrupulously" exploited the disaster "to accumulate a new fortune."[8] Robert Pastor, director of Latin America and Caribbean Affairs on the National Security Council under President Jimmy Carter, also knew that Somoza had turned a national disaster into an opportunity for personal enrichment. He explained how Somoza expanded his wealth by "channeling aid through his companies and purchasing the parts of the city where he planned to undertake reconstruction."[9]

It is a tenet of faith among all non-Somocista observers that Anastasio Somoza exploited the earthquake relief and reconstruction effort for personal gain. Tachito, however, refuted these charges by citing the testimony of Terence A. Todman, assistant secretary of state for Inter-American Affairs. Todman reported in March 1978 that no conclusive evidence of misuse or misappropriation of funds had been revealed after twenty-eight major audits, two congressional staff surveys, and a General Accounting Office investigation. Somoza asked, "How many other relief operations in other parts of the world have been investigated twenty-eight times?"[10]

Somoza may not have violated U.S. or Nicaraguan law or regulations, but he and his associates did in fact profit from the reconstruction effort that he directed. The perceptions of widespread postearthquake corruption, recounted in virtually every account of Nicaragua's current history, are due, in no small part, to the fact that the Somoza family controlled at least 25 percent of the Nicaraguan economy by 1972. When the earthquake leveled Managua, the family already occupied an economic position from which it could easily exploit the massive influx of foreign aid after the national tragedy. The Somoza family owned or controlled a vast network of enterprises that included the National Development Institute (INFONAC), the National Bank of Nicaragua, the National Cement Company, coffee and sugar plantations, cattle ranches, a savings and loan corporation, and the Mercedes Benz dealership. The Conservative party's economic interests associated with the Banco de América (BANAMER) and the Liberal party's network of business interests associated with the Banco de Nicaragua (BANIC) competed and collaborated with the Somoza network. But Tachito, with a fortune estimated at several hundred million dollars, controlled the National Guard and the national government, giving him the power to direct and profit from the reconstruction effort more than all other economic interests in Nicaragua.[11]

The Somoza family had amassed its fortune before the earthquake by diverting state resources into private bank accounts, extorting from investors, and using extralegal means to harass and eliminate political and economic rivals. Nicaraguan and foreign investors typically faced Somocista demands for a share in any profitable enterprise. Tachito, ruling with impunity like his brother and father before him, could demand a quid pro quo from any potential investor, ranging from direct cash payments to a share in the projected enterprise. According to International Business Machines executive Arthur K. Watson, the Somozas "blatantly demanded a payoff" when the company decided to expand its operations in the early 1960s. Another U.S. businessperson informed the *Wall Street Journal* that graft was built into the system: "I don't care who you're dealing with—whether it's an assistant minister or the chief himself—you have to cut him [Somoza] in if you're going to close a deal."[12]

Even multinational powerhouse U.S. Steel had to play by Somoza's rules of the game. The company purchased a 54 percent interest in METASA, a factory producing galvanized sheet metal, pipes, and bars, with Somoza as its partner. By 1977, Somoza had forced U.S. Steel to sell out at twenty cents on the dollar of its investment. According to a knowledgeable but anonymous source, Somoza "took U.S. Steel to the cleaners." Somoza was not averse to using physical intimidation to achieve his economic ambitions. One U.S. investor in Somoza's Concreto Premezclado de Nicaragua was squeezed out of his $1 million investment after receiving a physical beating from Somoza's Cuban-born associate.[13]

Given this entrepreneurial culture, foreign creditors could have predicted that Somoza would misappropriate or redirect reconstruction assistance in ways that would benefit his family's enterprises. The first charges of large-scale corruption surfaced in June 1973, when *La Prensa* exposed a massive land swindle associated with a low-cost housing project financed by the Agency for International Development (AID). The Nicaraguan Housing Bank purchased 340 acres of land on the outskirts of Managua from Cornelio Hueck, president of the National Assembly and a close political and economic associate of Tachito. Hueck purchased the land for about $20,000 and sold it two days later for $1.2 million.[14]

The *Miami Herald* picked up the story of the Hueck land deal and added two more allegations of Somocista improprieties. The Nicaraguan government awarded a $1 million contract to construct an orphan's home to a Miami-based firm linked to Somoza called Panelfab, even though Nicaraguan firms bid less than half that amount. Another government contract for the purchase of trucks went to the Mercedes Benz dealership, which, of course, Somoza owned. Tachito denied any wrongdoing in any of the three cases, explaining that Hueck sold his land prior to the earthquake. Yet even his good friend Ambassador Shelton recognized the improprieties. Shelton explained that the price of the land deal, not the timing, was the critical issue. He reported to Washington that a local businessperson had purchased better land nearby for a much lower price, at roughly the same time Hueck purchased his tract of land.[15]

In February 1974, the Agency for International Development approved a $15 million loan to Nicaragua to convert eleven thousand temporary shelters in four provisional colonies in Las Americas district into eight thousand homes for low-income families. The price of the land purchased from Hueck therefore became an issue of great concern to the United States, for the government of Nicaragua was required to contribute $15 million toward the project. Arthur Mudge, AID director in Nicaragua, explained, "If there are cases where sales of land to the Government have been used as a means of siphoning funds to supporters, we will have to insist on an adjustment of the Nicaraguan counterpart contribution."[16]

Any illegal conduct in Las Americas housing project would have serious implications for the entire AID-financed reconstruction program. The agency therefore hired a Nicaraguan law firm to investigate the allegations of land being sold by Somocistas to the Nicaraguan government at artificially swollen prices. The investigation, completed in December 1976, confirmed that four of the five land purchases were indeed completed prior to the earthquake. The Nicaraguan lawyers also confirmed that the

Nicaraguan Housing Bank paid nine hundred thousand for the first site on December 3, 1971, from an individual who had paid only thirty-five thousand on November 24, 1971. However, AID took no punitive actions against the Nicaraguan government, recognizing that the wide discrepancy in prices was probably due to the typical practice of undervaluing land at the time of transfer to minimize the tax obligation.[17]

In this case, Somoza may not have violated Nicaraguan laws or regulations of the Agency for International Development. Contemporary critics today would certainly convict them of insider trading, a common means by which the Somoza family acquired its fortune prior to the earthquake. Tachito and his associates, like his brother and father before him, bought land cheap and sold it high to institutions they controlled. The fact that they purchased the properties before the earthquake doesn't reveal any great foresight on their part; they probably intended to develop these properties using state institutions all along. The earthquake only increased the value of their property and exposed their crass indifference to public suffering.

In September 1973, Somoza accepted a reconstruction plan prepared by a team of Mexican consultants. The "Mexican Plan" called for rebuilding Managua in a deconcentrated pattern, spreading out over a wider geographical area and thereby avoiding the fault lines that lay under the old commercial center. The basic recommendation of the Mexican Plan, accepted by Somoza, was that "Managua should be developed as a multi-center city with several different service and employment centers rather than just one center as existed before the quake."[18]

Although the Mexican consultants provided a firm geologic rationale for the decentralization of Managua, Somoza's decision to rebuild on the outskirts of Managua, principally in the southeast section along the highway to Masaya, carried serious political and economic consequences. Somoza claimed that Nicaragua's traditional elites had owned much of the commercial district prior to the earthquake. By rebuilding Managua on the perimeter of the old city, all these downtown properties would be rendered worthless.[19] Their grievances against Somoza would only increase when they discovered that the new developments in the western, southern, and southeastern portions of the city were built on properties owned by Somoza and his closest associates.

The Somocista land grab infuriated the entrepreneurial class because it violated a tacit agreement that had allowed the Nicaraguan bourgeoisie to profit. As banker Arturo Cruz explained, "Tachito's free enterprise system had allowed the local bourgeoisie to manage significant elements of the economy while the Somoza clan ran the country." During the 1960s, the Nicaraguan economy grew at an impressive annual rate of 7.2 percent, fueled in part by $92.5 million in U.S. development assistance.[20]

The earthquake slowed this impressive rate of economic growth, coming on the heels of a severe drought that had already impacted Nicaragua's agricultural exports. To Somoza's rivals in the BANIC and BANAMERICA groups, Somoza's exploitation of land sales and government contracts, diverting Nicaraguan and foreign funds into projects that profited his family, represented a blatant attempt to enrich himself at the expense of both Nicaragua's impoverished majority and the traditional economic elites. The reconstruction program therefore produced catastrophic political results for Somoza. Enrique Dreyfus, a leader of the Nicaraguan Development Institute (INDE) and the Superior Council of Private Enterprise (COSEP) explained that Somoza's brazen attempt "to make himself a billionaire [was] the political spark" that activated a business community that had long been silent.[21]

It also alienated the Catholic Church. Priests, missionaries, and relief workers moved into the poorer neighborhoods of Managua to help with the reconstruction effort. For a time, they worked closely with government officials. Within weeks, however, Somoza began to channel relief aid and supplies through institutions that he controlled. Church officials saw firsthand the consequences of government corruption; relief supplies failed to reach the poor neighborhoods. Somocistas, they learned, were hoarding relief supplies and reselling them at high prices for personal profit. As a result of Somoza's corrupt practices, the Christian communities in the poorer neighborhoods of Managua became centers of political protest after the earthquake.[22]

Somoza's addiction to profiteering combined with his crass indifference to the pain and suffering of the Nicaraguan people to produce the scandal that cost him the last remnants of what little popularity and legitimacy he ever enjoyed. He apparently invested in and conferred benefits on a firm called Compañía Centroamericana de Plasmaféresis, which was technically owned by a Cuban-American associate of the Somozas named Pedro Ramos. Poor Nicaraguans could earn about thirty-five córdobas (roughly five U.S. dollars) for donating a half-liter of blood to the firm, which would then sell plasma products to the United States. Nicaraguans called the plant, allegedly the largest blood bank in the world, the "House of the Vampires," for it embodied the greed of a regime that literally profited from the blood of its citizens. According to Violeta Barrios de Chamorro, future president of Nicaragua, the Somoza family not only protected this firm, it actually held shares in the company.[23]

Pedro Joaquín Chamorro, a prominent Conservative and editor of *La Prensa* newspaper, exposed this sordid business in a series of *La Prensa* articles known as the "Vampire Chronicles." Taking advantage of a temporary relaxation of censorship rules, Chamorro condemned the unethical commercialization of Nicaraguan blood as a violation of international health standards. Without naming the family, Chamorro left no doubt that he held the Somozas personally responsible for sucking the very lifeblood out of poor Nicaraguans. Chamorro explained, "We all know, I repeat, who is behind this lucrative and despicable business, which exists for the purpose of exploiting the public need."[24] Somoza's public standing could not have sunk any further . . . but it did.

On January 10, 1978, two men pumped three shotgun blasts into Pedro Joaquín Chamorro as he was driving to work. His body, riddled with buckshot, slumped over the steering wheel of his Saab. Within hours of Chamorro's assassination, riots broke out on the streets of Managua, followed by protests and demonstrations throughout the country. The police quickly arrested two men for the murder, but within two weeks a Somocista judge released them. Tachito condemned the assassination, denied any involvement, and charged that Pedro Ramos ordered the killing. In the absence of an impartial investigation and a prosecution, most Nicaraguans believed the rumors that began to circulate soon after Chamorro's assassination. It is widely believed that Tachito's son, El Chigüin, conspired with Pedro Ramos to murder Chamorro. The motive apparently was to eliminate the younger Somoza's most popular rival for the presidency and avenge the slanderous articles about the blood bank that Chamorro had published.[25]

The Collapse of the Old Political Order

Somoza lost what was left of his political legitimacy long before the assassination of Chamorro. He lost it, in fact, in the hours after the Managua earthquake. By dawn of December 23, 1972, he had declared martial law and made himself the chair of a National Emergency Committee without consulting the other two members of the governing junta, demonstrating that he had long been the de facto ruler of Nicaragua. The National Emergency Committee, composed of prominent politicians and businesspeople appointed and therefore controlled by Tachito, subsequently met on a weekly basis on the tennis courts at his El Retiro estate.[26]

Somoza regarded himself as an effective manager with a clear vision. Educated at West Point, he had developed his administrative skills as head of the National Guard since his father's assassination in 1956. With the linguistic skills to curse as fluently in English as in Spanish, he knew U.S. political, economic, and social life better perhaps than that of his own country. He recognized the underdeveloped character of his impoverished country and promoted policies designed to develop Nicaraguan industry and new agroexport commodities. He personally owned or indirectly controlled many of the new enterprises made possible by these policies, a fact that he attributed not to corruption but to his superior business skills. He saw himself as an example of the modern entrepreneur Nicaragua lacked, trained in, inspired by, and supportive of the North American model of development.

He quickly recognized the opportunities created by the complete devastation wrought by the natural disaster. The tragedy had created, in his words, a "revolution of opportunities." From the ruins of the old Managua he intended to create a new capital and, by extension, a new country. Somoza described his vision to his most important political ally, U.S. ambassador Turner Shelton, who endorsed Somoza's efforts to rebuild *and* redesign old Nicaragua. After one of their regular meetings in March 1973, Shelton reported that

> Somoza said that it was clear to him that many of the patterns that existed prior to the earthquake would never be reestablished—that the individuals who had been small entrepreneurs more or less tied to a wealthy class which owned the buildings and facilities of downtown Managua, were now finding themselves able with the assistance of small loans and more flexible areas of opportunity to establish their own small businesses on a more independent basis and that this would inevitably create a much larger and more important middle class without ties to the wealthy classes and that this new middle class would have the opportunity to rise rather rapidly in the economic and social life of Nicaragua.[27]

Somoza's new Managua would look much like the increasingly suburban and commercialized United States that he so admired. He envisioned a sprawling new city that ironically would resemble the Managua that came into being in the 1990s, long after his death. In his memoirs he described the future capital: "The new Managua would bear no resemblance to the old. Shopping centers, service centers, office buildings, and all those facilities which are required in any major city would be built several kilometers from the epicenter of the earthquake. Also, this new construction would be spread out over a wide area."[28]

Somoza saw these developments as desirable and inevitable, and intended to lead and profit politically and economically from the construction of a decentralized Nicaragua. Somoza had little use for democratic institutions anyway, so he quickly discarded an awkwardly constructed executive structure, a three-person governing junta that had been formed by agreement between the Liberal and Conservative parties on March 29, 1971. Tachito had been elected to the presidency in 1968, but the constitution barred him from seeking reelection in 1972. To pave the way for his constitutional reelection, he arranged to step aside temporarily while the two major parties rewrote the constitution so that he could return to the presidency through the presidential elections of 1974. Somoza persuaded the minority Conservatives to go along with the maneuver by offering them a power-sharing agreement whereby an executive body of two Liberals and one Conservative would govern Nicaragua between 1972 and 1974, while the two parties accepted a 60-40 apportionment of seats in the National Assembly. Opponents of the pact, most notably Pedro Joaquín Chamorro, challenged the legality of this bipartisan pact, to no avail.

To only the most naive observers, the creation of the junta represented a limited democratic opening and a challenge to the Somoza dynasty. More astute observers recognized the pact as a Somocista plan to continue that dynasty, with the Conservatives officially bought out by their agreement to appoint a member of what critics labeled the "Junta of the Three Little Pigs." The genuine national crisis created by the natural disaster ended the political facade earlier than scheduled, but it also accelerated the demise of Somoza himself. Tachito's assumption of dictatorial powers exposed the junta for what it was—a thinly disguised cover for a Somoza dictatorship—and mobilized the opposition political forces that would ultimately bring Somoza down.[29]

As commander of the National Guard and leader of the Liberal party, Somoza had always controlled the triumvirate and, by extension, the entire government. The Conservative party denounced Somoza's militarized response to the national crisis and called for a return to civilian rule. Fernando Agüero, the lone Conservative member of the old junta, publicly criticized Somoza for playing politics with the tragedy and charged that he had violated the terms of the Liberal-Conservative pact. Within weeks, Agüero had been removed from the ruling junta and replaced as leader of the Conservative party and member of the triumvirate by Edmundo Paguagua, a man willing to collaborate with Somoza in exchange for whatever political and economic favors Somoza cared to dispense.[30]

The reconfiguration of the governing junta did more than simply change the players at the table. It also splintered the Conservative party. According to political scientist Mark Everingham, the politics of reconstruction split the Conservative party into four factions, the most important of which followed the leadership of Pedro Joaquín Chamorro. Somoza weakened the strongest and best-organized opposition to his regime, giving the short-term appearance of clearing a path for his indefinite return to power. Within three years, however, Chamorro had emerged as Somoza's most popular critic and the Conservative party—thoroughly discredited by its collaborationist policies—no longer provided the democratic facade for Somoza's dictatorial regime. Nicaragua's two-party political system, marked by violent political rivalries and personal animosities for over a century, was coming apart. Without the political stability that had allowed for economic growth in the 1960s, Nicaragua's new social classes, entrepreneurs as well as labor unions, saw an opportunity to topple the dynasty that had been shaken to its foundations by the natural disaster. Everingham explains, "The business community, political parties, and the few existing labor unions saw the disappearance of the traditional structure of the Liberal-Conservative rivalry as an opportunity to redefine the national agenda in terms of political pluralism and more democratic economic policies."[31]

A new class of entrepreneurs first began to press their interests outside the traditional political party structure in March 1974, when Alfonso Robelo, Felipe Mántica, William Baez, and Enrique Dreyfus convened the First Convention of the Private Sector. The conference, organized under the auspices of COSEP and INDE, represented the first private sector initiative to check the growing power of Somoza's Liberal party, according to Baez. The fragmented Conservative party, which had clearly abdicated that responsibility by collaborating with Somoza, no longer possessed the will or the ability to challenge Somoza's power, despite mounting evidence that he was already diverting reconstruction projects toward businesses controlled by his family or his supporters. In August 1973, compelling evidence surfaced in newspaper reports that Somoza and his political associates had already begun to profit from unethical if not illegal land sales and government contracts associated with rebuilding Managua.[32]

The businesspeople associated with COSEP and INDE complained then and thereafter of Somoza's unethical use of state institutions to further his private economic interests. Charging him with "unfair competition," the entrepreneurs boldly criticized Somoza's misappropriation of reconstruction funds. They offered a political remedy that foreshadowed the neoliberal ideology that would blossom in the 1990s, calling for the liberation of private enterprise from state interference so that free market forces could work their magic. The role of the state, these businesspeople argued, should be limited to the maintenance of public order, infrastructural development, and the provision of social security, all of which should be done in a fair and transparent process based on competitive bidding within a free market system. The Somocista state, by favoring a particular family and those who collaborated with it, represented an antiquated political system that was increasingly incompatible with the needs and interests of a growing entrepreneurial sector. In the aftermath of a devastating earthquake, businessmen like Robelo and Dreyfuss could no longer tolerate Somoza's notoriously corrupt practices. Somoza ignored the criticisms and dismissed the private businesspeople as "schoolchildren."[33]

By all appearances, Somoza was secure in his position. He controlled the National Guard, dominated the Liberal party, co-opted the Conservatives, and still enjoyed the unwavering support of the United States. He had no reason to suspect any immovable obstacles in his path to the presidency through a "democratic" election in September 1974. Even the notoriously noncritical U.S. ambassador Turner Shelton could see through Somoza's political plans. In January 1974 Shelton explained to his superiors in Washington how Somoza, whom he described as the de facto ruler of Nicaragua, would engineer his election.

> Combining money, organization, and hard work, in 1974 the
> Somoza political machine is expected to insure a victory for the

general by effectively rounding up the voters, hauling them to the polls and giving them food, drink and small cash payments. An extensive pre-campaign has been underway for the past six months featuring proxy-campaigners who keep Somoza's name at the fore of party politics. Shortly before the PLN National Convention, Somoza is expected to submit a pro forma resignation from active military duty to enable him to accept his party's nomination and take control of his own campaign.[34]

Events unfolded just as Shelton predicted, suggesting that he was privy to, if not one of the architects of, Somoza's political plans. A new constitution was promulgated in March 1974. Although it prohibited the reelection of a president, Somoza would be allowed to run in the elections scheduled for September 1974 because he was not then the president; executive power technically resided with the "Three Little Pigs." So the presidential campaign got underway in mid-1974, with the Conservatives nominating Edmundo Paguagua to contest Somoza's bid for a second presidential term. Even Ambassador Shelton recognized the electoral campaign as a farce. He described Paguagua as a "neutralized opponent, happy to be second best," and eager to accept forty seats in the legislature as a reward for his collaboration. So even before the votes were tabulated, Ambassador Shelton predicted that "General Anastasio Somoza Debayle, at the head of the majority Liberal Party (PLN), will be triumphantly elevated from his position as the unquestioned de-facto ruler of Nicaragua to a six year term as constitutionally elected president—probably by a margin of about 80 percent of the official returns."[35]

Somoza won the elections and was officially inaugurated in December 1974. In retrospect, the victory came at a high political price, but few contemporary observers detected the changing political landscape of postearthquake Nicaragua. The Paguagua faction of the Conservatives happily took their forty seats in the legislature, but others, most notably the faction led by Pedro Joaquín Chamorro, rejected the collaborationist policies of their former colleagues and adopted increasingly aggressive tactics. Chamorro joined forces with seven opposition groups in an abstention campaign, encouraging voters to reject both candidates. Somoza had responded to this moderate challenge by filing suit against Chamorro and the other twenty-six people who promoted the abstention campaign. The abstention campaign did nothing to prevent Somoza from claiming a legitimate victory in the national polls, but it presaged an end to public confidence in elections as a means of challenging Somoza, let alone removing him from the presidency.[36]

Somoza also began to lose support in the U.S. Embassy because of his electoral sham, a significant indicator of the extent to which the earthquake transformed the political, economic, and social realities of Nicaragua. A political-economic counselor in the embassy, James Cheek, reported Somoza's corrupt and undemocratic practices to Washington and pressed for a reversal of U.S. policy. Using diplomatic back channels to avoid Shelton, Cheek argued that "the earthquake had changed the economic and social landscape of the country and inevitably a political earthquake had to come and that that was going to be the rub and challenge for Somoza and, therefore, Somoza was going to have to change or there would be no long-term stability."[37]

Somoza, however, was not about to change. To the bitter end he claimed to have been elected in a free and fair election. In his memoirs he summarized the political results succinctly: "Nicaragua had an honest election and I was elected."[38] Even Ambassador Shelton saw through Somoza's false promises of political reform, arguing that his promise to respect civil liberties and human rights was encouraging only "in light of the history of the Somoza dynasty."[39] Even Ambassador Shelton, Somoza's most loyal supporter in the United States, knew that Somoza held a tenuous claim to democratic and constitutional authority. Somoza's assumption of dictatorial powers and the abuse of disaster relief after the earthquake weakened the most important pillar of the Somoza dynasty, the support of the U.S. government.

The Collapse of the Alliance with the United States

The traditional alliance between the United States and Nicaragua began to unravel in the two years after the Managua earthquake. While President Jimmy Carter generally receives credit for imposing a human rights policy on Somoza's Nicaragua and thereby undermining the regime, the first signs of substantial change occurred during the administrations of presidents Nixon and Ford. The need to rebuild and democratize Nicaragua began to overwhelm U.S. policy makers in the State Department in the mid-1970s, who recognized the need to reform or remove Somoza long before the Sandinistas accomplished that feat.

Ambassador Turner Shelton, both symbol and architect of U.S. policy toward Nicaragua, had been in his hilltop home when the earthquake struck. The temblors severely damaged his home and the nearby embassy, causing the death of a secretary who had been trapped inside. Despite the devastation and the hour, Shelton managed to drive over to El Retiro and apparently encouraged Somoza to declare martial law and request U.S. military assistance before sunrise. The National Guard virtually disintegrated overnight, as police officers, soldiers, and military officers left their posts to check on their families, leaving Managua, and Somoza himself, defenseless. To maintain law and order, preserve the regime, and keep in power a close U.S. ally, Shelton requested emergency military assistance from the U.S. Southern Command in Panama. A battalion of U.S. paratroopers soon arrived in Managua along with medical teams and engineers.[40]

Tachito Somoza, like his father, had enjoyed exceptionally close and supportive relations with the United States. Through World War II and the cold war, the United States regarded the Somozas as loyal friends and allies, and U.S. ambassadors publicly supported the Nicaraguan bosses, who derived great political advantage over their domestic opposition as a result. The U.S. ambassador—Shelton and all his predecessors—wielded enormous influence over the Somozas, partly because the family built its domestic and foreign policies on complete devotion to the United States. Domestic and foreign observers perceived that real power rested with the U.S. ambassador to Nicaragua, regarded as a viceroy or proconsul in a virtual colony. Shelton perhaps carried the policy to its extreme, offering such public displays of support for Tachito that many Nicaraguans and even some U.S. diplomats regarded him as more of an advisor to Somoza than a representative of the United States. Anonymous foreign diplomats reported that Shelton spent at least ten hours a week with Somoza, often in private meetings, offering friendly advice and support, especially in times of crisis.[41]

Shelton did little to press Somoza for democratic reforms or honest administration publicly even as postearthquake political and social forces gathered enough strength to challenge U.S. interests in the region. Shelton studiously avoided the signs that Somoza's dictatorial and corrupt response to the earthquake had undermined his legitimacy to such an extent that influential members of the procapitalist, pro-U.S. entrepreneurial class demanded an end to the Somocista political order. Despite

Somoza's well-earned reputation for brutal, corrupt, and undemocratic practices, Shelton did not think that it was necessary or appropriate to criticize Somoza publicly:

> It's the job of an ambassador to establish the best possible rela-
> tionship with the president of a friendly country. I don't think of it
> in terms of a personal relationship, but I think President Somoza
> is a very nice man. He is friendly to the United States, he does
> a good job and he's a hard-working leader who has done a lot to
> improve things in this country. I'm sure if there were elections
> supervised by the United Nations, Somoza would win.[42]

Shelton was insensitive to the needs and interests of those Nicaraguans pressing for democratization. His character and relationship with the Nicaraguan people was revealed in the immediate aftermath of the earth-quake. Though his palatial residence atop a hill overlooking Managua had suffered extensive damage, the first floor remained intact. The U.S. Embassy had been rendered unsafe by the quake, so Shelton transferred his staff to the lawn outside his residence. He and his wife refused to allow the staff, which included a few Nicaraguans, to use the ground floor of their residence as temporary office space. Their workers were not even allowed to jump in the pool to cool off. Before he would allow such indig-nities to be inflicted on his person, Shelton requested money to lease office space at a nearby country club. The State Department rejected his request with a strong rebuke: "a part of the spacious ground-floor rooms of the residence could be adapted to provide all the office space required until the temporary chancery is erected, and with minimal inconvenience to the Sheltons. . . . Until this alternative has been thoroughly explored, your new proposal to rent the La Cuesta country club . . . can not be considered."[43]

Shelton was the last of the "ugly Americans" to serve in Managua. Speaking no Spanish, dismissive of both U.S. and Nicaraguan critics, Shelton won many enemies in Managua and Washington. He was consid-ered a Nixon man, a political appointee with little or no preparation for the Foreign Service. Nixon's resignation on August 8, 1974, as a result of the Watergate scandal, weakened Shelton's and Somoza's defenses, leav-ing them increasingly vulnerable to the growing number of opponents in Nicaragua, the U.S. Embassy, and the State Department, including the newly appointed assistant secretary of state for Inter-American Affairs,

William D. Rogers. "The day I went into office," Rogers explained later, "the first task was to get rid of Turner Shelton. It was not an easy task on which Larry Eagleburger [executive assistant to Secretary of State Kissinger] and I conspired almost daily because he had a lot of friends and he was persistent in involving them."[44]

The effort to replace Shelton and change U.S. policy toward Nicaragua gained considerable strength in the spring of 1975 during the administration of President Gerald Ford. Officials in the State Department and the National Security Council of the United States, apparently eager to adapt U.S. policy to the new political realities of Nicaragua, concurred. Shelton's style and policies had identified him too closely with Somoza personally, and, as Tachito's position deteriorated, U.S. officials worried that the United States' interests could also suffer if they did not change their policies. The opposition to Shelton therefore reflected a change in U.S. policy toward Nicaragua, not just a change in personnel. Stephen Low of the National Security Council explained the rationale for a new Central American policy:

> We have had a number of very conservative ambassadors to Nicaragua who have become closely associated with Somoza in the minds of many in Nicaragua, the U.S. and elsewhere in Central America. Somoza has used this relationship very astutely for his own benefit. Meanwhile his position in Nicaragua has markedly suffered and there is a growing question about how long he can maintain himself in power. I feel strongly that this is not the time for a political conservative to be named to Nicaragua. On the contrary, we should take this occasion to appoint a professional who can keep a proper distance. This has importance for us throughout Central America.

Somoza's friends and lobbyists in Washington did their best to persuade President Gerald Ford to keep Shelton and U.S. policy in place. Congress representative Jack Murphy of New York pleaded with Secretary of State Henry Kissinger, arguing that Somoza was the "staunchest ally of the United States in Latin America." The replacement of Shelton, Murphy recognized, might indicate a significant change in U.S. policy toward Nicaragua, with predictably negative political repercussions for Somoza in Nicaragua.[45]

The reformers eventually prevailed. President Ford removed Ambassador Shelton and replaced him with James Theberge. Assistant Secretary of State Rogers instructed Theberge to implement a new policy and traveled to Managua to deliver that message personally to Somoza. Rogers explained, "I accompanied Theberge either the first time he met with Somoza or shortly thereafter to underline the point that we were sending a new Ambassador down to open a new era of American-Nicaraguan relations and that Theberge was instructed to avoid any action that would give the impression that we favored any particular regime and to open channels of communication with the political opposition."[46]

Somoza got the message and he didn't like it. Ambassador Theberge presented his credentials on August 22, 1975, the same day that newspaper columnist Jack Anderson published the last of three incendiary articles about Somoza, citing unnamed sources in the U.S. Embassy. The series began with an article titled "Nicaragua Ruler Is World's Greediest" and was followed by two more exposés of Somoza's corrupt business practices. Citing secret U.S. government documents, Anderson and Les Whitten claimed to have evidence showing that Somoza used his control over the government to channel reconstruction projects into his many family enterprises. "For the impoverished populace, it [the earthquake] was the worst natural disaster of the century." For Anastasio Somoza, however, "the earthquake offered another opportunity to stuff his pockets," Anderson and Whitten wrote.[47]

Somoza expressed his outrage to Theberge shortly after he formally accepted the new ambassador's credentials. He apparently did not dispute Anderson's allegation that he had exploited the national disaster to expand his personal fortune, but he took exception to Anderson's references to secret U.S. government documents and his extramarital affairs. Theberge described Somoza "thrashing about looking for scapegoats and ways to ameliorate a situation which is being viewed with glee by his opposition."[48]

The coincidence of Theberge's appointment and the Anderson articles suggested a significant change in personnel as well as policy, a message that outraged Somoza and pleased his critics. Somoza undoubtedly suspected that an informant in the U.S. Embassy provided Anderson with the damning information. Theberge, more knowledgeable about Latin American affairs than his predecessor, recognized that the Anderson articles would seriously undermine public perceptions of Somoza's invincibility. Theberge warned,

Owing to the almost mystical belief by many that the key to the
end of the Somoza dynasty lies in the attitude of the U.S., the
Anderson articles have had a definite, albeit, incalculable effect,
on the internal political situation. The articles have encouraged
the simplistic hope that U.S. public opinion will force the USG
[U.S. government] to abandon Somoza and that this will render
him vulnerable to a determined effort to oust him. There are
indications that Somoza himself is aware of these ominous perceptions and is not likely to ignore them.[49]

Somoza's official response to Anderson's allegations of his corrupt business practices did nothing to refute public perceptions that those charges
were, in fact, true. Nicaraguan ambassador to the United States, Guillermo
Sevilla-Sacasa, Tachito's brother-in-law and dean of the Washington diplomatic corps, delivered the official response in the *Washington Post* on
August 29, 1975. He denied that Somoza held any economic interest in the
Inter Continental Hotel or prostitution rings, but he affirmed the extent
of Somoza's wealth. "May I point out," Sevilla-Sacasa wrote, "that it is a
matter of long standing record that President Somoza has never denied
his wealth. In fact, the President's ownership of properties and company
interests is a matter of public record in Nicaragua."[50]

Even as Somoza's perceived strength and legitimacy slipped away, the
Ford administration remained publicly supportive of Somoza. Somoza
traveled to the United States in April 1976 to visit his mother, who was
recuperating in a Washington hospital from a broken leg. He attempted
to exploit the personal travel for political gain by requesting a meeting
with President Ford. The State Department rejected a personal meeting
with the president but persuaded Ford to telephone Somoza to convey his
gratitude for Somoza's staunch support for U.S. policies. It was yet another
indication that high-ranking officials in Washington wanted to put some
distance between the Ford administration and Somoza, whose political
position at home was deteriorating.[51]

At the same time, human rights advocates in the U.S. Congress, led
by Senator Thomas Harkin (Democrat, Iowa) were pressing the Ford
administration for a more substantial change in U.S. policy. Harkin had
successfully lobbied for legislation requiring the State Department to cer-
tify that recipients of U.S. military and economic assistance respected
human rights. Nicaragua, as one of the largest recipients of U.S. economic

assistance since the 1972 earthquake, would not long be able to resist the increasingly powerful human rights lobby. As long as Henry Kissinger controlled the State Department, however, little would be done to enforce the human rights policy on Somoza's government. According to Morris Morley, "the policy of the Kissinger period was to do what was necessary to satisfy Congress on human rights but not to take any measures to distance the U.S. from governments helpful to us."[52]

The human rights policy eventually prevailed, of course, with the election of Jimmy Carter in 1976. The implementation of Carter's human rights policy shook the Somoza dynasty to its foundations, eliminating a pillar of a dynasty that had reacquired supreme political and economic power by brazenly exploiting the opportunities created by a natural disaster. By making an undisguised bid for absolute control, however, Somoza also alienated previously acquiescent Nicaraguan Conservatives. They did not necessarily embrace Carter's human rights policies, but they quickly recognized the opportunity it gave them to unseat a government that had failed to reconstruct and develop Managua in a fair and equitable way.

One can only speculate on the course of Nicaraguan history if nature had not destroyed downtown Managua on December 23, 1972. The earthquake did not inevitably lead to the Sandinista Revolution, but Somoza's response to it exposed him for what he was, a brutal and corrupt dictator who ruled Nicaragua as if it were his private fiefdom. The earthquake leveled a city, but it also set in motion the events that ultimately led to the overthrow of Somoza and the creation of a new political, economic, and social order in Nicaragua.

The assassination of Chamorro is frequently cited as the catalyst for the Sandinista insurrection of 1978–79. While there is no doubt that it outraged the Nicaraguan public and led the upper class into an uncomfortable alliance with the FSLN, the anti-Somoza coalition had been in formation since the Managua earthquake of 1972. This natural disaster had indeed created a "revolution of opportunities," just as Somoza had predicted. While he had hoped to lead this revolution, his corrupt and authoritarian response to the national crisis alienated the traditional elites in the Conservative party and the diplomatic corps of the United States, both of them previously supportive or co-opted by the Somoza regime. In the seven years after the earthquake, these traditional elites moved into an alliance with labor unions, students, women, peasant organizations, and eventually the Sandinistas. With Sandinista rebel forces leading the way, this multiclass coalition destroyed what the earthquake had left wobbly but still standing: the Somoza family dynasty. U.S. officials, led by James Cheek in the U.S. Embassy, recognized that a "political earthquake" would inevitably follow the natural disaster.[53]

For over forty years, the United States had maintained friendly relations with a Nicaraguan government dominated by the Somoza family. Six U.S. presidents, from Roosevelt to Nixon, had ignored Nicaraguan pleas for help in reforming or overthrowing the Somoza government. In the aftermath of the Managua earthquake, with international aid and attention focused on efforts to rebuild Managua, the United States could no longer tolerate the corrupt and authoritarian practices of the Somoza family. The earthquake was a natural disaster and a political earthquake. It destroyed a city, Somoza's alliance with business elites and the Conservative party, and Somoza's friendly relations with the United States.

✤ NOTES ✤

1. Quoted in Jay Mallin, "The Great Managua Earthquake," www.ineter.gob.ni/geofisica/sis/managua72/mallin/greato1.html (accessed February 15, 2009).

2. "Thousands Dead as Quakes Strike Nicaraguan City," *New York Times*, December 24, 1972.

3. Agency for International Development, U.S. Department of State, "Nicaragua: Low Cost Housing," capital assistance paper, proposal and recommendations for the review of the Development Loan Committee, February 12, 1974 (Washington, DC: Department of State, Agency for International Development).

4. David Maraniss, *Clemente: The Passion and Grace of Baseball's Last Hero* (New York: Simon and Schuster, 2006), 301–5.

5. Ibid., 317–29.

6. Jack Anderson and Les Whitten, "Somoza's Christmas," *Washington Post*, August 22, 1975.

7. Mauricio Solaún, *U.S. Intervention and Regime Change in Nicaragua* (Lincoln: University of Nebraska Press, 2005), 79.

8. Anthony Lake, *Somoza Falling: The Nicaraguan Dilemma; A Portrait of Washington at Work* (Boston: Houghton Mifflin, 1989), 19.

9. Robert Pastor, *Not Condemned to Repetition: The United States and Nicaragua*, 2nd ed., (Boulder, CO: Westview, 2002), 31.

10. Anastasio Somoza, *Nicaragua Betrayed* (Boston: Western Islands, 1980), 6–7.

11. For detailed analyses of the Somoza family holdings and the structure of the Nicaraguan economy see Mark Everingham, *Revolution and the Multiclass Coalition in Nicaragua* (Pittsburgh: University of Pittsburgh Press, 1996), 72–85; North American Congress on Latin America, "Nicaragua: Somoza's Dictatorship," *Latin America and Empire Report* 10, no. 2 (February 1976); Jaime Wheelock, *Imperialismo y dictadura* (Managua: Nueva Nicaragua, 1985).

12. Quoted in Morris Morley, *Washington, Somoza and the Sandinistas: State and Regime in U.S. Policy toward Nicaragua, 1969–1981* (Cambridge: Cambridge University Press, 1994), 47.

13. Charles Stafford, "Bill Cramer and the Nicaraguan Connection," *St. Petersburg Times*, October 30, 1977.

14. Bernard Diederich, *Somoza and the Legacy of U.S. Involvement in Central America* (New York: Dutton, 1981), 100–103.

15. "Nicaragua Strongman Somoza Accused of Profiting from Quake Relief Aid," *Miami Herald*, August 23, 1973; Somoza, *Nicaragua Betrayed*, 17; Turner Shelton to State, August 31, 1973, U.S. Department of State, RG 59, General Records of the Department of State, Central Foreign Policy Files, National Archives, Washington, DC (hereafter referred to as State Department Cables). Access to archival databases available at http://aad.archives.gov/aad/series-description.jsp?s=4073 (accessed March 4, 2009).

16. Alan Riding, "Nicaraguans Accused of Profiteering on Help the U.S. Sent after Quake," *New York Times*, March 23, 1977.

17. General Accounting Office, "Nicaragua: An Assessment of Earthquake Relief and Reconstruction Assistance," report of the comptroller general of the United States, app. 6. (Washington, DC: General Accounting Office, 1977).

18. U.S. Department of State, Agency for International Development, "Nicaragua—Urban Sector Loan (Managua Reconstruction)" (capital assistance paper, June 14, 1974), 11.

19. Somoza, *Nicaragua Betrayed*, 16.

20. Arturo Cruz, *Memoirs of a Counterrevolutionary* (New York: Doubleday, 1989), 57; Pastor, *Not Condemned*, 36.

21. Everingham, *Revolution*, 114.

22. Michael Dodson and Laura Nuzzi O'Shaughnessy, *Nicaragua's Other Revolution: Religious Faith and Political Struggle* (Chapel Hill: University of North Carolina Press, 1990), 124.

23. Violeta Barrios de Chamorro, *Dreams of the Heart: The Autobiography of President Violeta Barrios de Chamorro of Nicaragua* (New York: Simon and Schuster, 1996), 112; Douglas Starr, *Blood: An Epic History of Medicine and Commerce* (New York: Knopf, 2002), 231–49.

24. "Todos sabemos repito quién está detrás de ese lucrativo y despreciable negocio, cuya base es la explotación de la necesidad social," Pedro Joaquín Chamorro, "Detrás de la sangre," *La Prensa* (Managua), November 18, 1977.

25. The assassination of Chamorro and the aftermath are best followed on the pages of *La Prensa*; see in particular the editions of January 13, 16, 18, and 20, 1978; see also Somoza's account in *Nicaragua Betrayed*, 109–22; George Black, *Triumph of the People; The Sandinista Revolution in Nicaragua* (London: Zed, 1981), 107–8; John Booth, *The End and the Beginning: The Nicaraguan Revolution* (Boulder, CO: Westview, 198), 159–60.

26. Diederich, *Somoza*, 97.

27. Shelton to State, March 17, 1973, State Department Cables.

28. Somoza, *Nicaragua Betrayed*, 21.

29. Diederich, *Somoza*, 89–90.

30. Marvin Howe, "Managua Parties Resume Politics," *New York Times*, December 31, 1972; David Wigg, "Ruling Family Strengthened by Nicaraguan Disaster," *Times* (London), January 10, 1973; Everingham, *Revolution*, 111.

31. Everingham, *Revolution*, 111.

32. Ibid., 111–12; Diederich, *Somoza*, 100–103; Shelton to State, August 31, 1973, State Department Cables.

33. "Nicaragua: Two Faces of UNO," *Envío Digital* (Managua, Nicaragua), no. 108 (July 1990); Everingham, *Revolution*, 114.

34. Shelton to State, January 24, 1974, State Department Cables.

35. Shelton to State, September 3, 1974, State Department Cables.

36. Shelton to State, December 5, 1974, State Department Cables.

37. Interview with James Cheek, quoted in Morley, *Washington*, 70–71.

38. Somoza, *Nicaragua Betrayed*, 36.

39. Shelton to State, December 3, 1974, State Department Cables.

40. Somoza, *Nicaragua Betrayed*, 8; Maraniss, *Clemente*, 296; Diederich, *Somoza*, 94–95.

41. Alan Riding, "Hopes of Nicaraguan Opposition Rise with Shift of the U.S. Envoy," *New York Times*, August 11, 1975.

42. Ibid.

43. Jack Anderson and Les Whitten, "Rebuke, Denied by Envoy, is Quoted," *Washington Post*, March 31, 1975.

44. Interview with William D. Rogers, quoted in Morley, *Washington*, 75.

45. John M. Murphy to Honorable Henry A. Kissinger, May 16, 1975, folder "Nicaragua," CO 111, Subject Files, White House Central Files, Gerald R. Ford Library and Museum, Grand Rapids, MI.

46. Morley, *Washington*, 76.

47. Anderson and Whitten, "Somoza's Christmas," *Washington Post*.

48. James Theberge to State, "Reaction to Anderson Columns on Somoza," August 25, 1975, folder "Nicaragua-State Department Telegrams to SECSTATE-EXDIS," box 5, NSA Presidential Country Files for Latin America, 1974–1977, Ford Library.

49. Ibid.

50. Guillermo Sevilla-Sacasa (ambassador of Nicaragua), "Nicaragua: The Ambassador Replies," *Washington Post*, August 29, 1975.

51. Brent Scowcroft (State Department), Recommended Telephone Call, National Security Adviser, folder "Nicaragua," box 5, Presidential Country Files for Latin America, 1974–1977, Ford Library; C. Arthur Borg to Brent Scowcroft, "Vice President Rockefeller's Meeting with President Somoza of Nicaragua," April 19, 1976, folder "Nicaragua," Ford Library.

52. Morley, *Washington*, 81.

53. Ibid., 70–71.

CHAPTER SIX

Under God's Thumb

The 1976 Guatemala Earthquake

VIRGINIA GARRARD-BURNETT

❧

⸭ INGA STOOD ON THE BALCONY OF HER ELEGANT HOUSE THAT overlooked Guatemala City's vast *barranca*—a deep ravine that divided the capital city.[1] The barranca separated rich from poor, long-established residents from new urban immigrants, and rich foreigners and members of the planter class from poor ladinos and the indigenous. From her second-story view in the wealthy area known as Vista Hermosa, she could see the dim lights of poor makeshift dwellings that snaked up the hill on the other side of the divide, some lit by candles and lanterns, others illuminated by illegally pirated electrical wiring. It was nearly three in the morning, and Inga could not sleep—it had been a late night, and, although she was tired, the constant and frantic barking of dogs—including her own, who failed to respond to her usual administrations of comfort—kept her awake. As she gazed out on the barranca, the lights suddenly began to go out—she described it later as if "a giant hand had swept across the hill and wiped the lights away." Seconds later, the balcony she was standing on began to shake wildly.

That same night, in Chimaltenango, a predominantly indigenous town located up in a high plateau of the Sierra Madre some thirty-five miles

156

away, Juan also could not sleep. The constant barking of the dogs had kept him awake, although his wife and infant son slept comfortably beside him in their common bed. The dogs were an annoyance, to be sure—they had barked wildly and incessantly for more than a day, but it was not the noise alone that bothered him. Juan, like most of the Kakchikel Maya who make up the majority of people who live in Chimaltenango, knew that dogs are able to predict natural disasters, and he suspected that they were trying to issue some sort of warning. He got up to go to the bathroom. While he was there, the earth began to shake for what seemed like many minutes, although he later learned that the tremor had lasted for only thirty-nine seconds. The walls of his adobe house began to loudly collapse around him. When he was able to regain his footing, Juan raced back through the rubble into his bedroom to check on his wife and child. A huge rock that had been part of the wall of their house had fallen on the bed, crushing Juan's wife and baby, as well as the pillow where his own head had lain only moments before. At that moment, Juan regretted that he had gotten up in the night, only to survive to bear witness to the collapse of his entire world.

At 3:05 a.m. on February 4, 1976, a devastating earthquake measuring 7.5 on the Richter scale struck Guatemala. A second powerful 5.5 after-shock rattled the country again two days later, on February 6, bringing even further damage, especially to Guatemala City.[2] The earthquake, its epicenter portentously located in Chimaltenango—soon to be an epicen-ter of the armed conflict as well—by official count killed 22,545; wounded 74,000; and displaced more than a million people. These numbers, though substantial, probably underestimate those killed, injured, and left home-less in the nameless shantytowns that ringed Guatemala City and in the remote rural areas.[3] Even Guatemala City, located fifty-four kilometers from the epicenter, was seriously affected: its water supply, telephone sys-tem and electrical grid so damaged that even after repairs they would function erratically for many years to come.

Like so many natural disasters, the earthquake disproportionately affected the poor, whose substandard housing, especially adobe, collapsed and crushed those inside, or whose insubstantial homes located on mar-ginal lands, such as the sides of ravines and barrancas, tumbled down the hillsides to ruination.[4] One makeshift neighborhood of Guatemala City, for example, the ironically named Colonia 4 de febrero, was reduced to an unrecognizable wasteland of plastic sheeting, wood, tin, and cardboard—the materials that had once composed the resident's homes.[5]

In the town of Chimaltenango, the quake's epicenter, every building in the town was destroyed except three made from reinforced concrete: the local health clinic, the town hall, and one private home. All the other buildings in town, including every single other house—all of which were made out of adobe, cornstalk, tile, thatch, or corrugated tin—collapsed, often killing the entire extended family that was sleeping inside.[6] Over nine thousand residents of Chimaltenango died immediately in the earthquake, while more succumbed in the coming weeks to injuries and trauma associated with the disaster.[7] Over ten thousand people died in the department of Chimaltenango alone, and more than thirteen towns in the region suffered the loss of greater than 80 percent of their buildings.[8] Of those who perished, the very young and the very old were least likely to survive, as were people who lived in dwellings that were home to seven or more people, where overcrowded conditions and body weight proved to be an unusually lethal combination.[9]

As both a natural catastrophe and metaphor, the earthquake shattered the fragile social and political infrastructure of the country. In 1976 Guatemala had been at war with itself for fifteen of what would eventually be thirty-six years of an asymmetrical struggle between Marxist guerrillas and a virulent anticommunist military government. This struggle had emerged as a response to the CIA-sponsored overthrow of the revolutionary, and democratic, government of Jacobo Arbenz in 1954. The war, which ebbed and flowed between periods of relative calm alternating with phases of severe state-sponsored violence against the guerrillas and other "enemies of the state," had entered a period of relative calm in the late 1960s. In the early 1970s, however, the guerrilla movement had started to resurge, recruiting and organizing in the largely indigenous western highlands, where levels of poverty and inequality were among the worst in the entire country, even before the earthquake.

The gateway to the western highlands is Chimaltenango, and it was here, of course, where revolution and natural disaster would especially converge. Indeed, the earthquake added such unprecedented momentum to the growing popular resistance that social scientist Philip Berryman has described the 1976 earthquake as a "detonator" of revolution, and so it was, as the earthquake set off a contagion of social and political processes that brought the nation's civil war to a head.[10] The earthquake also set off a social revolution, opening the door to new forms of identity and metaphors of meaning (especially in the religious sphere) that vested what

Typical street view in Patzicia, showing adobe block rubble that is all
that remains of the houses that formerly lined this street. The adobe
block buildings had very little resistance to horizontal forces and most
of them were completely destroyed. Collapse of the heavy adobe walls,
roof tiles, and beams caused most of the casualties (SLIDE 43, OPEN-FILE
REPORT 77-165, U.S. GEOLOGICAL SURVEY PHOTOGRAPHIC LIBRARY).

would otherwise be incomprehensible loss and violence with a coherent
logic and purpose. While it is nearly impossible to untangle these factors
one from another, all shared in the 1976 earthquake a proximate cause.

The Earthquake as History: Part I

Lying as it does on the tectonically active Motagua Valley fault, the
"young" fault line is still subject to many of what geologists call "displace-
ments." Earthquakes are nothing new to Guatemala and are as much a
part of that nation's history as fire and blood. Earthquakes play a role even
in the Mayan creation story. The ancient Maya sacred text, *Popol Vuh:
The Mayan Book of the Dawn of Life*, describes a confrontation between
the Hero Twins, Hunahpu and Xbalanque, and a celestial being named

Earthquake. Earthquake, the "destroyer of mountains," is the second son of the fearsome and cunning Seven Macaw, whom the Hero Twins nonetheless are able to successfully dupe and vanquish.[11]

During colonial times, Spanish officials on three separate occasions ordered the capital of the province moved to a new location, so that they could either rebuild after a quake or try to relocate in a region of the country less prone to such natural disasters. (One geographic consideration for relocating the city was the presence of nearby ravines, which Guatemalans long believed helped to insulate a locale from an earthquake's worst effects.)[12] Such was the case in the aftermath of the great earthquake of 1773, perhaps the most devastating of all the colonial temblors. It was in the wake of that disaster that Bourbon administrators took the opportunity to move the capital of Guatemala from the lovely, but earthquake-prone, town that is now known as Antigua to its present location in the Almolonga Valley. There they aspired (with limited success) to build a modern city that, through architecture and spatial planning, would reflect Bourbon values and sensibilities.[13]

Since independence, Guatemala has been afflicted either by a series of earthquakes caused by tectonic shifts, as in the 1976 quake, or by the more common but usually milder "volcanic front," the type that shook the Central American region on average every two and a half years during the twentieth century.[14] Guatemala suffered particularly serious earthquakes in 1816, 1902, and 1917. Prior to the 1976 event, Guatemalans remembered 1917–1918 as the worst earthquake "season" on record, when a series of major earthquakes rattled the capital city over a period of seven weeks starting in early December 1917 and continuing on through January 1918. The earthquakes were accompanied by massive landslides and followed by the eruption of the Santa María (Santiaguito) volcano in 1922, which, taken together, brought the country nearly to a standstill.[15]

Yet even by the standards of a country accustomed to earthquakes, the 1976 event was unparalleled both for its seismic and social extremity. First among these was the quake's intensity: it released thirty times more energy than the December 1972 earthquake that destroyed Managua, Nicaragua, and killed twenty thousand people.[16] The 1976 Guatemalan earthquake, moreover, involved the most extensive "surface faulting" (highly destructive bolts and cracks that rise to the earth's surface during a displacement) on record since the disastrous 1906 San Francisco earthquake.[17] Such faulting is unusually devastating to buildings and other structures, especially to

Southward of a newer part of Guatemala City where shaking damage was relatively light. Few of the typical reinforced concrete homes and multistoried buildings in this area were significantly damaged, and there were no building collapses or casualties (SLIDE 44, OPEN-FILE REPORT 77-165, 1976, U.S. GEOLOGICAL SURVEY PHOTOGRAPHIC LIBRARY).

the modest adobe-and-cornstalk housing used back then in most of rural Guatemala.[18] Not surprisingly, many of the buildings in the capital city, which were constructed of rebar and reinforced concrete, fared much better, and suffered, for the most part, relatively minimal damage. (Modern building materials did not provide an absolute guarantee of security, however, as evinced by the "pancaking"—the collapse of multiple floors, one on top of the other, that completely destroyed Guatemala City's Terminal Hotel, and by the overall structural damage that took place in the elite and well-built Hotel Camino Real.) Nevertheless, building quality did significantly affect the quake's impact, making the disaster, at its root, a class-based crisis.[19] As one member of the U.S.-based Earthquake Engineering Research Institute (EERI) team, which did a preliminary assessment of damage to the city (a project that focused almost entirely on the capital rather than on the deeply afflicted countryside) in the days immediately

following the quake, noted, "Even the poorly built brick buildings performed significantly better than the adobe dwellings."[20]

 To make matters worse, because many of the poor who lost their
houses were artisans or self-employed workers, they lost their livelihoods
and incomes as well as their homes.[21] As one scholar has noted, with only
slight exaggeration, the earthquake "left the upper and middle classes virtually unscathed. This was the first major earthquake widely recognized
as having had such a markedly selective impact, hence its designation by
an American journalist as a 'class-quake.'"[22]

The Earthquake as Detonator of Revolution

The 1976 earthquake struck a country that was already in the midst of serious social and political upheaval. In the late 1960s, the military government of Guatemala had launched a massive counterinsurgency campaign
against the Cuban-inspired revolutionary movement that had operated
in the eastern part of the country since the early years of that decade,
virtually annihilating both the guerrillas and their civilian supporters in
1967. The strategies of counterinsurgency had not only involved an armed
confrontation that had killed nearly eight thousand people, but had also
incorporated the use of state terror—disappearances, assassinations, and
the extreme suspension of civil rights—to "safeguard the nation" from a
Marxist takeover.

The Guatemalan military government had also tried to ward off the
guerrillas' advance through the use of "soft power," which in this case
included making considerable investment in the economy and introducing
new agricultural lands and technologies to the poverty-stricken rural populace. This carrot-and-stick approach had kept the population relatively
in check until the early 1970s. However, neither the government's efforts
at development nor its exercise of raw power through terror had managed
to solve the considerable problems and inequities—racism, inequality,
severe poverty, lack of representation for the majority of the people in the
country—that had spurred the formation of the revolutionary movements
in the first place.[23]

By 1972, the armed resistance had begun to retrench, forming new
guerrilla groups and organizing among sectors it had not previously tried
to incorporate into the popular struggle. This included, most importantly,
the indigenous population. In addition, new kinds of social movements

were emerging that were not directly associated with the guerrillas, including a Catholic population recently politicized through Liberation Theology and new (if still covert) militant campesino organizations such as the Comité de Unidad Campesina (CUC). Taken together, this multidirectional mobilization added up to a population that was, in historian Deborah Levenson's words, "already relatively radicalized" when the earthquake struck.[24] Thus, while the earthquake precipitated many serious problems of its own, it also cast Guatemala's preexisting problems into high relief and aggravated an already volatile social and political situation.

The Government Responds

Against this backdrop, the Guatemalan military government under the president and general, Kjell Eugenio Laugerud García, determined that one of the first priorities of the recovery would be to distribute relief in such a way as to safeguard powerful interests and to preclude the further mobilization of progressive social and political movements. On the night of the disaster, Laugerud, looking "tired," as one observer described him, offered words of encouragement: *"Estámos heridos pero no de muerte"* (We are wounded but not mortally) and added, perhaps a bit prematurely: *"¡Guatemala está en pie!"* (Guatemala is on its feet!).[25] Relief flowed into Guatemala almost immediately—the government began to distribute emergency food rations within hours; medics who were already working in the countryside were able to establish field hospitals on the very afternoon of the day the quake took place; and the U.S. Army installed a hundred-bed medical facility in Chimaltenango within forty-eight hours of the catastrophe.[26] The international community also rose to the occasion, with thirty-five nations contributing to the cause. (This excluded Great Britain, whose offer of aid the Guatemala government declined because of England's continuing claims on Belize, which Guatemala still considered to be part of its sovereign national territory).[27]

Despite this outpouring, once aid arrived into the country, it did not always make it into the areas of greatest need quickly or expeditiously.[28] This was due in part to logistics—the quake itself and the *derrumbes* (landslides) that followed it had made many roads and bridges impassable—but it also had to do with political considerations that impelled the government to privilege some groups over others in the administration of aid.

Collapse of three central spans of the Agua Caliente bridge, kilometer
36 on the road to the Atlantic Ocean. The image shows the damage to
Guatemala's infrastructure, isolating quake victims from relief efforts
(PHOTO BY A. F. ESPINOSA, FIGURE 64, PROFESSIONAL PAPER 1002, 1976,
U.S. GEOLOGICAL SURVEY PHOTOGRAPHIC LIBRARY).

(U.S. government agents, nevertheless, heaped praise upon the Guatemalan government for the speed and efficiency of its relief effort).[29] One of the Guatemalan government's first decisions was to turn over the bulk of recovery efforts to a mixture of government agencies, private groups, and even wealthy families to distribute relief to afflicted areas.[30] A second decision that weighed heavily in the aftermath of recovery was that which placed the Guatemalan Army in charge of a civilian agency, the government's National Reconstruction Committee (CNR), the central coordinating committee for all relief efforts that would take place in the months and even years after the quake. Later, in the early 1980s, the CNR would assume the paradoxical role of coordinating government relief to communities that had been destroyed in the government's own counterinsurgency campaigns.

Although many of the international agencies that came to Guatemala to offer relief after the 1976 earthquake were private or faith-based (including many Protestant organizations from the United States), the military demanded that even private agencies award aid to victims based at least in part upon their loyalty to the government. Historian Deborah Levenson has documented specifically how this worked in the case of *lámina*, the corrugated metal or fiberglass sheets that aid agencies provided as roofing to replace the traditional red tile that had performed so dismally in the earthquake. The military impounded lámina imported by aid agencies until they agreed to distribute the building materials to zones that the CNR specifically chose to be rewarded for their political acquiesce and compliance. Although the level of corruption and political favoritism in Guatemala never reached the depths it did in Nicaragua—where dictator Anastasio Somoza sold blood plasma donated to earthquake victims by the Red Cross after the 1972 quake for personal profit on the open market— the political use of emergency aid helped to undermine a government that many already regarded as unresponsive and even illegitimate.

The Earthquake as Political Opportunity

Certainly, the earthquake provided new opportunities and challenges for both the guerrillas and for the military. For the armed Left, the earthquake offered an unprecedented opening to recruit and develop a revolutionary consciousness among sectors of the population that were fed up with the nation's inequities and the government's venality. Both the timing and location of the quake was propitious for the armed movement, as the revitalized guerrilla movement, specifically the Ejército Guerrillero de los Pobres (EGP) and the Organización del Pueblo en Armas (ORPA), had recently established itself in the area in and around Chimaltenango, as well as elsewhere in the western highlands.[31]

While the guerrillas—secular Marxists that many of them were—decided against playing up the metaphorical qualities of the earthquake, they did use it as an opportunity to emphasize the need for a new social-ist, classless society in Guatemala. Whether or not it was this approach that resonated with local people, or their newly straitened circumstances drove them to consider more revolutionary alternatives, the influence of the guerrilla groups expanded significantly in rural Guatemala in the wake of the earthquake. In the capital, organized labor also used the cri-sis of earthquake to fuel the flames of discontent against the government by putting out pamphlets and radio broadcasts that posed the simple but piquant question: "What's there to reconstruct?"[32]

Although it is difficult to parse exactly how large a role the earthquake itself played as the political drama unfolded, the disgust and discontent that people felt in the wake of the cataclysm must surely account in some large part for the substantial increase in influence and support the popular movements received as they expanded dramatically across the Guatemalan highlands between 1976 and 1981. Not surprisingly, Chimaltenango, the epicenter of the quake, also become one of the chief battlegrounds in the wars of insurgency and counterinsurgency during that same period. After 1976 the armed movement expanded its presence dramatically in rural areas, especially in the Ixcán region of the northern El Quiché depart-ment and in and around Chimaltenango. There it won significant support among some of the civilian population, which provided the "mucha-chos" with material and strategic support, such as food, communications, and help in navigating the local terrain. But as the guerrilla movement expanded, so did the government's violent response. With the election of General Romeo Lucas García to the office of the presidency in 1978, the stage was set for the downward spiral of terror, violence, and scorched-earth counterinsurgency policies that would result in the period of the greatest killing in Guatemala since the Spanish conquest.

It is clear that the Guatemalan military understood some of the larger ramifications of the earthquake from the beginning. Social anthropolo-gist Sheldon Davis has observed that "for the Guatemalan government,

the chaos created by the earthquake presented a military r
social problem." Hoping to start a preemptive strike against ῑ
advances in the midst of the upheaval, the army launched it
cant offensive in the Ixil region of the department of El Quiche a mᴇɪᴄ
two weeks after the earthquake. This initial attack killed several Catholic
activists and a bilingual teacher. Between February 1976 and December
1977, government forces would assassinate sixty-four cooperative members in the same area, a bloody prelude of events to come.[33]

In 1982, when General Efraín Ríos Montt took power in a *golpe de
estado* (coup d'état), the war turned against the popular movement, as the
Guatemalan army launched a scorched-earth campaign against the Maya
population to eliminate any real or potential support for the guerrillas.[34]
This period, now known as "la violencia," took place between 1978 and
1983, and represents the bloody nadir of Guatemala's thirty-six-year-long
civil war, when the Guatemalan Army declared the Maya to be "internal
enemies" of the state. Guatemala's truth commission reports estimate that
as many as 40 percent of the two hundred thousand killed over the course
of the nation's entire armed struggle died during this period.[35] Although
these events fall outside the scope of this particular chapter, they are in
some regards a legacy of the 1976 earthquake. Had it not been for the
earthquake and the way that it brought the basic fissures of Guatemalan
society to the fore, unleashing new movements of resistance, perhaps—
perhaps?—this might have all played out differently.

The Earthquake as Metaphor: Some Catholic Responses

As for mobilizing resistance, the 1976 earthquake also galvanized Catholic
grassroots organizations around the country. This is not to suggest that
the national church as an institution lent any particular support to the
relief effort. To the contrary, Guatemala's deeply conservative archbishop,
Mario Casariego (whose support of the Guatemalan military project was so
absolute that he had famously remarked that had he not become a bishop,
he would have liked to have been a general) offered a concise theological explanation of the disaster.[36] This was to place blame for the geologic
event squarely on the shoulders of Guatemala's people, who, the bishop
argued, deserved God's punishment for getting involved in demonstrations, strikes, and radical mobilization against the government. In a pastoral address to the traumatized nation on the evening of February 4, the

archbishop was explicit in his condemnation. "God placed his finger over Guatemala," he scolded, "and I hope he will not put his whole hand."[37]

In this respect, Casariego's words complemented the ruling elite's reaction to the quake, which was to focus its response on Guatemala City and to do its best to ignore the suffering in the countryside. A mere three days after the disaster—at a time when the earthquake was still actively claiming victims who were dying of shock, injury, and trauma—CACIF (the Comité Coordinador de Asociaciones Agrícolas, Comerciales, Industriales, y Financieras; the most powerful sector of businesspeople and planters in the country) issued a reassuring, if patently untrue, statement that economic production was already almost back to normal. In the same notice, CACIF admonished the general population to stop whining and to "reconstruct by working and not clamoring and crying." In the same document, CACIF also took the opportunity to remind the suffering Guatemalan people that "God is on our side."[38]

The chiding and unsympathetic tone of the upper echelon of the church, the military government, and the planter class notwithstanding, the elite sectors were not alone in conceptualizing the earthquake in theological and theodic terms. Indeed, many Guatemalans echoed the archbishop's assessment of the earthquake as a direct and effable message from God. Not all, obviously, agreed with his interpretation, although they did concur with CACIF that God, in fact, was a partisan in the recovery effort.

Local Metaphors of Meaning: Santa María Cauqué

At the village level, local knowledge also tended to explain the earthquake in religious or spiritual terms, although specific explanations naturally differed from one locality to another. By way of example, we can see this clearly demonstrated in a survey conducted just little more than a week after the earthquake took place, in the Kakchikel village of Santa María Cauqué. This community is located in the central highland department of Sacatepequez, some thirty miles west of the capital and not terribly far from Chimaltenango and the quake's epicenter.

Santa María Cauqué had been the subject of a series of longitudinal public health studies conducted since the 1960s, so there happened to be researchers in the village at the time of the quake who were readily equipped to evaluate the disaster's impact from a social science perspective almost as soon as the ground stopped shaking.[39] The town, which had a population of 1,577, lost 5 percent (79 people) of its population in the earthquake.[40] Most of the victims were children. The temblor destroyed every single house in the town; the only surviving buildings were the village clinic, the city hall, and the local slaughterhouse, which was the center of the village's main industry, the raising and selling of poultry. Most of the town's livestock also perished in the earthquake. In short, the earthquake left its survivors bereft of almost every basic human necessity: housing, food, livelihood, children, or hope for the future.

Against a backdrop of such desolation, the survey, which researchers associated with the Pan American Health Organization's Division of Environmental Biology of INCAP (Instituto de Nutrición de Centroamérica y Panamá) conducted over a three-day period from February 16–19, 1976, posed a series of questions in which they requested that villagers think about their expectations for the future, conceptualize their immediate and medium-term needs, and frame their understanding of what had happened to them. To this last point, the survey asked heads of households a single question: what do you think caused the earthquake? In an open-ended response, the villagers' answers reveal a profoundly theodic worldview—*theodicy* speaks to the question of why and how an omnipotent God permits evil to happen—that explained the earthquake not simply as a metaphor for God's action, but as God's direct intervention on the earth. Among the survey's 101 respondents, of whom 75 percent were Catholic and 25 percent were Protestant, the responses to the question of what caused the earthquake were as follows:

God's command	26
God's punishment	21
Only God knows	17
God's Word	11
God's lesson	2
Because of a volcano	10
Geological fault	1
No response	11
Total	101 families

Taken as a whole, as we can clearly see, more than 75 percent of respondents attributed the earthquake, in one way or the other, to God's will.[41] Perhaps surprisingly, this perspective also seems to have provided the survivors with a modicum of stoicism and even optimism, given their belief that the disaster had not been a random act of nature but part of an unfolding divine plan. Confident in the wisdom of God's purpose, almost all of the residents of Santa María Cauqué expressed a desire to remain in the town and rebuild their lives there.[42] Although Santa María Cauqué is no more and no less representative of local attitudes toward the earthquake than any other central highland village, it nonetheless illustrates how quickly the immediate physical crisis of the earthquake acquired a metaphoric narrative that allowed villagers to imbue the horrific event with some kind of logic and higher meaning.

The Popular Church Responds

Within other sectors, the earthquake carried other metaphors of meaning. In particular, one significant group who assigned religious meaning to the quake was Catholic clergy and laypeople who were engaged with Liberation Theology. This was the movement that emerged in the Latin American church during the mid-1960s and that called upon Catholics to work for justice among the poor and oppressed, particularly through political activism. Although the term "Liberation Theology" per se was not widely used in Guatemala at that time, the ideas that drove the movement—that the church should take a "preferential option for the poor" and demand social justice—had begun to take root in the late 1960s and early 1970s there among many of the clergy and lay activists in the Catholic Action, a movement that worked among and helped to organize young and dynamic community leaders.

Foreign priests and "religious" parties, particularly members of the Maryknoll order, an U.S. clerical order that associated strongly with social justice issues, made up a significant proportion of Catholic clergy in Guatemala in the 1970s. This demographic consideration added to the administrative distance between the conservative Catholic hierarchy and the progressive clergy at work in the *campo*. Among these lower clergy, Catholic social activism at first followed a *desarrollista* (developmentalist) model that favored land reform and agricultural innovations over more radical remedies, but by the mid-1970s, the glacial pace of reform had begun to frustrate many of the activist clergy.[43] It would be the crisis of the earthquake, however, which laid open so many of the deep fissures in Guatemala society—further exaggerated by the government's erratic and uneven efforts at recovery—that would eventually push a significant minority of activist Catholic clergy and laypeople into the radical camp.

In the immediate wake of the earthquake, however, Liberationist clergy read the catastrophe as a clarion call to action on behalf of social justice. The destruction of the earth was God's sign that it was time for Guatemalans to build a *"tierra nueva."* This was to be, quite literally, a new land, based on a radical, but also very biblical, Christian foundation of economic and social justice. As Deborah Levenson has shown in her excellent article about the 1976 earthquake, Catholic clergy in Guatemala City were quick to respond to the challenge of the recovery. For them, the call for the tierra nueva translated into land invasions (*asentamientos*) led by priests, nuns, and lay workers who in the days following the quake immediately began to organize seizures of property in the name of homeless and displaced people. As one priest explained, "the intense joining together of people [and] church in relation to the housing problem resulted from our theological contextualization of the earthquake. We said that the earthquake was God's signal that we should leave the ravines to search for a communal identity."[44]

The land invasion movement took off in the months immediately following the quake; between February and May 1976, church groups established 126 such communities in and around Guatemala City. Because the asentamientos involved both (1) the seizure of what was technically private property and (2) large numbers of people who were strongly motivated for social change (a church-founded community known as Tierra Nueva located on a deserted *finca* [farm] on the outskirts of Guatemala City, for example, eventually became home to eight hundred families), they posed a serious threat to the status quo.[45] Moreover, despite repeated condemnation by Archbishop Casariego, the land invasion movement publicly signaled the Guatemalan church's embrace of Liberation Theology and its aggressive advocacy for the rights of the poor, marking a clear separation between the institutional Catholic Church and the "popular church" at the grassroots.

It was in the earthquake's aftermath that the government, already dubious of Catholic organizing among the rural poor, would come to regard Catholic activists as enemies of the state. It was around this time that Mario Sandoval Alarcón, one of the founders of the ultra right-wing political party, the Movimiento de Liberación Nacional (MLN), and vice president under General Kjell Laugerud, observed, "The Church propagates communism."[46] Within the year, the government initiated a policy to staunch the rising power of the popular church, policy that included the selective killing of Catholic activists, ranging from local lay leaders to the assassination of Guatemalan and foreign clergy. By the war's end, religious leaders would constitute one of the single largest sectors of victims killed during the entire conflict, second only to campesino political leaders.[47]

The Earthquake as Metaphor: The Protestant Response

In the years immediately following the 1976 earthquake, another religious movement, Protestantism, expanded quite dramatically in Guatemala, especially among the Maya population. As the Catholic Church constricted due to repression by the state in the late 1970s and early 1980s, Protestant churches grew by leaps and bounds. Although the statistics are imperfect, Guatemala's Protestant population mushroomed between 1960 and 1980, growing from approximately 5 percent of the population in 1960 to nearly a quarter of the overall population in 1980.[48] During this period of expansive growth, it was not Protestantism in general so much as one branch of Protestantism, Pentecostalism, that grew like wildfire in the wake of the earthquake's destruction.

Pentecostalism's rapid advance in Guatemala dated roughly, but not precisely, from the time of the earthquake, but Protestant missionaries from mainline denominations such as the Presbyterian Church and Central American Mission had worked in the country for a century, with relatively modest success.[49] Despite the missions' substantial contributions toward building institutions such as hospitals, schools, and clinics, few Guatemalans converted to Protestantism before the mid-1960s. At that time, bolstered by missionary divestitures (as U.S.-based missions, fearing expropriation, turned their work over to native leadership) and a wave of evangelization campaigns sponsored by foreign organizations seeking to offer a "spiritual alternative to communism," Guatemalan Protestantism began to assume a local character. In addition to appealing to a much larger constituency than had the mission churches, the new Guatemalan denominations also embraced a different theology, known as Pentecostalism, a variation of Christianity that emphasizes the miraculous experience of God, manifest through the "baptism in the Holy Spirit" expressed in ecstatic behavior such as faith healing and speaking in tongues.[50] By the early 1980s, many, perhaps the majority of, Mayan

Protestants would belong to locally based Pentecostal denominations, which had few direct ties to foreign missionary organizations.[51]

This, however, would all come much later. In the days immediately following the earthquake, international Protestant aid agencies, mostly from the United States, poured into Guatemala, offering spiritual succor along with relief supplies. In all, just over a dozen large Protestant relief agencies, most affiliated with mainline U.S. denominations and nondenominational faith-based organizations like World Vision, came to Guatemala in the weeks that followed the disaster, where their efforts fell under coordination of an umbrella board begun by the National Council of Church and Church World Service, called the Consejo Cristiano de Agencias de Desarrollo (CONCAD).

Although some Protestant aid agencies were linked to progressive denominations, many were not. A number of these conservative church-related groups, sponsored by evangelical and fundamentalist groups in the United States, declined to join CONCAD because of its affiliation with the liberal National and World Council of Churches. Although these groups' primary object at this point was to provide physical relief to the stricken, their long-term objective was to "saturate with Scripture," winning converts by word and example.[52] Aid workers who belonged to conservative denominations, though by no means blind to Guatemalans' suffering and tragedy, nonetheless saw the earthquake as providing an opportunity to help rebuild Guatemala physically and spiritually in such as way as to inoculate it from further influence of the armed Left and other "godless" elements.

Regardless of their varying political views, however, Protestant aid agencies, well funded and well staffed (at least by Guatemalan standards), worked quickly to rebuild communities, placing an emphasis on replacing community structures such as schools, clinics, and churches to help restore the institutions that they believed might help bring some sense of normalcy back to people's shattered lives. They also distributed goods—food, clothing, and building materials—to families and individuals, usually free of cost other than an invitation to attend church services. The recipients of the aid, grasping the quid pro quo, readily complied, and within a few months of the earthquake evangelical church membership throughout Guatemala jumped by 14 percent.[53] Critics sneered at such timely conversion, mocking it as "*lámina por ánima*" (a soul for new roofing).[54]

This clever bit of word play did not tell the whole story, however; Guatemalans in the postearthquake period proved by and large to be more

than "rice Christians."[55] Obviously, some "converts" were simply oppor-
tunists, claiming to be born-again only as long as the concrete blocks
and potted meats held out. Others joined Protestant churches explicitly
because they believed them to offer a safe haven against the government's
assault against activist Catholics. But these explanations only go so far in
explaining the continued meteoric growth of Protestant churches after
the immediate emergency had passed. By 1982 the annual growth rate
of Protestant conversion in Guatemala had risen to nearly 24 percent per
year, nearly four times what it had been a decade earlier.[56]

By far the greatest growth in the postearthquake period took place
among the Pentecostal groups. In the days immediately following the
earthquake, this was largely due to the widely discussed experience of El
Calvario Church, a Guatemalan-based church that had started up in the
1960s. The parishioners of El Calvario underwent a group conversion to
Pentecostalism in 1965, after one member of a small charismatic prayer
group within the church had a terrifying prophetic vision that a major
earthquake would destroy Guatemala at some time in the near future.
This specter of destruction so horrified the member's prayer circle that
they persuaded the entire congregation to convert to Pentecostalism en
masse and stockpile supplies for the impending disaster.

When the earthquake did strike, El Calvario was ready for it. Within
days of the quake, the congregation began to actively proselytize and distribute supplies in the most stricken parts of the country, particularly in
the densely populated and ruined region around Chimaltenango. Cynics
scoffed that anyone with even a passing knowledge of Guatemalan history could predict a future earthquake with a fair degree of confidence,
but to the many quake victims who began to rebuild their lives with provisions from El Calvario's well-stocked warehouses, the evidence spoke for
itself. The church seemed to have a direct line to a higher power that many
Guatemalans could simply not ignore, prompting whole extended families
and even *aldeas* to join El Calvario and other Pentecostal churches like it.[57]

(The case of El Calvario, in fact, also helps to illustrate the arc of
Pentecostal church growth in Guatemala. Although it was a small congregation in 1976, membership in El Calvario grew very rapidly after the
earthquake. In 1978, it spun off a new Pentecostal church that took the
name Fraternidad Cristiana, which met for some years in a converted movie
theater in Guatemala City. Today, Fraternidad Cristiana claims to be the
largest Pentecostal church in Guatemala. In May 2007, it inaugurated

its mammoth new church building, the "Megafrater," which can hold its entire fifteen-thousand-member congregation at one time.)[58]

Beyond the drama of El Calvario's experience, however, purely secular side effects of the earthquake contributed to the growth of evangelical churches in the months and years to follow. One factor was urbanization, in part the result of increasing population pressures that worsened significantly when the earthquake pushed rural people into the city in search of jobs and sustenance. In the capital, immigrants joined evangelical churches in substantial numbers, as religious organizations became one of the few forms of urban voluntary associations accessible to low-income families.[59] Of particular importance were small Protestant-run neighborhood organizations, such as women's support groups, youth fellowships, and Alcoholics Anonymous, which often met in church buildings or members' homes. These types of associations provided important supportive relationships that helped newcomers to the city avoid the kinds of social ills—family disintegration, gangs, alcoholism—most commonly associated with low-income urban migration.

At one time, immigrants to the city would have looked to the Catholic Church to provide these kinds of services, and, given the fact that the vast majority of urban immigrants in the 1970s were at least nominally Catholic, one might have expected the church to play a significant role in their resettlement. But the official Catholic Church did not, largely because of increasing government repression against clergy and lay activists who were engaged in social justice efforts at the grassroots level. A second reason for the institutional church's reticence was Guatemala's conservative archbishop, Mario Casariego, who feared that social action projects would push his flock down the slippery slope to Liberation Theology. Casariego tried to limit Catholic response to the most traditional sorts of Catholic charities, thus leaving the more innovative and, indeed, more dangerous work, to the clergy and laypeople of the emerging popular church in rural and poor urban communities.[60] Yet it would be within these very settings that they would find themselves head-to-head with new Protestant communities.

Living in the Latter Days

Aside from practicalities and social factors, the earthquake brought Guatemalans to Pentecostal belief for theological reasons as well. Although the crisis of the event alone was enough to drive many to religion in a kind of "trench faith" to see them through hard times, the basic tenets of Pentecostalism also seemed to resonate with the disaster. Many Pentecostals, including Mayan converts, became attracted to the doctrine of premillennialism, an apocalyptic theology that places emphasis on the immediacy of the earth's temporal end, heralding Christ's return. For a people whose traditional spirituality was closely tied to the cycles of the cosmos and the calendar—where the end of a Maya Long Count calendar cycle in ancient thinking threatened (or promised) the end of the present creation—the Protestant Christian teaching of premillennialism fell on fertile ground.[61]

As subscribers to this doctrine, converts to Pentecostalism readily gave themselves over to the teaching that the Second Coming of Christ was imminent, but only after a period of signs, wonders, suffering, and trials for God's people. For them, the 1976 earthquake marked the start of this Great Tribulation, a period of great suffering that reached its prophetic climax in the early 1980s. By the time of the administration of General Efraín Ríos Montt (1982–1983), when political violence and the military's policies of counterinsurgency had reached an apex, the similarities between the biblical descriptions of this prophetic ordeal and the reality that so many Guatemalans were living were almost too numerous to mention; as biblical literalists, the descriptions of earthquake, violence, and famine were as descriptive as they were visionary. "There was a violent earthquake and the sun went black . . . the whole population . . . took to the mountains to hide in caves among the rocks . . . For the Great Day of His anger has come and who can survive it?" (Rev.6:12–17). This, indeed, was no allegorical reading of the final book of the Bible, but a literal roadmap for the days ahead.

By the early 1980s, Guatemalan Pentecostals had begun to actively prepare for the End Times. The sense of impending apocalypse was so acute that an urban Pentecostal group briefly published a newspaper (prudently undated) to cover the end of the world. Its final edition, the third of a Trinitarian three, probably published in late 1982, carried the headline, written in the present tense: "*El Señor Viene* [The Lord Comes]: His return is imminent, this is an alert." Within this issue, articles carried titles such as "Earthquake: Plagues, general commotion, and many afflictions, the sun and moon will be darkened, and the mountains will fall," "The final cataclysm," "Know the signs: The sound of the trumpet, declares Paul of Tarsus," and, reassuringly, "The Teacher: Do not be afraid; Trust in me."[62] To many Pentecostals, this, indeed, was Guatemala's *kairos*: to bear witness to the Great Tribulation but to rise, faithful and triumphant, with the Lord on the day of his final coming. For the faithful, this interpretation vested logic and meaning in what was otherwise inexplicable suffering, a theodic answer to the riddle of overwhelming loss.

The Earthquake as History: Part II

The 1976 earthquake as a seismic event was one of the worst in recorded history, the physical destruction it wrought so profound that it would have rattled the foundations of even a country that was much more stable and peaceful than Guatemala was at that point in its history. Yet the earthquake's effects reached far beyond the overwhelming and immediate humanitarian crisis. In the words of Guatemalan politician/historian Francisco Villagrán Kramer, "the major effect of the earthquake, without doubt, was to expose to the light of day the crude reality of [a] country . . . that operated on a base of clearly-established hierarchies that [up until that time] were observed and respected."[63] Or, as Levenson cogently observes, "Although the military never claimed that the earthquake was a turning point in its history, it was."[64]

In Chinese history, there is the Confucian concept called the "mandate of heaven" (*t'ien ming*) that explains that good and moral leadership is given and mandated by heaven, which can and does bring an end to a regime or dynasty when it no longer rules wisely.[65] Heaven heralds the end of the era by putting forth portents in the physical world—earthquakes, famine, floods—that summon the people to rise up and overthrow bad government. In a very real sense, the 1976 Guatemalan earthquake, with its mulitvalenced and redolent metaphors of meaning, played a similar role, signaling to Guatemalans of all stripes that the moment for change—political, metaphysical, or otherwise—had come. The earthquake was an overwhelming natural disaster, but it was also much more than that. The earthquake served notice that society's authorities—the military government, the institutional Catholic Church, and the planter class; indeed, the old system of living—had at last lost their mandate. At the same time, Guatemalans also derived from the quake a series of metaphoric narratives for new systems and ways of being for both the near and distant future.

For some people, the change that the earthquake demanded was broad, political, and communitarian, while for others it was social or, especially,

religious and personal. But for virtually no one who lived through that
night was the earthquake "just" a natural disaster. For those who were
alive in 1976, the earthquake—when time stopped, then started up
again—represents the beginning of Guatemalan's modern history, when
the nation began to imagine itself as not only under God's thumb but also
in the palm of his hand. There is not (yet) a happy ending to this story; the
years following the earthquake were among the most violent and traumatic
in that nation's long and troubled history. But even at that, Guatemala has
managed to survive—as a postage stamp from the 1980s commemorating
the earthquake declared, echoing President Laugerud's words, the nation
was "wounded but not dead" (*herido pero no muerto*). More importantly,
Guatemalans themselves continue, even now, to find metaphors of hope
within what others might regard to be hopeless circumstances. This, too,
is one of the earthquake's lasting legacies.

✦ NOTES ✦

1. Inga and Juan are pseudonyms, but their stories are real, as they were told to
   the author.

2. C. J. Langer and G. A. Bollinger, "Secondary Faulting Near the Terminus
   of a Seismogenic Strike-Slip Fault: Aftershocks of the 1976 Guatemala
   Earthquake," *Bulletin of the Seismological Society of America* 69, no. 2 (April
   1979): 427–44.

3. Deborah Levenson, "Reaction to Trauma: The 1976 Earthquake in
   Guatemala," *International Labor and Working-Class History* 62 (Fall 2002):
   60–68.

4. See Andrew A. Morrison and Rachel A. May, "Escape from Terror: Violence
   and Migration in Post-Revolutionary Guatemala," *Latin American Research
   Review* 29, no. 2 (1994): 111–32. Morrison and May aptly describe the
   earthquake as a "class earthquake."

5. Noel W. Solomons and Nancy Butte, "A View of the Medical and Nutritional
   Consequences of the Earthquake in Guatemala," *International Health* 93, no. 2
   (March–April 1978), 169.

6. Roger I. Glass, Juan J. Urrutia, Simon Sibony, Harry Smith, Bertha Garcia,
   and Luis Rizzo, "Earthquake Injuries Related to Housing in a Guatemalan
   Village: Aseismic Construction Techniques May Diminish the Toll of Death
   and Serious Injuries," *Science* 197, no. 4304 (August 12, 1977): 638–43.

7. W. H. Smith, "'The Guatemala Earthquake of February 4, 1976,' Preliminary Report from EERI Reconnaissance Team Member W. H. Smith," Earthquake Engineering Research Institute, www.eeri.org/site/content/view/183.35 (accessed September 1, 2008).

8. These communities included Chimaltenango, Tecpán, Patzicía, Sumpango, Santa María Cauqué, San Pedro Sacatepequez, San Juan Sacatepequez, Zaragoza, Comalapa, San Martín Jilotepeque, Sanarate, and El Progreso. (Note that not all of these are in the department of Chimaltenango.) Solomons and Butte, "Consequences of the Earthquake," 163.

9. Glass, Urrutia, Sibony, Smith, Garcia, and Rizzo, "Earthquake Injuries," 638–43.

10. Philip Berryman, *Christians in Guatemala's Struggle* (London: Catholic Institute for International Relations, 1984), 24; Gustavo Berganza, ed. "El terremoto de 1976: drama y convulsión política," *Compendio de Historia de Guatemala, 1944–2000* (Guatemala City: ASEIS, 2004), 41–42.

11. Dennis Tedlock, trans., *Popol Vuh: The Definitive Edition of the Mayan Book of the Dawn of Life and the Glories of Gods and Kings* (New York: Touchstone, 1985), 99–101.

12. Marshall H. Saville, "The Guatemalan Earthquake of December 1917 and January 1918," *American Geographical Review* 5, no. 6 (June 1918), 459–69; see also Oscar Guillermo, *Nueva Guatemala de la Asunción y los terremotos de 1917–18* (Guatemala City: Centro de Estudios Urbanos y Regionales, Universidad de San Carlos de Guatemala, 1994).

13. See Rafael V. Álvarez P., *Terremotos en Antigua: secuencias y secuelas* (Guatemala City: Centro Editorial Valle, 2001) and María Cristina Zilbermann de Luján, *Aspectos socioeconómicos del traslado de la Ciudad de Guatemala (1773–1783)* (Guatemala City: Academia de Geografía e Historia de Guatemala, 1987).

14. Randall A. White and David H. Harlow, "Destructive Upper-Crust Earthquakes of Central America since 1900," *Bulletin of the Seismological Society of America* 83, no. 4 (August 1993): 1115–42.

15. Saville, "Guatemalan Earthquake," 459.

16. C. del Valle de Coyet and E. Jeannée (Centre de Recherche sur Épidémiologie des Désastres École de Santé Publique), "Earthquake in Guatemala: Epidemiological Evaluation of the Relief Effort," *Emergency Planning Digest* (January–February 1977), 2.

17. George Plafker, "Tectonic Aspects of the Guatemalan Earthquake of 4 February 1976," *Science* 193, no. 4259 (September 24, 1976): 1201–8.

18. Glass, Urrutia, Sibony, Smith, Garcia, and Rizzo, "Earthquake Injuries," 638–43.

19. Ibid.

20. Earthquake Engineering Research Institute, "General Summary: EERI Reconnaissance Team Efforts, Guatemala, February 6, 1976 to February 12, 1976," www.eeri.org/site/content/views/1831351 (accessed September 5, 2008).

21. Levenson, "Reaction to Trauma," 61.

22. Piers M. Blaikie, *At Risk: Natural Hazards, People's Vulnerability, and Disasters* (London: Routledge, 1994), 170.

23. See Kate Doyle, "The United States and Guatemala: Counterinsurgency and Genocide, 1954–1999," in *Guatemala and the United States, 1954–1999: Death Squads, Guerrilla War, Covert Operations, and Genocide* (Ann Arbor, MI: ProQuest Information and Learning, 2002).

24. Levenson, "Reaction to Trauma," 1.

25. Solomons and Butte, "Consequences of the Earthquake," 164.

26. Ville de Coyet and Jeannée, "Earthquake in Guatemala," 3.

27. Solomons and Butte, "Consequences of the Earthquake," 164.

28. Ville de Coyet and Jeannée, "Earthquake in Guatemala," 4.

29. U.S. Agency for International Development (AID), "Disaster Relief Case Report: Guatemala—Earthquake February 1976, Section D; Action Taken by the Government of Guatemala and the Guatemalan People; Part I," (Washington, DC: USAID, July 1978).

30. Ibid., part 2.

31. Comisión de Esclarecimiento histórico, *Guatemala: causas y orígenes del enfrentamiento armado interno* (Guatemala City: F and G, 2000).

32. Levenson, "Reaction to Trauma," 63.

33. Sheldon H. Davis and Julie Hodson, *Witness to Political Violence in Guatemala: The Suppression of a Rural Development Movement* (New York: Oxfam, 1983), 164.

34. For more on these attacks, please see Virginia Garrard-Burnett, *Terror in the Land of the Holy Spirit: Guatemala under General Efraín Ríos Montt, 1982–1983* (New York: Oxford University Press, forthcoming).

35. Patrick Ball, Paul Kobrak, and Herbert F. Spirer, *State Violence in Guatemala, 1960–1996: A Quantitative Reflection* (Washington, DC: AAAS, 1999).

36. Phillip Berryman, *Stubborn Hope: Religion, Politics, and Revolution in Central America* (Maryknoll, NY: Orbis, 1994), 117.

37. In his radio address to the victims of the earthquake on February 4, 1976, Casariego offered these words of comfort: "Dios había puesto el dedo sobre Guatemala y ojalá no fuera a poner la mano" (*Recuperación de la Memoria Histórica*, vol. 3. Proyecto Interdiacano de Recuperación de la Memoria Histórica, Oficina de Derechos Humanos de Arzobispado de Guatemala), 131.

38. Levenson, "Reaction to Trauma," 61.

39. See Leonardo Mata, *The Children of Santa María Canqué: A Prospective Field Study of Health and Growth* (Cambridge, MA: MIT Press, 1978).

40. Glass, Urrutia, Sibony, Smith, Garcia, and Rizzo, "Earthquake Injuries," 638.

41. Berta García and J. Urrutia, "Damages Caused by the Earthquake in Santa María Cauquí [*sic*]," Biblioteca CIRMA D-1260, 7.

42. Ibid., 8.

43. For a sense of this process, see Susan Fitzpatrick Behrens, "From Symbols of the Sacred to Symbols of Subversion to Simply Obscure: Maryknoll Women Religious in Guatemala, 1953 to 1967." *The Americas* 61, no. 2 (October 2004): 189–216.

44. Levenson, "Reaction to Trauma," 64.

45. Ibid., 64–65.

46. Fernando Bermúdez, *Historia de la Iglesia Católica* (Guatemala City: Diocesis de San Marcos, 2003), 193; see also *Recuperación*, vol. 3, 132.

47. See Ball, Kobrak, and Spirer, *State Violence*, 77.

48. Proyecto Centroamericano de Estudios Socio-Religiosos, *Directorio de Iglesias, organizaciones y ministerios del movimiento protestante: Guatemala* (San Francisco de Dos Ríos, Costa Rica: Instituto Internacional de Evangelización, 1981).

49. Virginia Garrard-Burnett, "Tongues People and Convolutionists: Early Pentecostalism in Guatemala, 1915–1940" (unpublished paper presented at the Latin American Studies Association, Washington, DC, September 2001).

50. For more on this subject, see Garrard-Burnett, *Protestantism in Guatemala: Living in the New Jerusalem* (Austin: University of Texas Press, 1998). The first Pentecostal mission to Guatemala actually opened in 1916, but its fortunes as a missionary church were similar to that of the mainline denominations in that it did not attract a large number of converts. In addition, the Pentecostal mission faced considerable opposition from the non-Pentecostal Protestant missions.

51. Ibid., chap. 8.

52. The most notable of these relief agencies include the following: World Vision, Partners in the Americas, a nonsectarian group that unofficially helped channel aid from the U.S. Embassy into the altiplano in and around Chimaltenango; Christian Children's Fund; the World Relief Committee of the Association of Evangelicals; Episcopal Presiding Bishop's Fund for World Relief; Norwegian Church Aid; Baptist World Relief; and Wycliffe Bible Translators / Summer Institute of Linguistics. Major local organizations that emerged to cope with the disaster include the Coordinadora Cakchiquel Desarrollo Integral (CODAPI), a nondenominational agency that provided technical and health aid around Chimaltenango; and the Fundación Cristiana para la Educación y Desarrollo (FUNDACED), which originally provided housing to victims of the earthquake and later shifted its focus to reforestation and community development in highland areas affected by the civil war. PROCADES (Proyecto Centroamericano de Estudios Socio-Religiosos), *Directorio de iglesias, organizaciones y ministerios del movimiento protestante* (Guatemala City: Servicio Evangelizador para América Latina, 1981), 385–90; interview with Julian Lloret, March 5, 1985, Guatemala City; interview with Harris Whitbeck, February 18, 1985, Guatemala City; "Consejos cristianos de agencias de desarrollo," *Esfuerzo* 84, no. 2 (1983): 14.

53. Enrique Dominguez and Deborah Huntington, "The Salvation Brokers: Conservative Evangelicals in Central America," *NACLA* 17, no. 1 (1984): 26.

54. Marlise Simons, "Latin America's New Gospel," *New York Times Magazine*, November 7, 1982, 112.

55. The term "rice Christians" came out of the missionary experience in Asia in the interwar period, where church attendance and "conversions" ran high only so long as missions gave out food aid.

56. The church membership statistics that appear in this and the following chapter (unless otherwise noted) are those compiled by PROCADES (Proyecto Centroamericano de Estudios Socio-Religiosos) and its sister organization, SEPAL (Servicio Evangelizador para América Latina). The directory lists 210 different evangelical denominations (as opposed to individual congregations) and estimates the overall Protestant population of the country to be 1,337,812, based on a formal report of 334,453 adult members multiplied by a factor of four. In his book *Is Latin America Turning Protestant? The Politics of Evangelical Growth*, David Stoll offers a more conservative estimate of 18.92 percent Protestant population in Guatemala in 1985 (Berkeley: University of California Press, 1990), 337–38.

57. Clifton L. Holland, ed. *World Christianity: Central America and the Caribbean* (Morovia, CA: Missions Advanced Research and Communications Center, 1981), 79.

58. See Israel Ortiz, "Social Change and Neo-Pentecostalism: A Socio-Religious Analysis of the Neo-Pentecostal Churches in Guatemala with Special Reference to Their Presence and Social Role from 1976–96" (PhD diss., Oxford Centre for Mission Studies, University of Wales, 2008).

59. See Bryan Roberts, "Protestant Groups and Coping with Urban Life in Guatemala City," *American Journal of Sociology*, 73, no. 6 (1968): 753–67; Ruth A. Wallace, "A Model for Change for Religious Affiliation," *Journal for the Scientific Study of Religion* 14, no. 4 (December 1975): 345–55.

60. Agustín Estrada Monroy, *Datos para la historia de la iglesia en Guatemala*, vol. 3 (Guatemala City: Sociedad de Geografía e Historia de Guatemala, 1979), 672.

61. For more on ancient and modern Mayan beliefs on the significance of the calendar cycles in Mayan cosmovision, see Barbara Tedlock, *Time and Highland Maya* (Albuquerque: University of New Mexico Press, 1982) and Jean Molesk-Poz, *Contemporary Maya Spirituality: The Ancient Ways Are Not Lost* (Austin: University of Texas Press, 2006).

62. *El Señor viene: inminente su regreso, esté alerta; sucesos extraordinarios*, no. 3, ca. 1982.

63. Francisco Villagrán Kramer, *Biografía política de Guatemala*, vol. 2 of *Años de guerra y años de paz* (Guatemala City: Editorial de Ciencias Sociales, 2004), 105.

64. Levenson, "Reaction to Trauma," 63.

65. S. J. Marshall, *The Mandate of Heaven: Hidden History in the I Ching* (New York: Columbia University Press, 2001).

CHAPTER SEVEN

Economic Fault Lines and
Middle-Class Fears

Tlatelolco, Mexico City, 1985

LOUISE E. WALKER

❧

✢ IN THE EARLY MORNING ON SEPTEMBER 19, 1985, AN EARTHQUAKE
shook the heart of Mexico City. The next evening, a second earthquake hit.
Together, they left approximately 10,000 dead, 50,000 injured, and 250,000
homeless.[1] On that first day, in less than three minutes, the city center was
in utter disarray. Thousands of buildings had fallen or been damaged; the
pavement had cracked open; the water distribution system had ruptured;
and live electrical lines dangled from their posts.[2] Doomsayers appeared in
the city's streets and meeting places, proclaiming the end of the world.[3]

The state desperately needed to get in touch with residents. Radio
broadcasts provided information and instructions; pamphlets circulated
throughout the city urging residents to stay in their homes: "Citizen: The
priority is to save lives. . . . Allow the rescue workers to do their jobs. Stay
at home. . . . Your solidarity is valiant. Read this and pass it along."[4] Official
rescue workers did not appear, though, and it fell upon residents to dig
through the rubble for their loved ones and neighbors. In the context of
official incompetence, residents did much of the rescue work. Chronicler
of the earthquake Elena Poniatowska describes the scene:

Around the ruins, enormous chains of people of all ages begin to form. The debris and broken concrete are passed from hand to hand in buckets, pots and pans, all sorts of kitchenware, any container at all. The spectacle of a single arm stretching for the air among the masonry and iron rods seems intolerable.[5]

That first night, without electricity, darkness fell upon the downtown and danger appeared in many forms. Buildings that had been severely damaged teetered, threatening to fall with the smallest aftershock. Relief workers distributing blankets and milk armed themselves, and bands of looters roamed the streets.[6]

In the aftermath of the earthquake tens of thousands of victims organized a social movement of unprecedented scale in Mexico City's history. They demanded help with the rescue work and a say in how the city would be rebuilt. In the weeks and months following the disaster, these demands grew to encompass calls for economic reforms. Many scholars and public intellectuals who have written about this victims' movement concentrate on the political effervescence in poor and working-class neighborhoods.[7] Through close examination of a new historical source, this article documents middle-class political mobilization following the earthquake.[8]

In this article, the middle classes are studied through the analytic category of neighborhood residence. Certainly, the middle classes can be traced through a number of different categories, such as income, education, occupation, consumption, lifestyle, values, and self-identity.[9] This creates a dynamic, sometimes volatile, spectrum that the plural term *middle classes* appropriately conveys. Strict delineations of the middle class are unsatisfactory: many people could be considered middle class; the same people might be labeled something else. E. P. Thompson's definition of class as a historical experience and relationship, rather than a thing, helps to glean the process by which an array of interests constitute and define the middle classes.[10]

By approaching the middle classes through the analytic category of urban residence, this article focuses on one of Mexico City's emblematically middle-class neighborhoods, the Tlatelolco apartment complex. One of the areas hardest hit by the earthquake, Tlatelolco became a nucleus of subsequent political activism. Often referred to as a city within the city, on the eve of the earthquake the complex consisted of 102 buildings, with over twelve thousand apartments housing approximately a hundred thousand

residents—the largest of its kind in Latin America. It had its own commercial locales, schools, sporting centers, cultural centers, and medical clinics.
In total, it covered over 750,000 square meters. Built by the government
between 1962 and 1965 to house the middle classes, these apartment high-
rises symbolized the growth of this class in post–Revolutionary Mexico.
Many of its residents were government bureaucrats, doctors, university
professors, and other professionals.[11]

This study of the middle-class earthquake victims in Tlatelolco dif-
fers from much of the scholarship on the Mexico City earthquake and
its aftermath. Here, middle-class political mobilization takes center stage.
This article connects middle-class mobilization to the contemporaneous
economic crisis. This focus on the middle classes, and on Tlatelolco in
particular, stems from research in recently opened archives. The middle
classes emerge as a prominent theme in declassified documents in Mexico's
Department of Federal Security archive (Dirección Federal de Seguridad),
which contains thousands of government spy reports on the victims' movement.[12] These documents reveal as much about the state's perceptions and
worries as they do about the activities of groups deemed subversive.

This study argues that middle-class political discontent caused serious concern for the Party of the Institutional Revolution (Partido Revolucionario Institucional, or PRI), which governed Mexico for seventy-one
years until its defeat in the 2000 elections.[13] Of all the affected neighborhoods, the state worried most about the political fallout in middle-class
areas. Tlatelolco in particular generated a wealth of documents: government spies reported copiously on activities in the complex, and internal
government discussions after the earthquake focused disproportionately
on Tlatelolco. Drawing upon these documents, this article charts the
immediate aftermath of the earthquake and the political mobilization in
Tlatelolco, which reveals the importance of middle-class residents in the
victims' movement. It then analyzes this discontent in the context of the
economic crisis, a crisis so severe that the 1980s became known as the "lost
decade." It argues that this crisis provided important impetus for middle-
class residents to take to the streets. We will then turn to the concern that
these politicized middle classes inspired in the highest echelons of the PRI.
Indeed, internal discussions between the president (Miguel de la Madrid,
1982–1988); the head of Urban Planning (Guillermo Carrillo Arena,
replaced by Manuel Camacho Solís in February 1986); and the city's mayor
(Ramón Aguirre) concentrated on Tlatelolco and are documented in the

presidential archives. Concerns regarding political fallout in Tlatelolco, it appears, overshadowed their worry about discontent and mobilization in poor and working-class neighborhoods. Finally, this article concludes with a consideration of the significance of this middle-class story.

Tlatelolco, Mexico City, September 19, 1985

From parking space Z-650, at the corner of the Nuevo León building, I saw the tremor unleashed. . . . I saw as clear as day how the building fell over, but what can you do? Turn into Superman and stop it? My children were waiting for breakfast to go to school. . . . The first thing I thought was, "My children, my children, God of mine!" And the building came down, nothing but a screech, and when it hit the ground as if yanked out from the roots, it raised black smoke, really black smoke. . . . I sprinted like everyone, going to look for their family, their loved ones, their relatives, their acquaintances.

—Testimony of a Tlatelolco resident,
collected by Elena Poniatowska, *Nothing, Nobody*

For many, it began as a bombardment of sounds: the shrill shattering of glass; the rumble of crumbling cement as it hit the ground; the deep groan, "a sort of *boooooo*" of the earth moving; the unnatural moans of the buildings as they stretched beyond the limits of their established forms; then, a moment—seconds or minutes, no one is sure—of surreal silence, soon filled by the muffled voices of those trapped beneath the rubble and the desperate screams of their loved ones for help.[14] Within half an hour, hundreds of survivors in Tlatelolco organized a rescue effort. Thin young men squeezed through narrow passages, following voices to enclaves of open space; many lost their lives trying to save others. Doctors and nurses who lived in the complex set up makeshift medical stations. As the day progressed, residents from other areas of the city sent food and blankets. Volunteers worked for hours—ten, twelve, or more—without food or rest.[15]

Tlatelolco quickly emerged among the principal national and international symbols of the devastation. The Nuevo León building, thirteen stories tall, had toppled and lay on its side. In the first hours of the disaster, residents asked one another if the emergency services had been called because they did not hear the wail of ambulance sirens. There was no sign

Nuevo León fifteen-story reinforced concrete structure. Part of the building was only slightly damaged, while another part of it collapsed (IMAGE 21,
MEXICO CITY, 1985, U.S. GEOLOGICAL SURVEY PHOTOGRAPHIC LIBRARY).

of official rescue workers and residents dug through the rubble, directed
traffic, organized food distribution and made lists of the survivors and
the dead. Almost immediately, residents and volunteers clashed with the
state over the rescue work. Many residents accused the state of shirking its
responsibility. In the days after the earthquake, they took to the streets to
demand that the state help those still alive under the debris. Men, women,
and children wore placards in the city's main streets:

> Mr. President and functionaries [of Mexico City], help us.
> Our parents are trapped.
> My wife is trapped; I need help.[16]

Rescue workers in Tlatelolco complained that the state was impeding
their work. They told NBC news that they could hear voices calling from
under the fallen buildings, but that the machinery sent from the United
States was sitting in a custom's warehouse.[17] The state's handling of the
disaster frustrated foreign rescue brigades. An Israeli team complained,

"Up to now we haven't had a chance to use our air cushion that can lift up to 50 tons of concrete. . . . We're waiting to be coordinated. We're under the authority of Dr. Aries, but we haven't seen her. Do you know who Dr. Aries is?"[18] Little organization and a lack of information characterized the work: the city did not provide rescuers with blueprints of the buildings or maps of the area. While initial chaos might be expected in such an event, the incapacity of the state to organize the workers likely cost countless lives. A professor of architecture and a volunteer described the situation:

> Even after two or three days everyone was working chaotically, without any system. The desperation to save loved ones led to great inefficiency. I believe that the lack of coordination and organization made it impossible to save a great many people. There was even a lack of communication between soldiers and their captains. It's not for nothing that most countries have offices to deal with emergencies and people trained for such events.[19]

The city's Prevention of Disasters and Management of Risk Office had been closed the year before, in a round of budget cuts related to the austerity measures agreed on by the PRI and the IMF. In 1981 this office, as part of the Department of Urban Planning, had published a short document on the impact of strong earthquakes on Mexico City. It anticipated, nearly point-by-point, what actually happened on September 19, 1985. It also offered recommendations to avoid such a tragedy—none had been followed; instead, the government liquidated the office in 1984. As this became known, indignation ran high and residents demanded to know how this could have happened.[20]

The official emergency plan, "DN-3," became an infamously well-kept secret. No one knew what it contained or what the PRI's plans were for a disaster of that magnitude. Residents, opposition political parties, and civil associations demanded that the PRI make public the DN-3 plan, so that they might have a document against which to evaluate the actions of the military and police.[21] While soldiers had flooded into the capital city only hours after the disaster, they arrived bearing weapons instead of shovels and picks; instead of helping dig for survivors, they cordoned off the area and tried to prevent residents and volunteers from continuing their work.[22] At best, residents regarded the police, military, and state officials as onlookers; at worst, they viewed them as bullies and thieves who

Urbana Suárez Apartment Complex completely collapsed (IMAGE 21,
MEXICO CITY, 1985, U.S. GEOLOGICAL SURVEY PHOTOGRAPHIC LIBRARY).

sought to benefit from the tragedy.[23] Residents in the Colima building
in Tlatelolco reported soldiers stealing valuable goods from abandoned
apartments.[24] At certain points, city officials tried to force eviction of residents in Tlatelolco, stealing electronics and threatening them with physical disappearance (*desaparición física*).[25]

Scandals surrounded the state's initial handling of the disaster. Rumors
spread that the president, Miguel de la Madrid, had refused to accept foreign aid in an attempt to present a "good image of the state" to the international community, an illusory vision of a self-sufficient Mexican state able
to handle the disaster.[26] Victims resented the PRI's preoccupation with its
international image, but, with Mexico scheduled to host the 1986 World
Cup, the party needed to assure the international community and FIFA
(International Federation of Association Football) that the event would
proceed as planned. Indeed, it was rumored that one of de la Madrid's first
telephone calls on the morning of the earthquake was to the soccer association. Victims complained that the state worried more about the World
Cup than it did about them:

Bravo, Mr. President, we have the World Cup, but no housing for the victims![27]

When national and international aid poured into Mexico, victims accused the PRI of corruption and demanded more transparent distribution of the donations. They accused the officials in charge of siphoning the aid to PRI sycophants and members of the elite. For instance, it was reported that cheese sent by the Swiss government as part of an aid package—the highly coveted Swiss cheese—was being sold in Polanco, one of Mexico City's most exclusive neighborhoods, which was not located in the disaster zone.[28] Messages on banners at a protest on September 27 capture victims' gratitude to those who helped and their fury directed at the PRI:

> Mexican brothers, thank you.
> The children demand the foreign aid.
> Where is the national and international aid?
> The national and international aid is for the victims,
> not for government offices.[29]

"To the Chamber of Deputies!"

Faced with official recalcitrance, residents decided to take action. The PRI's mishandling of the disaster in the first crucial days and the perception that the president valued the respect of the international community over the respect and lives of his citizens provoked victims to demand change. Hundreds gathered in Tlatelolco's Plaza de las Tres Culturas to analyze the situation, and leaders argued that it was imperative to put pressure on the authorities.[30] Banners went up around the city. At first, they simply demanded help with digging and shelter; quickly, though, the breadth of their demands grew. Residents organized protests, calling upon citizens to come together: "Once again they want to stain Tlatelolco with blood; those who speak of reconstruction have their hands and pockets full! Thursday, the 26th, 11:00: To the Chamber of Deputies!"[31] Four days after the earthquake, the residents' organizations wrote a letter to architect Enrique Ortiz Flores, the head of the National Housing Fund (Fondo Nacional de Habitación Popular, or FONHAPO), one of the principal state agencies responsible for the complex:

We write to you with strong feelings of pain, rage, impotence, and uncertainty. Pain for our dead brothers; rage because this tragedy could have been avoided if the necessary preventative measures had been taken; impotence for not being able to rescue more survivors buried in the rubble; and uncertainty for the present and the future of our housing complex.

We are Tlatelolcas [residents of Tlatelolco]. We are proud to be Tlatelolcas and we will fight for our patrimony and our dignity, with the pain of our dead and the courage it inspires in us to move forward.[32]

Importantly, the earthquake hit after years of fighting between residents and the state agencies responsible for the complex. Residents had written letters to these agencies, detailing the poor maintenance of many buildings and requesting repairs. This history of struggle in Tlatelolco would prove fundamental to shaping the social movement that emerged after the earthquake. We will analyze this history by focusing on four primary demands that emerged after the disaster: first, punishment of those responsible for the shoddy construction and maintenance of the buildings, especially the Nuevo León; second, reconstruction in Tlatelolco, not another part of the city; third, indefinite suspension of the plan to change the property rights pertaining to the complex; and fourth, no decision about Tlatelolco be made without consulting the residents' organizations.[33] We will address each of these in turn.

To begin with, residents demanded an investigation into the collapse of the Nuevo León building. Since at least 1983 the state agencies had refused to repair the buildings, or when pressured, undertook only the most superficial repairs. "How much," residents asked, "is the cost of rementing the foundation of a building, compared to the lives of those who live in it?"[34] For example, by 1979 the Nuevo León building was leaning seventy centimeters. This exceeded the maximum allowed by city safety regulations: for a building of its height, the maximum horizontal inclination ought to have been thirty-two centimeters. By early 1982, the Nuevo León leaned over one hundred centimeters. In March of 1982 repair work reduced the inclination to eighty centimeters.[35] At one point during the bureaucratic back-and-forth regarding the safety of the Nuevo León building, one activist recalled that authorities had "displayed blueprints and sketches, using technical terms far beyond the reach of our understanding, telling us in sum that 'the Nuevo León is the safest building not [only] in Tlatelolco, but in Mexico City.'"[36]

The attitude of state functionaries exacerbated the frustration of residents. For example, on October 9, Carrillo Arena (the head of Urban Planning) claimed, "We still don't know why the Nuevo León fell. We must consider that many people modified their apartments and this could have altered the structural integrity of the building. We know who they are and we will proceed against them."[37] His insinuation that residents who may have taken down a wall in their apartment might have altered the structural integrity of the building inspired disbelief and fueled the anger of Tlatelolcas. Residents appeared on television and described a "collective psychosis of terror"; only a trustworthy inspection of the entire complex—by foreign technicians—could begin to calm the fear of further buildings collapsing.[38] This emphasis on foreign technicians reveals a profound distrust of the state.

Survivors accused city functionaries of criminal negligence in the construction of many of the fallen buildings. Of all the destroyed buildings, the majority were schools, hospitals, and housing units built by or for the state between 1950 and 1970.[39] Corruption in the construction industry had been a known problem. Before a project began, the contractor had to apply for a license and submit the architectural and structural plans. City authorities then filed these but rarely confirmed that the building had been built according to specifications; often contractors used lower-grade materials than those originally proposed. The seven-story Ministry of Labor building that fell during the earthquake offers one example of the disregard for safety standards: it had been built on a concrete base designed to hold only three stories.[40] Residents complained that there was no system in place to check this corruption and that without democratically elected officials, nepotism and incompetence riddled the system.[41] Until 1997, the president named the mayor of Mexico City, who in turn appointed his ministers.[42] These were the public officials responsible for approving building licenses and performing inspections. Residents demanded to know who would be held responsible for the fallen buildings: "If the government itself built many of these buildings, who would judge it?"[43]

In the weeks following the disaster, the victims' movement organized massive protests against the construction industry and the corruption in these state contracts; meantime, the state, engineers, and contractors closed ranks. They claimed that because there were so many parties involved in any given project, it was impossible to assign blame. A lawyer who lived in one of the hardest-hit neighborhoods complained that the rubble had been removed too quickly: "When should we assign blame? After the rubble has been removed? How can we look for proof of poor construction when there is a garden growing in every vacant lot?"[44] Indeed, lucrative demolition contracts had been awarded to powerful consortiums in the building industry that pressured for the demolitions to begin before proper surveys could be conducted to evaluate whether demolition was even necessary. Residents in Tlatelolco filed a complaint with the Federal Attorney's Office (Procuraduría General de la República), and an official investigation into the Nuevo León building was opened. However, many of the very men responsible for the construction of Tlatelolco were charged with the investigation.[45]

Secondly, residents in Tlatelolco—and in many of the affected neighborhoods—demanded that the state rebuild on the same site. Rumors flew around the city about the state's intentions for the affected areas. State plans to create more green spaces met with anger from residents: "Mr. Mayor, it was a brilliant idea to build gardens in the Roma; how about we build houses in your garden?"[46] In Tlatelolco, organizers complained that residents were being pressured to move and that the PRI intended to use the buildings for its own offices. Residents worried that the area would be converted into a tourism center, complete with casinos, and demanded immediate reconstruction of residential housing.[47] Residents did not want to leave; their attachment was emotional and their protests reveal a strong sense of place: "We are Tlatelolcas, we are proud to be Tlatelolcas, and we want to stay in Tlatelolco."[48] They also had economic motivation to stay: Tlatelolco was centrally located and well connected to the city's public transportation. Had residents been forced to move—likely to the outskirts—their cost of living would have increased.[49] Residents sent telegrams to the president, trying to move him with personal pleas: "I am a pensioner. Minimal resources. Supporting my family. Asking you respectfully for your intervention. Rebuild Tlatelolco on the same site."[50]

The third demand involved a debate over property rights (*régimen de propiedad*) in the complex. The earthquake struck during a prolonged battle between residents and the National Housing Fund. For several years, the Housing Fund had been trying to force a change in property rights that would convert the buildings into condominiums. This violated the spirit of the original contracts, which were meant to be nontransferable and nonnegotiable for ninety-nine years.[51] Under these contracts, residents did not own the apartments; they owned certificates of real estate participation with an array of government agencies. According to the contracts, these agencies were responsible for the maintenance and upkeep of the buildings. The proposed change in property rights would place the burden of maintenance upon residents. It would also introduce the complex into the housing market.[52]

Although faced with intimidation, campaigns of misinformation, and sometimes blackmail, many residents had refused to consider the proposal until the National Housing Fund undertook the needed repairs. The agency had delayed and tried to make the change in property rights a precondition for repairs. This bureaucratic wrangling went on for years. In the last round before the earthquake, the director of the Housing Fund promised concrete replies to residents' demands by September 15, 1985. On September 18, residents were still awaiting his reply and on the morning of the 19th it became evident why the Housing Fund wanted out.[53]

In the months before the earthquake, residents of the Nuevo León building had hung a large banner on an outside wall of their building, calling upon the Housing Fund to maintain the minimum safety requirements: "Residents of the Nuevo León building are in danger because FONHAPO is not maintaining the control panels."[54] Tlatelolcas recalled this history with bitterness and fury, and wrote that if earthquakes were not predictable, it could well be predicted that buildings with poor foundations would fare poorly in such an event. One resident of the Nuevo León building, Jorge Coo, wrote that "In total, FONHAPO saved—*saved?*— 21 million pesos; 472 residents died and over 156 were disappeared, who for us are also dead."[55] In the aftermath of the disaster, when the state tried to force the change in property rights as a condition of reconstruction, rage exploded in Tlatelolco.[56] With their letters unanswered and their demands unmet, the nature of protest changed and Tlatelolcas took to the streets.

Finally, residents demanded to be consulted on every decision regarding reconstruction. Here, we will analyze the structure and strategies of the protest movement, which demonstrates how quickly the initial outpouring of rage became organized into a formidable force that challenged the status quo of urban politics. Residents did not channel their demands through the PRI's standard procedures. Instead, they formed powerful organizations outside the party and demanded to negotiate the terms of reconstruction with the PRI. In Tlatelolco most buildings had committees and there were several complex-wide groups, joined together under the Front of Tlatelolco Victims. The PRI claimed that activists did not enjoy majority support in the complex and accused leaders of agitating among residents. It is difficult to determine the degree of support for activist groups in Tlatelolco; they themselves admitted they did not have "overwhelming" support. They described an ongoing battle against apathy and conservative and conformist tendencies.[57] Indeed, the fight was scattered and complicated. Many buildings had not been damaged and resisted joining the political activism; some building leaders signed agreements with the state, only to have them challenged by residents. Accusations of intimidation abounded.[58]

In mid-October, these Tlatelolco groups united with other organizations to form the CUD (Overall Coordinating Committee of Disaster Victims). Based in Tlatelolco, many residents from the complex held prominent positions in this umbrella organization, which incorporated organizations from other neighborhoods as well as other specific groups, such as garment and hospital workers whose workplaces had been destroyed.[59] Each group continued to work toward its particular goals: the garment workers successfully organized for recognition of their union, and the poorer neighborhoods won a historical expropriation decree in which the state took control of thousands of abandoned or empty lots to further the interests of public housing. These groups coordinated their efforts to express solidarity with one another and apply maximum pressure on the state. Although residents from all of the affected areas worked together, class tensions emerged between different groups of victims. One leader from Tlatelolco described how the CUD had emerged because the media-savvy protest in Tlatelolco, which harnessed the national and international press to further its cause, impressed the victims' organizations in other neighborhoods.[60] In contrast, residents of the poor and working-class Tepito and Morelos neighborhoods resented the media coverage of the disaster, which focused almost exclusively on the luxury Regis Hotel and the middle-class neighborhoods of Roma and Tlatelolco. They claimed the media had forgotten the victims from the marginal classes.[61]

Cross-class alliances in the CUD were often difficult; some residents of Tlatelolco considered themselves not just middle class but upper middle class, and they disdained the notion of working alongside residents from lower classes. Indeed, class tensions emerged within Tlatelolco as victims who lived (either as subletters or squatters) in the service rooms on the rooftops of the buildings had to fight to be considered victims and Tlatelolcas.[62] Many of the poorer neighborhoods had strong traditions of urban protest that predated the earthquake, which compounded their resentment of Tlatelolco's emergence as a national and international symbol of the devastation. In turn, Tlatelolcas claimed that their case was unique, due to its long-documented, bureaucratic history. This distinguished them from the extensive history of urban protest in proletarian neighborhoods, and they often identified as middle class with a sense of pride and entitlement.[63]

Leaders of the movement often came from the ranks of the middle classes (many had a degree from the National Autonomous University of Mexico, or UNAM) and many had experience in urban protest before the earthquake. A large number had participated in the student movement of the 1960s, and some ex–student leaders organized in poor and working-class neighborhoods during the 1970s and 1980s. They later appeared as activists after the earthquake.[64] In addition, organizers from a wide array of political parties appeared on the ground in Tlatelolco in the first few hours after the disaster, helping with the rescue work. This earned them respect in the eyes of many residents and indeed some of the political leaders were themselves residents of the complex. This legitimacy, combined with their experience in political organizing and access to the necessary equipment (most residents did not own mimeographs or loud-speakers), led to the participation of many leftist opposition parties in the protest movement.[65]

After the earthquake the experience of these leaders, combined with the history of bureaucratic protest in Tlatelolco, helped shape a powerful culture of political protest that transformed the victims' movement into an organized and formidable force in urban politics. The middle classes, and especially Tlatelolco residents, provided much of the drive behind this movement. Tactics included banners, newsletters, flyers, open-air meetings, marches to the presidential residence of Los Pinos, demonstrations that reclaimed historic sites such as the Angel of Independence monument, and interventions in the Chamber of Deputies.[66] Local artists proposed street theater and artistic festivals, and although initially received with scepticism by activists, these events became an important channel of protest and release.[67] As the weeks passed and their demands were still not addressed, residents' ideas for protest became more radical, such as a possible hunger strike by housewives, with leftist political parties as observers.[68]

Why did Tlatelolco, among all the devastated areas, become a nucleus of protest? And why did a natural disaster spark such a strong protest movement? The initial participation of middle-class residents in the protest movement could be largely attributed to the randomness and vehemence with which the earthquake devastated the neighborhood. The history of struggle between Tlatelolco residents and state agencies such as the Housing Fund helps to explain the specific demands that emerged in the complex. But it does not explain why the movement quickly embraced issues beyond specific concerns related to reconstruction and began to call for economic reforms. Nor does it entirely explain the massive outpouring of middle-class discontent. After all, many of the points of contention, such as scandals around corruption in the construction industry, had been known for some time. To better understand the motivations of the middle-class protestors, we must consider the contemporaneous economic crisis that set the stage for widespread discontent.

Middle-Class Fears and Economic Crisis

The earthquake acted as a catalyst for middle-class discontent—it provoked, increased, and sped it up. The natural disaster struck during the worst economic crisis Mexico had experienced in decades. Following the 1982 oil shock, economic growth had slowed to a standstill; inflation spiraled out of control; and Mexico faced a balance-of-payments crisis.[69] The urban middle classes felt the brunt of this economic crisis; with declining real wages they could no longer afford to maintain their lifestyles and consumption patterns.[70] Indeed, in her celebrated account of the tremors' immediate aftermath, Poniatowska writes, "The Plaza de las Tres Culturas [in Tlatelolco] is a battlefield. . . . Broken television sets, sewing machines, typewriters, canned goods, tablecloths, sheets, and mattresses form small pyramids."[71] These material goods of middle-class lives represented decades of economic growth and prosperity; but this growth had slowed during the 1970s and come to an abrupt stop in 1982, when Mexico inaugurated the Latin American debt crisis. This economic crisis helps explain the emergence of middle-class protest after the earthquake.

The economic crisis hit the middle classes particularly hard and their

Damaged upper floors of the Lacsa building (IMAGE 27, MEXICO CITY, 1985, U.S. GEOLOGICAL SURVEY PHOTOGRAPHIC LIBRARY).

lifestyles changed drastically.[72] Until the crisis, the Mexico City middle classes—especially the public employees, university professors, and doctors living in Tlatelolco—had benefited from decades of economic expansion and enjoyed a lifestyle that included job security, upward mobility, and varying levels of luxury consumption.[73] This changed with the debt crisis and subsequent high inflation rates, peso devaluation, and salary cuts. According to sociologist Diane Davis, the middle classes began "to feel the pinch in several critical areas of urban consumption . . . including the rising cost of luxury imports, a scarcity of affordable housing, steep increases in gas prices, and cutbacks in expenditures on education, including up to 100 percent increases in the costs of private education."[74]

In his study of the middle classes during the economic crisis of the early 1980s, anthropologist and historian Claudio Lomnitz contends that the middle classes became embarrassed to admit their dreams of upward mobility and vacations abroad—but they still held onto these dreams. Lack of access to credit was perhaps the most difficult change for the middle classes; they needed it to imagine a better future for themselves.[75] The short-term effects of the crisis combined with a fear that changes in Mexico's economic development model might render permanent these circumstances. As Lomnitz describes, "During the 1980s . . . the great rift between free trade and national economy, between pro- and anti-globalisation, affected national identity, with parties struggling either to monopolise or to retain their claim on national identity."[76]

When he took office in December 1982, President Miguel de la Madrid had faced an unenviable situation: crippling foreign debt and no way to pay it.[77] His administration struck a deal with the IMF, a "shock treatment" of fiscal austerity that cut wages and government spending. In turn, Mexico received further financing and its foreign debt payments were rescheduled. However, by mid-1985, Mexico had failed to meet the agreed-on targets and faced another balance-of-payments crisis, whereupon the IMF suspended funding. When the earthquake struck, debates raged over Mexico's economic development, and the natural disaster provided an opportunity for the different sides to fortify their positions. The victims' movement entered these debates as it became stronger and better organized: demands moved beyond immediate concerns such as rescue work and shelter, and beyond urban issues such as housing, property rights, and indemnification payments. Residents clamored for a say in the country's political economy. Indeed, reconstruction necessarily raised questions about the country's economic development. Among the most contested issues was the future of Mexico's foreign debt: some challenged the policies of the de la Madrid administration and called for a moratorium on the foreign debt; others argued for further austerity measures.

Before the earthquake, a panoply of political parties and social organizations had been calling for a renegotiation of the debt, arguing that austerity measures had made life unbearable for most Mexicans. The economic effects of the earthquake worsened the state of public finances. The estimated cost reached US$4 billion, equivalent to 11 percent of the government's spending budget for 1985.[78] Anger boiled up against groups of industrialists who worked against any possibility of a moratorium. "Wouldn't it be better," asked one activist, "if these industrialists—servants and representatives of foreign capital—stopped thinking of their foreign masters and instead thought for a moment of their brothers and joined the widespread demand for a one-year moratorium?"[79] Speaking of economic planning, activists argued, "If we do not have the capacity to change while facing a catastrophe of this magnitude, then we do not have the moral capacity to survive as a nation."[80]

The earthquake allowed activists to draw connections across Latin America. Leftist activists referred to the example of Managua, Nicaragua, where an earthquake played a role in the triumph of the Sandinista revolution. Activists argued that, should the state not address their demands, they might organize on all levels and spark a social revolution similar to Nicaragua's.[81] Indeed, the earthquake hit as debates over foreign debt raged across the continent. In September 1985, Cuba hosted an international conference on the foreign debt and Fidel Castro called on Latin American countries to go on strike against its payment.[82] On October 23, 1985—the International Day against Debt—the victims' movement led a march of ten thousand residents from the statue of the Angel of Independence to the presidential residence in Los Pinos. The placards and banners in this march demonstrate the escalating frustration and rage:

First Nicaragua, then El Salvador, Liberation for Latin America.
Tlatelolco, we love you and will defend you.
Moratorium on debt payment.
Death to Carrillo Arena.
Miguel de la Madrid, surrounded by corrupt rats.
Miguel de la Madrid, you don't have the pants to make decisions.[83]

The expansion of demands from immediate concerns to include economic reforms reveals residents' worries about Mexico's changing political
economy. The economic crisis gives context to the middle-class political
mobilization after the earthquake. The wells of discontent went deep and
one of the victims' oft-repeated demands was for an intangible dignity
(*dignidad*). The political mobilization tapped into this discontent. The scandals that emerged after the earthquake appeared in the context of an economic crisis that had eroded decades of middle-class hopes and dreams.

Official Neurosis

The PRI feared that the economic crisis had generated an explosive atmo-
sphere in which it would be easy to spark, in its words, "one of the worst
social situations."[84] The PRI understood that there was much at stake and
monitored the political protest closely, desperate to counteract any support
the natural disaster might have generated for its opposition among the
middle classes.[85] The PRI's concern over middle-class discontent must be
understood in the context of recent history. Mexico City's middle classes
had thrived in the economic boom from the 1940s to the 1970s and, until
the late 1960s, largely upheld the PRI's one-party rule. During these
decades, the PRI had maintained its rule through a combination of repression and co-optation. Some sectors of society, such as railway workers or
peasant activists, had experienced firsthand the repression upon which
the party's rule depended.[86] Mexico City's middle classes, however, had a
mutually beneficial working consensus with the PRI, based largely upon
economic prosperity.[87]

In the late sixties, a countercultural movement emerged in the capital
and other cities; middle-class and aspiring middle-class students began to
challenge the authoritarian nature of the PRI regime. The party responded
to this challenge with repression, and on October 2, 1968, the state gunned
down hundreds of students at a peaceful meeting in the Plaza de las Tres
Culturas in the Tlatelolco apartment complex.[88] Many scholars and public
intellectuals point to this as a moment of rupture of the working consensus between the PRI and the middle classes, a consensus that had never
been complete or permanent. After continued repression and, some would
argue, successful co-optation of the student movement, 1985 stands out as
a moment when thousands of protestors, many from the middle classes,
marched through Mexico City's streets to challenge the PRI.

In a meeting with the president, the head of Urban Planning, Manuel Camacho Solís, acknowledged that activists had successfully generated an image of political incapacity, authoritarianism, and abuse on part of the state, an image linked to symbols such as the 1968 student massacre.[89] Nearly six months after the earthquake, he remained worried about the political ramifications in Tlatelolco. Camacho Solís perceived three main areas of contention: first, the accusations that building representatives had signed illegal contracts with the state regarding the change in property rights; second, disagreement over inspections; and third, the attorney general's investigation into responsibility for the collapse of the Nuevo León building. De la Madrid and Camacho Solís hoped to address the first two issues with a program of democratic reconstruction. This involved a clear definition of reconstruction as a service to the community, a campaign to counteract the rumors that the government had other uses for the buildings and land, and resident participation and supervision of the program. It also created a high-level technical committee to address disagreements over the inspections, including members of the faculties of architecture and engineering at UNAM, representatives from the construction industry, and internationally renowned leftist urbanists.[90]

Regarding the official investigation into responsibility for the Nuevo León building, the president and his highest advisors wanted to do the minimum, as quietly as possible, to comply with their duty. In the attorney general's report, they were willing to admit civil responsibility, not crime. Camacho Solís and the president worried about political fallout upon the release of the report in May 1986, fearing that activists—especially women—would succeed in converting the issue into a referendum on the government and the PRI's very legitimacy, a referendum they feared they would lose. Thus, they sought to prevent the Nuevo León building from becoming a glaring symbol of official corruption and ineptitude. Camacho Solís suggested to the president that they scapegoat one of the engineers who had made technical mistakes in the repairs to the building's cement foundations. Beyond that, the official position should be that there were too many entities and people involved to assign blame, including residents who had been unwilling to pay a minimal amount for the maintenance of their building.[91]

The state also sought to reach out to residents and reestablish on-the-ground legitimacy. In another meeting, Camacho Solís and de la Madrid considered which residents of Tlatelolco would be best suited to represent the state within the complex; their criteria included neighbors who were generally regarded as honest, without close ties to the state, and who did not look down on people of less education.[92] Their desire for such representatives betrayed their awareness that residents commonly met with corrupt and arrogant party cronies in their day-to-day dealings with the state. In a similar fashion, the PRI functionaries attempted to control the victims' movement. They created brigades of youth, but their vision was bureaucratic, top-down and, antidemocratic, illustrated in the programs they conceived.[93] One of the reconstruction subcommittees proposed a program called "organized civil solidarity" to give coherent form and content to all levels of social mobilization and to be run through neighborhood and building committees, the city's boroughs (*delegaciones*), schools, unions, political parties, universities, businesses, and religious organizations. Their desire to control "civil solidarity" reveals their perception that they had already lost control of it.[94]

The state also used tactics of intimidation and repression when dealing with the victims' movement. Leaders were kidnapped. Tlatelolco was under surveillance as unmarked Dodge Darts drove through the complex. Officials attempted to discredit leaders by accusing them of drinking and taking drugs in the parking lots of the complex. Leaders were also accused of dealing in arms, thereby laying the groundwork for a more widespread, violent repression. Indeed, before the movement's protest marches, the state routinely spread rumors that the activists were armed.[95]

Why did Tlatelolco worry the state so much? No doubt, the government worried about the shift in middle-class protest from writing letters to marching in the streets. In a group interview two months after the earthquake, prominent political organizers in Tlatelolco told how, for the first time, wide sectors of the middle classes were suffering from the government's policy of pressure and coercion. For middle-class residents, the mobilization became "a political school of the highest order."[96] While members of this class might have been involved in urban social movements before the earthquake, it was often as leaders or organizers. After the earthquake, throngs of middle-class residents in the rank-and-file of a protest movement marked a significant change in the city's history of urban protest. For the first time since the late 1960s, large numbers of middle-class residents took to the streets to demand change. Speaking with activists, Camacho Solís admitted that Tlatelolco was the state's priority because of the noisy and troublemaking (*escandalosa*) middle classes.[97] Residents still penned bureaucratic letters to government agencies, but they were now also marching in the streets and contemplating hunger strikes by housewives.

Less than a year after the earthquake, the PRI developed a program entitled Project Middle Classes, designed to regain their support. PRI officials believed the middle classes were "demonstrating their repudiation or disagreement with the political system." The goal of the project was to better identify this elusive class and strengthen its connections with the party. In the project's founding document, the PRI asks itself, "What is their [the middle classes'] attitude toward the Mexican Revolution, the government and the PRI?"[98]

The PRI worried intensely about the political straying of the middle classes and connected it directly to declining economic conditions. Project Middle Classes depicts them as particularly sensitive to any change that might alter their expectations of upward mobility or force them to modify their lifestyles. In conditions of economic crisis, the document argues, the middle classes are the ones who manifest most quickly and acutely a greater sensation of insecurity and anguish, which aggravates levels of "malaise, irritation, [and] social inconformity, and propitiates authoritarian attitudes." From the state's point of view, these "pessimistic" attitudes manifest in a lack of confidence, indifference, or even frank rejection of official policies and programs. In this context, the PRI considered it of utmost importance to acquire information on the socioeconomic changes that affect the middle classes:

> To what extent has the real quality of life of the middle classes deteriorated? . . . Are they becoming proletarianized? . . . How intense is their malaise in any given moment? What do they perceive to be the causes of their discontent? What are their expectations and fears? . . . And, more than anything: WHAT WILL BE THE LONG TERM EFFECTS OF THESE PHENOMENA ON THE SOCIAL DYNAMICS OF THE MIDDLE CLASSES?[99]

The objective of Project Middle Classes was to provide a profound diagnostic of the middle classes, which would serve as the basis for a series of political, economic, and social actions:

> What should be their link to the party in power? What should a government policy for them look like? How could the social

communication with the middle classes be improved? What alternatives can be offered them that would change their view of the
economic crisis?

The rapidly changing economic structure provided the imperative for this
project. The state foresaw that its economic readjustment programs would
continue at a rapid pace through the end of the de la Madrid presidency
in 1988—and indeed through the end of the century—and anticipated
that the accompanying changes in social and political structures would
generate dangerous tensions among the middle classes. The state needed
trustworthy data on this class. The sense of urgency conveyed by these
strings of questions, and the document as a whole, suggests that the state
felt a keen sense of estrangement from its archetypal social class. This
desperation to apprehend, woo, and control the middle classes betrays the
self-perceived vulnerability of the state as well as the power it accorded to
the middle classes.[100]

A Reckoning

While the middle-class mobilization was center stage in the eyes of the
state, it is largely absent from analyses of the earthquake and its aftermath.
The dearth of scholarly attention to middle-class protest has resulted in a
static and unchanging vision of the political cultures and strategies of the
city's higher-income sectors. The historical experience that emerges from
the archives is strikingly different: the politicized, middle-class multitude
that marched through the city streets marked a profound change in urban
politics; it certainly captured the PRI's attention. Before the earthquake
these residents had lobbied the state to address their interests but had
normally restricted themselves to standard, bureaucratic channels.[101] The
economic crisis set the stage for widespread middle-class participation in
the protest movement. Had the earthquake struck ten or twenty years earlier, it would likely not have generated such a fierce outcry.[102]

Much of the scholarship on the earthquake has focused on poor and
working-class neighborhoods. While helpful in illuminating the history
of urban protest in these areas, these studies do not explain middle-class
protest; indeed, little importance is attributed it. This is due to the dominant place of the poor and the working class in social movement studies.
Many scholars state that their aim is to study the urban poor because they

are largely absent from the literature. But it is actually quite the contrary—the urban poor dominate scholarship on the urban history of Mexico City. This lopsidedness in the literature flattens the historical experience, and our understanding, of the Mexico City middle classes. For example, in her study of the victims' movement in the Centro neighborhood, sociologist Susan Eckstein casts the middle-class participants and leaders of the CUD as a foil for the poor and working-class residents of the Centro. Poor residents, she claims, saw the CUD "as primarily a middle-class organization whose concerns differed from theirs." While this may well have been the case, and helps to tease out nuances in the political strategies of poorer residents, this reading leads to a one-dimensional vision of middle-class political culture:

> The middle-class *damnificados* [victims] who dominated the CUD lived in high-rise condominium apartments. Many of them had property title problems and no strong commitment to their place of residence. By contrast, the people of El Centro were tenants in rent-controlled buildings and had strong ties to their community.[103]

The repeated invocations of Tlatelolco as an emotional and historically charged site in the protest previously discussed ("We are Tlatelolcas, we are proud to be Tlatelolcas, and we want to stay in Tlatelolco") belies Eckstein's depiction and underscores the strong sense of place that pervaded middle-class demands.[104]

This chapter has offered a recuperation of the middle classes. This adds nuance to narratives of recent Mexican history, which attribute a prominent place to the earthquake and its aftermath. Indeed, these events have been marshaled to chart the history of civil society and the transition to democracy in Mexico. Scholars argue that the natural disaster augured a new form of urban politics in the capital city. Writing in the immediate aftermath of the shocks, some of Mexico's most prominent public intellectuals described the victims' movement as nothing less that the spontaneous "birth of civil society." Carlos Monsiváis is perhaps the best-known proponent of this interpretation:

> Civil society exists, as a latent necessity, in those who don't even know the expression. Its first and most insistent demand is the

redistribution of power. . . . On the 19th [of September] and in response to the earthquake victims, Mexico City experienced a taking of powers of the noblest kind in its history. It transcended the limits of mere solidarity and converted the people into government and official chaos into civil order.[105]

What was most alive in Mexico City was the presence of a new social actor whose more appropriate name is "civil society."[106]

Elena Poniatowska, chronicler of the earthquake, also evokes the "birth of a civil society":

In many of us, the earthquake gave birth to a desire to participate responsibly in permanent brigades, to systematize our efforts, to create a national network of volunteers. Let the enthusiasm of all the señoras who distributed thousands of meals every day not be lost. Let the bags of food and clothing be accompanied by a will to know each other, the will to build a strong civil society that will know how to overcome the inept and corrupt government, a society that can say with Carlos Monsiváis: democracy is the sudden importance of each individual.[107]

Nevertheless, in the aftermath of the earthquake many contested the "civil society" narrative. Some argued that the so-called social movement was a natural response to crisis: residents simply did what they had to do. Others adopted a more moderate stance, emphasizing that the earthquake opened a space in Mexican political culture that offered the potential for change, that Mexican society had been infused with hope for the future, that a new horizon had opened. This debate raged in the daily newspapers, as public intellectuals and scholars tried to make sense of the disaster and perhaps discern a silver lining amid the rubble.[108] Another, perhaps more lasting, popular interpretation of the victims' movement holds it as the origins of democracy in Mexico. To understand this, we must return to the story of the protest movement, to the resolution of the conflict between victims and the state and the future of the victims' organizations. On May 13, 1986, after prolonged and escalating confrontation, as well as strained negotiations, the state and the victims' organizations signed the Pact of Democratic Agreement on Reconstruction (Convenio de Concertación Democrática para la Reconstrucción). The secretary of Urban Planning, the city government, and the official reconstruction organization, Renovation for Popular Housing (Renovación Habitacional Popular), represented the state. The CUD and many of the major victims' organizations—but not all—signed the pact. University institutes, technical groups, various business chambers, and an array of foundations and civil associations, all involved in reconstruction, also signed the accord. The pact was announced to great fanfare at a press conference in which representatives of these diverse organizations testified to their support. At its core, the pact guaranteed the democratic participation of victims' organizations in the reconstruction process. It emphasized transparency in the distribution of funds, prioritized the needs of victims for safe and affordable shelter, and underscored the importance of maintaining urban cultures and lifestyles. Sociologist Susan Eckstein argues that the process of negotiation and consensus that generated the pact ushered in a new type of conflict resolution in Mexico, one that emanated from below as well as above.

What was won and what was lost? In some ways, everyone won something. The pact was intended to complement other agreements between the state and specific neighborhoods or groups, and there was a separate decree for reconstruction in Tlatelolco. Residents and the state agreed on which buildings would be demolished, those that needed repairs, and the schedule for reconstruction, with the state bearing all costs. The change in property regime would not be a condition for reconstruction.[109] Residents, then, won a seat at the decision-making table.

However, the buildings that had signed contracts with the National Housing Fund agreeing to a change in property regime would receive information manuals that purported to teach residents how to live under the Regime of Property in Condominium (Régimen de Propiedad en Condominio). These didactic manuals explained how to properly maintain and administrate the units. One comprehensive illustrated manual emphasized that residents should be respectful of neighbors and not make much noise. It was perfectly clear that, in these buildings, residents would be responsible for all maintenance and that everyone would have to pay a monthly upkeep fee.[110] Further, with the exception of certain buildings in Tlatelolco, most of the housing built in the reconstruction program fell under the new property regime, and the state emphasised that residents would be responsible for all maintenance, after the expiry of a six-month guarantee against structural deficiencies.[111] In this way, the state also emerged victorious.

What was lost? While residents had mobilized successfully for concrete issues surrounding housing, reconstruction, and urban services, no clear victors emerged on matters such as urban democratic representation and economic planning. The victims' movement had raised questions about urban democracy and challenged the state's economic development strategies. Nevertheless, instead of granting Mexico City's residents the right to elect their mayor, the state established an elected Representative Assembly (Asamblea de Representantes) that had no legislative power. On the economic front, Mexico did not lead Latin America to defy international creditors. Just as some victories might have been illusory; likewise, it may be counterproductive to interpret the lack of success on issues such as democracy and economic development as failures. The impact of such "failures" could indeed signify more profound accomplishments. The most profound reverberation of the earthquake may be that it opened the space for debate of these issues and brought a wider array of citizens into the debate.

While there is no precise date on which the CUD dissolved, it had largely achieved its goal as the victims began to receive their new homes and the reconstruction programs neared completion.[112] However, as some victims gained their housing, others remained in need. Some were earthquake victims who had fled the city, but many were urban residents who had needed housing before the earthquake, who were, in a sense, permanent victims. These victims approached the CUD and neighborhood organizations for advice and help. Just when some organizers thought they had won the battle, they were obliged to begin another fight.[113]

After much deliberation, a group of organizers from the CUD formed the Assembly of Barrios (Asamblea de Barrios) to address the concerns of the urban poor and the general problem of housing in Mexico City. When opposition candidate Cuauhtémoc Cárdenas lost the 1988 presidential elections amid denunciations of electoral fraud (the computers counting votes "went down" for several crucial hours), the Assembly of Barrios threw its support behind him:

> *The narrative that we began to invent* was that [19]85 was the outburst of citizen participation, the breaking of all the mechanisms of control in the city, and that 1988 was its political expression. You could not explain 1988 without 1985. . . . [P]eople had experienced autonomous political participation on the margins of the PRI's structures. . . . [T]hey had already won outside the PRI's schema.[114]

The former members of the CUD and leaders of the Assembly of Barrios assumed this representation (*"nos abrogamos esa representación"*) and brought it to the Cardenista movement. Importantly, the Cardenista movement and the controversial 1988 elections are generally regarded as the beginning of Mexico's transition to democracy. In this way, then, the CUD activists created a pervasive origins story of Mexico's democratic transition.

Conclusion

Enough to blast open the continuum of history.
—Walter Benjamin, "Philosophy of History"

In his study on earthquakes in Ancien Régime France, historian Grégory Quenet argues that natural disasters are historically constructed events, constituted not outside of history but in fact by scientific, religious, and political forces and by society's *imaginaire*. The physical characteristics of a natural disaster are not sufficient to transform it into a historical event. Earthquakes are, he argues, defined by intellectuals, managed by governments, remarked on by religious leaders, contextualized by writers, and mobilized by different social groups to advance their interests.[115]

The Mexico City earthquake offers a rare glimpse into historical processes. When it sheared open the city's fault lines, it threw the system into shock, and power relations became visible; it was, to borrow Walter Benjamin's words, "enough to blast open the continuum of history."[116] From the debris, the history of the disaster—the discursive event—emerged. Participants and leaders of poor and working-class neighborhood organizations, and scholars interested in the history of these movements, cast the earthquake as an organizing event in poor and working-class political mobilization. For others, it signified the birth of a so-called civil society or served as an origins story of democracy in Mexico. The earthquake has been marshaled to tell particular stories and this process—this transformation of a natural disaster into a discursive event—has obfuscated the middle-class story told here.

This middle-class story is lodged in both the Department of Federal Security and the presidential archives. In these documents another story of the earthquake, another discursive event, emerges. Residents of Tlatelolco experienced the incapacity, and even unwillingness, of the state to resolve their problems. The state perceived a threat emanating from the middle classes and faced that challenge with anxiety, dread, and fear; in this threat, the state saw the unraveling of its official Revolutionary project among its archetypal social group, the middle classes. The earthquake proved a formidable test for the state and its institutions. The state had failed specific groups many times before, but on September 19, 1985, its failure lay exposed on the streets of the nation's capital, undeniable to even the most casual observer.

Whatever remained on the eve of the earthquake of the mid-century consensus between the state and Mexico City's middle classes had vanished. In June 1986, at the opening ceremonies of the World Cup in Mexico City's Azteca Stadium, as President Miguel de la Madrid stepped out to greet the crowd, the entire stadium—over 110,000 middle- and upper-class fans—lustily booed their president in front of the whole world.

⊹ NOTES ⊹

1. The first earthquake measured 8.1 on the Richter scale; the second registered at 7.3. For stylistic reasons and following the practice of many writers, I conceptualize these two earthquakes as one event.

2. "Información del DDF," September 19, 1985, exp. s/n, 30.00.00.00, c. 1, Dirección General de Difusión y Relaciones Públicas, Departamento del Distrito Federal (hereafter DDF), Miguel de la Madrid Hurtado (hereafter MMH), Archivo General de la Nación (hereafter AGN), Mexico City.

3. Raúl Macín A., "Una lectura del apocalipsis," *Los Universitarios*, December 1985, exp. 11, 32.06.01.00, c. 7, MMH, AGN.

4. "Ciudadano," September 22, 1985, Dirección Federal de Seguridad (hereafter DFS) 009-031-003, AGN, 1-6.

5. Elena Poniatowska, *Nothing, Nobody: The Voices of the Mexico City Earthquake* (Philadelphia: Temple University Press, 1995), 11.

6. "Situación que prevalece en la Col. Morelos y zonas aledañas, respecto al movimiento telúrico ocurrido hoy," September 19, 1985, DFS 009-031-003, AGN, 1-5; "Situación que prevalece con motivo de los movimientos telúricos," September 23, 1985, DFS 009-031-003, AGN, 1-6.

7. "Victim" is a translation of the Spanish word *damnificado*, which is used to describe the earthquake victims. This is an imperfect translation because the Spanish word does not imply victimization, as its English equivalent

does. This is an important distinction: by referring to residents as "victims" this article does not mean to imply that they were victimized. Instead, it documents the agency and empowerment of so-called victims.

8. While many authors point to the participation of middle-class residents and to the unique multiclass alliances that emerged in the victim movement, they have not studied the reasons that drove these residents to march in protest through the city's streets. See, for example, Ligia Tavera-Fenollosa, "Social Movements and Civil Society: The Mexico City 1985 Earthquake Victim Movement" (PhD diss., Yale University, 1998), 95. Most scholarship on the earthquake has been based on the many firsthand accounts of the earthquake, such as observations and analysis by contemporary commentators and testimonies of survivors, volunteers, and activists. Scholars often complement these sources with scientific reports and interviews with government actors and participants in the social movement. For testimonies and contemporary analyses see, for example, Poniatowska, *Nothing, Nobody*; Carlos Monsiváis, *Entrada libre: crónicas de la sociedad que se organiza* (Mexico City: Era, 1987); Francisco J. Núñez de la Peña and Jesús Orozco, *El terremoto: una versión corregida* (Guadalajara: ITESO, 1988); Adolfo Aguilar Zinser, Cesáreo Morales, and Rodolfo F. Peña, *Aún tiembla: sociedad política y cambio social; el terremoto del 19 de septiembre de 1985* (Mexico City: Grijalbo, 1987); and Leslíe Serna and Coordinadora Única de Damnificados [hereafter CUD], *¡Aquí nos quedaremos! Testimonios de la Coordinadora Única de Damnificados: entrevistas* (Mexico City: Universidad Iberoamericana, 1995). For social science analyses of housing, health, and employment issues following the earthquake see, for example, Diane E. Davis, "Reverberations: Mexico City's 1985 Earthquake and the Transformation of the Capital," in *The Resilient City: How Modern Cities Recover from Disaster*, ed. Lawrence J. Vale and Thomas J. Campanella (Oxford: Oxford University Press, 2005), and articles in *Estudios Demográficos y Urbanos* 2, no. 1 (1987). This chapter builds on all of these works and especially on Jorge Coo's discussion of the Nuevo León building in Tlatelolco. "Después de la caída" in Aguilar Zinser, Morales, and Peña, *Aún tiembla*, 39–54.

9. It must be emphasized that because of high levels of poverty and inequality in Mexico, the term *middle class* does not describe those in the middle of the income distribution; rather, the middle classes reside in the top deciles, between the poor majority and an extremely small, wealthy minority.

10. Edward Palmer Thompson, *The Making of the English Working Class* (New York: Vintage, 1963), 9–14. The conceptualization of the middle classes in this chapter is further inspired by historian Robert D. Johnston's call for an "anti-definition." This chapter uses a panoply of criteria to speak of the this class: "To examine middling folks as they have constituted (or not constituted)

a class *over time* requires giving up the illusion that sociological abstraction can aid us much beyond providing interesting ideas to reflect upon and use in a highly flexible manner. We must therefore blend together an eclectic mix of occupation and ideology, gender and culture, property and politics, in order to bring out a middle class—really, middle class*es*—with any significant complexity and historical meaning." Robert D. Johnston, *The Radical Middle Class: Populist Democracy and the Question of Capitalism in Progressive Era Portland, Oregon* (Princeton: Princeton University Press, 2003), 12.

11. Rubén Cantú Chapa, *Tlatelolco: la autoadministración en unidades habitacionales gestión urbana y planificación* (Mexico City: IPN Plaza y Valdés, 2001).

12. The Department of Federal Security is part of the Secretaría de Gobernación. Gobernación is Mexico's Ministry of the Interior. This collection is housed in gallery 1 of the AGN, although it is administered directly by Gobernación. While these documents offer richly detailed accounts of public meetings and private conversations, excitement over this historical source must be tempered with caution. These reports are sometimes inaccurate and analysis often only scratches the surface. Agents' reporting would sometimes exaggerate the threat posed by groups or individuals, in an effort to curry favor with their superiors and justify increased government funds for the Department of Federal Security. For more on the history of this source, see Sergio Aguayo, *La charola: una historia de los servicios de inteligencia en México* (Mexico City: Grijalbo, 2001).

13. Originally called the National Revolutionary Party (Partido Revolutionario Nacional) and renamed the Mexican Revolutionary Party (Partido de la Revolución Mexicana) in 1938, it became the PRI in 1946.

14. Quotation from Serna and CUD, *¡Aquí nos quedaremos!*, 33.

15. This is a composite paragraph that draws from the testimonial literature. See note 6.

16. "Por medio de la presente," September 24, 1985, DFS 009-031-003, AGN, 1–7.

17. "Entrevista realizada por el corresponsal en México," September 25, 1985, DFS 009-031-003, AGN, 1–7.

18. Poniatowska, *Nothing, Nobody*, 73–77.

19. "Tras el porqué del por qué," *Obras*, November 1985, exp. 3, 32.05.00.00, c. 1, MMH, AGN.

20. "Ciudad de México: vulnerabilidad y alto riesgo," *Púnto crítico*, December 1985, exp. 6, 32.05.00.00, c. 2, MMH, AGN.

21. "Información del frente nacional contra la represión," September 25, 1985, DFS 009-031-003, AGN, 1–7.

22. Gustavo Suárez, "Movimiento del sistema," *Insurgencia Popular*, October 1985, exp. 17, 32.03.00.00, c. 2, MMH, AGN.

23. "Información del frente nacional," DFS.

24. "Actividades de militantes del PMT," September 26, 1985, DFS 009-031-003, AGN, 1–8.

25. Arbitrario desalojo en el Churubusco," *El Tlatelolca*, September 18, 1986, exp. 11, 32.01.00.00, c. 4, MMH, AGN.

26. "Al pueblo de México," October 1, 1985, DFS 009-031-003, AGN, 1–10.

27. "*¡No queremos goles, queremos frijoles!*" Promotora Democrática de Comunicadores Gráficos, November 1985, DFS 009-031-003, AGN, 1–20.

28. Aguilar Zinser, Morales, and Peña, *Aún tiembla*, 33.

29. "Los manifestantes que se dirigen a la residencia oficial de los Pinos," September 27, 1985, DFS 009-031-003, AGN, 1–8.

30. "Movimientos telúricos," DFS.

31. "¡De nuevo quieren manchar Tlatelolco!" September 22, 1985, DFS 009-031-003, AGN, 1–6.

32. "Al dirigirnos a usted," September 23, 1985, DFS 009-031-003, AGN, 1–8.

33. "Movimientos telúricos," DFS; "Al dirigirnos a usted," DFS; Frente de Residentes de Tlatelolco, "Como es de su conocimiento," October 7, 1985, DFS 009-031-003, AGN, 1–11.

34. "Al dirigirnos a usted," DFS.

35. "Tlatelolco: a la hora de los sismos," *Púnto Crítico*, December 1985, exp. 6, 32.05.00.00, c. 2, MMH, AGN.

36. Poniatowska, *Nothing, Nobody*, 255.

37. Coo, "Después de la caída," 43.

38. "Extracto de información," September 22, 1985, 009-031-003, AGN, 1–6.

39. See Davis, "Reverberations"; and CEPAL, *Daños causados por el movimiento telúrico en México y sus repercusiones sobre la economía del país* (Santiago: Comisión económica para América Latina y el Caribe, 1985).

40. "El terremoto: heroísmo y corrupción," *Contenido*, December 1985, exp. 7, 32.05.00.00, c. 1, MMH, AGN.

41. Indeed, this system persisted long after the earthquake. For example, a journalist living in the disaster zone called authorities to schedule a structural inspection of his home to ascertain whether it needed repairs. When the

inspector arrived, the journalist recognized him as one of the city's press liaison officials; the journalist had attended many press briefings delivered by this supposed technician. Countless such examples exacerbated the conflict between residents and the state as residents decried the state's unwillingness— even incapacity—to alter its ways after the effects of corruption made themselves so devastatingly manifest ("Se han detectado anomalías en las supervisiones de las construcciones afectadas por los sismos," October 7, 1985, DFS 009-031-003, AGN, 1–11).

42. On Mexico City's political structure see, for example, Diane E. Davis, *Urban Leviathan: Mexico City in the Twentieth-Century* (Philadelphia: Temple University Press, 1994) and Peter M. Ward, *Mexico City: The Production and Reproduction of an Urban Environment* (London: Belhaven, 1990).

43. Suárez, "Movimiento del sistema."

44. "El terremoto: heroísmo," AGN.

45. Núñez de la Peña and Orozco, *Terremoto*, 124.

46. "Mítin-plantón silencioso de la unión de vecinos y damnificados '19 de septiembre," October 8, 1985, DFS 009-031-003, AGN, l–12.

47. "Asamblea plenaria del PRS en el DF," September 28, 1985, DFS 009-031-003, AGN, l–9.

48. Frente de Residentes de Tlatelolco, "Conocimiento," DFS.

49. "Asamblea informativa en la Plaza de las Tres Culturas," October 3, 1985, DFS 009-031-003, AGN, l–10.

50. "Textos de telegramas que se enviarán mañana," October 23, 1985, DFS 009-031-003, AGN, l–19.

51. "Tlatelolco: a la hora," AGN.

52. For more on this, see Coo, "Después de la caída," 44–54.

53. "Al dirigirnos a usted," DFS.

54. *El Tlatelolca*, October 6, 1985, DFS 009-031-003, AGN, l–11.

55. Coo, "Después de la caída," 50, italics added.

56. "Al dirigirnos a usted," DFS.

57. "Un año después, hay que reforzar el trabajo organizativo," *El Tlatelolca*, September 18, 1986, exp. 11, 32.01.00.00, c. 4, MMH, AGN.

58. "Situación que prevalece en la unidad Nonoalco-Tlatelolco," October 18, 1985, DFS 009-031-003, AGN, l–17. This had also been a problem before the earthquake: an article in the July–August issue of a Tlateloclo newsletter, *Unidad Urbana*, reveals that many residents of the buildings who had signed

contracts to convert to condominiums refused to accept the legality of these contracts (*Unidad Urbana*, July–August 1985, DFS 009-031-003, AGN, l–31).

59. Of the many instances of corruption revealed by the earthquake, the discovery of semiclandestine sweatshops of garment workers in the city center was among the most notorious. In the immediate aftermath, the police and military helped factory owners rescue the sewing machines, as their workers lay buried underneath.

60. Serna and CUD, *¡Aquí nos quedaremos!*, 72–75. It also did not hurt that Placido Domingo had family who lived in the Nuevo León building and was on the ground in Tlatelolco in the aftermath.

61. "Movimientos telúricos," DFS; "Asamblea informativa del STUNAM," September 24, 1985, DFS 009-031-003, AGN, l–7.

62. Serna and CUD, *¡Aquí nos quedaremos!*, 49, 72–75.

63. "Movimientos telúricos," October 25, 1985, DFS 009-031-003, AGN, l–20.

64. "A las 12:45 hs. del día de hoy," September 24, 1985, DFS 009-031-003, AGN, l–7. During the 1970s and early 1980s, these leaders fought rises in rents and evictions in proletarian neighborhoods. Their tactics included taking buildings by force, illegally occupying them, and sometimes even collecting rent for the landlords. They did this, for example, on the rooftops of Tlatelolco. They also organized homeowners for urban services, as well as for education and health care, and, in the years before the earthquake, fought the rising cost of living due to inflation and economic crisis ("Antecedentes de los principales líderes y militantes en las colonias populares," October 1985, DFS 009-031-003, AGN, l–22).

65. Frente de Residentes de Tlatelolco, "Conocimiento," DFS; "Movimientos telúricos," DFS. The parties active in Tlatelolco ranged from what Barry Carr has called the "loyal left," such as the Popular Socialist Party (Partido Popular Socialista, or PPS), which adhered to a Marxist rhetoric but worked within the electoral arena determined by the PRI, to more radical parties such as the Unified Socialist Party of Mexico (Partido Socialista Unificado de México, or PSUM). For more on the history of leftist political parties in Mexico see, for example, Barry Carr and Ricardo Anzaldúa Montoya, eds., *The Mexican Left, the Popular Movements and the Politics of Austerity* (San Diego: Centre for U.S.-Mexican Studies, 1986); and Barry Carr and Steve Ellner, *The Latin American Left: From the Fall of Allende to Perestroika* (Boulder, CO: Westview, 1993).

66. "Frente de residentes de Tlatelolco," October 18, 1985, DFS 009-031-003, AGN, l–17.

67. Serna and CUD, *¡Aquí nos quedaremos!*, 45.

68. "Frente de residentes," DFS.

69. From 1983 to 1985, the annual inflation rate averaged 75 percent and Mexico's total external debt averaged US$95.7 billion, equal to 56.8 percent of the GDP. Nora Lustig, *Mexico: The Remaking of an Economy* (Washington, DC: Brookings Institute Press, 1998), 32–33, 40–41.

70. Indeed, during the crisis of the 1980s the middle classes were hit disproportionately harder than other groups (Lustig, *Mexico*, 71–95).

71. Poniatowska, *Nothing, Nobody*, 11.

72. A crucial caveat to this statement is that while the middle class might have lost *relatively* more than the working class and the poor, the smallest decline in the income of the poor can have devastating effects (Lustig, *Mexico*, 93).

73. Between 1940 and 1980 the annual growth rate of the GDP averaged over 6 percent. Gustavo Garza, *La urbanización de México en el siglo XX* (Mexico City: Centro de Estudios Demográficos y de Desarrollo Urbano, El Colegio de México, 2003), 41–43.

74. Davis, *Urban Leviathan*, 278.

75. Claudio Lomnitz, "Times of Crisis: Historicity, Sacrifice, and the Spectacle of Debacle in Mexico City," *Public Culture* 15, no. 1 (2003): 127–48.

76. Claudio Lomnitz, *Death and the Idea of Mexico* (New York: Zone, 2005), 454.

77. In 1982 the debt reached US$92.4 billion, 54.2 percent of the country's GDP; for comparison, in 1980 the debt was US$50.7 billion, 26.0 percent of the GDP. See Lustig, *Mexico*, 32–33.

78. *Daños causados*, CEPAL.

79. Francisco Ortiz Mendoza, "Terremoto, industriales y deuda externa," *Combatiente*, September 30, 1985, exp. 4, 32.03.00.00, c. 2, MMH, AGN.

80. Partido Laboral Mexicano (hereafter PLM), *Reconstruir y salvar vidas es la prioridad*, October 1, 1985, DFS 009-031-003, AGN, l–11.

81. "Información del frente nacional," DFS.

82. "Movimientos telúricos," DFS.

83. "Marcha plantón de la coordinadora única de damnificados," October 26, 1985, DFS 009-031-003, AGN, l–20.

84. "Informe de la dinámica post-sísmica macrosismos del 19 y 20 septiembre 1985," exp. 4, 30.00.00.00, c. 5, DDF, MMH, AGN.

85. "Extracto de información," AGN.

86. See, for example, Tanalis Padilla, "From Agraristas to Guerrilleros: The Jaramillista Movement and the Myth of the Pax Priísta" (PhD diss., University

of California, San Diego, 2001), on the repression of peasant activists in the state of Morelos. There is a rich body of literature on the PRI's mechanisms of control, its balancing act of coercion and compromise, and the myriad ways it negotiated its hegemony. See, for example, Gilbert Joseph and Daniel Nugent, *Everyday Forms of State Formation: Revolution and the Negotiation of Rule in Modern Mexico* (Durham, NC: Duke University Press, 1994).

87. For a discussion of middle-class consumption during the boom, see, for example, Julio Moreno, *Yankee Don't Go Home! Mexican Nationalism, American Business Culture, and the Shaping of Modern Mexico, 1920–1950* (Chapel Hill: University of North Carolina Press, 2003). For a discussion of consensus between the urban middle class and the PRI during the boom, see, for example, Eric Zolov, *Refried Elvis: The Rise of the Mexican Counter-Culture* (Berkeley: University of California Press, 1999). For a discussion of urbanization and urban economic growth during the boom, see, for example, Garza, *Urbanización de México*, 41–68. It is important, however, not to overestimate the stability of the mid-century boom. Alan Knight suggests instead that we think of the PRI as a "Swiss cheese" PRI, full of holes rather than all-encompassing; see "Historical Continuities in Social Movements," in *Popular Movements and Political Change in Mexico*, ed. Joe Foweraker and Ann L. Craig (Boulder, CO: Lynne Rienner, 1990), 93–100.

88. For discussions of the 1968 student movement, see, for example, Zolov, *Refried Elvis*; Elena Poniatowska, *Massacre in Mexico* (New York: Viking, 1975); and Leslie Jo Frazier and Deborah Cohen, "Defining the Space of Mexico '68: Heroic Masculinity in the Prison and 'Women' in the Streets," *Hispanic American Historical Review* 83, no. 4 (2003).

89. Secretaría de Desarrollo Urbano y Ecología [hereafter SEDUE], "Estrategia política en Tlatelolco," March 5, 1986, exp. 5, c. 161, MMH, AGN.

90. Ibid.

91. SEDUE, "Edificio Nuevo León," May 1986, exp. 2, c. 162, MMH, AGN; and SEDUE, "Edificio Nuevo León," September 9, 1986, exp. 4, c. 162, MMH, AGN.

92. SEDUE, "Movimientos internos," March 5, 1986, exp. 5, c. 161, MMH, AGN.

93. "¿Qué pueden hacer Las Brigadas Juveniles de Solidaridad Social?" October 1985, exp. 5, 30.00.00.00, c. 4, DDF, MMH, AGN.

94. Subcomité de Movilización Social para la Defensa Civil, Comité de Reconstrucción del Área Metropolitana, "Conclusiones," 1986, exp. 5, 30.00.00.00, c. 4, DDF, MMH, AGN.

95. "Coordinadora de Tlatelolco," November 20, 1985, DFS 009-031-003, AGN, 1–28; "Datos de los principales dirigentes," October 25, 1985, DFS; and "Conferencia de prensa del Dr. Cuauhtémoc Abarca Chávez," November 16, 1985, DFS 009-0310-003, AGN, 1–26.

96. "Entrevista con cinco dirigentes de Tlatelolco," *El tlatelolca semanal*, December 18, 1985, exp. 4, 32.01.00.00, c. 6, MMH, AGN.

97. Serna and CUD, *¡Aquí nos quedaremos!*, 95.

98. Secretaría de Programación y Presupuesto [hereafter SPP], "Proyecto de 'clases medias,'" August 1986, exp. 5, c. 215, MMH, AGN.

99. Ibid.; capitalization in original.

100. Ibid.

101. For more on previous struggles in Tlatelolco, see Cantú Chapa, *Tlatelolco*.

102. As historian Alan Knight suggests, "We should perhaps see the social protests of recent years chiefly as replications of earlier movements, now rendered more extensive, and perhaps more radical, by harsh economic circumstances" ("Historical Continuities," 94).

103. Susan Eckstein, *Power and Popular Protest: Latin American Social Movements* (Berkeley: University of California Press, 2001), 338.

104. Frente de Residentes de Tlatelolco, "Conocimiento."

105. Carlos Monsiváis, "Triunfó el valor de mostrar el propio pánico," *Proceso*, September 21, 1985, quoted in Núñez de la Peña and Orozco, *Terremoto*, 71.

106. Carlos Monsiváis, "Organizaciones populares y resistencia a su acción," *Proceso*, November 9, 1985, quoted in Tavera-Fenolloso, "Social Movements," 40.

107. Poniatowska, *Nothing, Nobody*, 310.

108. Aguilar Zinser, Morales, and Peña, *Aún tiembla*, 17, 320; and Núñez de la Peña and Orozco, *Terremoto*, 70–77. Many scholars sought to trace links between the earthquake protests and previous forms of urban protest, demonstrating that the so-called civil society did not emerge phoenix-like from the rubble but instead drew upon a long history of urban protest. Sociologist Ligia Tavera-Fenollosa's in-depth study of the victims' movement casts it as neither spontaneous nor novel; instead, she demonstrates how it emerged from a history of urban protest. She argues that civil society existed before the earthquake and that it was by drawing on an established ideology of protest that the victims' movement acquired its strength ("Social Movements").

109. "¡Por fin!" *El Tlatelolca*, March 13, 1986, exp. 3, 32.01.00.00, c. 6, MMH, AGN.

110. SEDUE, "Manual de organización y mantenimiento: conjunto urbano 'Presidente Adolfo López Mateos' Nonoalco-Tlatelolco," July 1987, exp. 10, 20.01.00.00, c. 5, MMH, AGN.

111. "Hoy te cumple," n.d., exp. 3, 30.00.00.00, c. 9, DDF, MMH, AGN.

112. Serna and CUD, *¡Aquí nos quedaremos!*, 150–53.

113. Ibid., 139.

114. Ibid., 142–47; italics added.

115. Discussing the November 1, 1755, earthquake in Lisbon, Grégory Quenet points out that while this was likely the first earthquake to have a Europe-wide effect, it was not the biggest nor most damaging natural disaster in modern history. He suggests that it was Voltaire's subsequent writings that transformed the Lisbon earthquake into a European event. As a discursive event, the Lisbon earthquake had profound reverberations; in February 1756, Frederick the Great of Prussia issued a decree forbidding earthquakes in his territory. *Les tremblements de terre aux XVIIe et XVIIIe siècles: la naissance d'un risque* (Seyssel: Champ Vallon, 2005), 9.

116. Walter Benjamin, "Theses on the Philosophy of History," in *Illuminations* (New York: Schocken, 1968), 262.

CONTRIBUTORS

JÜRGEN BUCHENAU is chair of the History Department at the University of North Carolina at Charlotte. He is the author of *In the Shadow of the Giant: The Making of Mexico's Central America Policy, 1876–1930*; *Tools of Progress: A German Merchant Family in Mexico City, 1865–Present*; *Plutarco Elías Calles and the Mexican Revolution*; and *Mexican Mosaic: A Brief History of Mexico*, as well as the editor of *Mexico OtherWise: Modern Mexico in the Eyes of Foreign Observers* and the coeditor of *Governors in the Mexican Revolution, 1910–1952: Portraits in Conflict, Corruption, and Courage*.

PAUL J. DOSAL is a professor of Latin American history at the University of South Florida, specializing in the modern history of Cuba and the Caribbean region. He is the author of four books, including *Comandante Che*, a study of the military career of the legendary Latin American revolutionary Ernesto Che Guevara, and *Doing Business with the Dictators*, a history of the infamous United Fruit Company in Guatemala in the early twentieth century. His most recent book is *Cuba Libre*, a brief introductory history of Cuba designed for the classroom as well as for a more general audience.

VIRGINIA GARRARD-BURNETT is an associate professor of history at the University of Texas, Austin, where she is also an affiliated faculty with the Teresa Lozano Long Institute of Latin American Studies and the Department of Religious Studies. She is the author of *Terror in the Land of the Holy Spirit: Guatemala under General Efraín Ríos Montt, 1982–1983* and *Protestantism in Guatemala: Living in the New Jerusalem*. She has written more than two dozen articles and chapters on Guatemalan history and religion in Latin America.

MARK ALAN HEALEY is an assistant professor of history at the University of California, Berkeley. He received his PhD from Duke University. His research interests are urban cultures, populist politics, and state power in modern Latin America, especially Argentina, and the making of modern citizenship across Latin America. His book on Peronism and the San Juan earthquake, *The Ruins of the New Argentina*, is forthcoming.

LYMAN L. JOHNSON is a professor of history at University of North Carolina at Charlotte. His most recent books are *Faces of Honor*, edited with Sonya Lipsett-Rivera, and *Death, Dismemberment, and Memory: Body Politics in Latin America*. Professor Johnson is also coauthor of *Colonial Latin America* and *The Earth and Its Peoples*. He is currently working on a study of Buenos Aires in the era of the Atlantic revolutions.

SAMUEL J. MARTLAND is an assistant professor of history and Latin American studies at Rose-Hulman Institute of Technology, Terre Haute, Indiana. He received his PhD from the University of Illinois at Urbana-Champaign in 2003. He has published articles on nineteenth- and early twentieth-century Valparaíso in the *Hispanic American Historical Review*, the *Journal of Urban History*, and *EURE* (Santiago de Chile), and an article on nineteenth-century street lighting in the Southern Cone in the *Journal of Urban History*.

STUART MCCOOK is an associate professor of history at the University of Guelph, Ontario. He received his PhD from Princeton University. His research focuses on the environmental history of Latin America and of tropical crops. He is the author of *States of Nature: Science, Agriculture, and Environment in the Spanish Caribbean, 1760-1940*, as well as several articles on related subjects.

CHARLES F. WALKER is the author of *Shaky Colonialism: The 1746 Earthquake-Tsunami in Lima, Peru, and Its Long Aftermath* and *Smoldering Ashes: Cuzco and the Formation of Republican Peru, 1780–1840*. He is a professor of history at the University of California, Davis, where he is also the director of the Hemispheric Institute on the Americas.

LOUISE E. WALKER is an assistant professor of history and international studies at Louisiana State University in Baton Rouge. Trained at Yale University, she is working on a manuscript based on her dissertation on middle-class politics and culture in Mexico City in the 1970s and 1980s.

INDEX

Agency for International
Development (AID), 136–37

Agüero, Ferdinand, 142

Aguirre, Ramón, 186

Alcántara, Pedro, 30–31

Amusquíbar, Mateo de (Inquistor), 13,
25–27, 38

Anderson, Jack, 149–50

Aragón, Diego de, 27, 29–30

Arbenz, Jacob, 158

Argentina: adobe construction,
111–14, 117, 120–21, 127n28;
building codes, 101, 110, 118, 123;
city of San Juan, 11, 100–124;
Commission for Restoration of the
Province, 109–110, 118; concrete
construction, 115–18; construction
methods, 101, 104; earthquake of
1861, 104; earthquake of 1894,
104; earthquake of 1954, 123; fault
lines, 105; property rights, 107–
110; quincha construction, 111–
114, 120–21, 123; Reconstruction
Council, , 122–24; regulations
regarding traditional building
materials, 101, 104, 110–14; social
conflict, 100–102; wine industry
of, 100, 107–109, 123. *See also*
earthquake of 1944

Baez, William, 142

Barroeta, Pedro de (Archbishop), 13,
21, 23–27, 38

Bermúdez, Enrique, 74–75, 81, 89

Berryman, Philip, 158

Bolívar, Simón, 9–10, 12, 46, 50–61,
64

Bonaparte, Joseph, 46

Bonaparte, Napoleon, 46

Buchenau, Jürgen, 1, 222

Buchenau, Nicolas, xi,

Bueno, Sebastián, 44

Caldera, Rafael, 64

Camacho Solís, Manuel, 186, 203–205

Cárdenas, Cuauhté, 210–11

Carrasco Palomino, Nicolás, 33–35

Carrillo Arena, Guillermo, 186, 193

Carter, Jimmy, 134, 145, 151

Casariego, Mario (Archbishop),
167–68, 171, 175

Castanera, Juan, 130

Castro, Fidel, 201

Catastrofe (Rodriguez and Gajardo
1906), 79

Chamarro, Pedro Joaquín, 139,
141–45, 151